P9-API-845

Goethe and Schubert

Goethe

and

Schubert

The Unseen Bond

KENNETH S. WHITTON

AMADEUS PRESS
Portland, Oregon

All music excerpts from *Schubert: Lieder* (ed. M. Friedlaender), reproduced by kind permission of Peters Edition, London.

Copyright © 1999 by Kenneth S. Whitton
All rights reserved.

ISBN 1-57467-050-6

Printed in Hong Kong

Published in 1999 by Amadeus Press (an imprint of Timber Press, Inc.)
The Haseltine Building
133 S.W. Second Avenue, Suite 450
Portland, Oregon 97204, U.S.A.

Library of Congress Cataloging-in-Publication Data

Whitton, Kenneth S.
Goethe and Schubert : the unseen bond / Kenneth S. Whitton.
    p.   cm.
Includes bibliographical references and index.
ISBN 1-57467-050-6
1. Schubert, Franz, 1797–1828. Songs. 2. Goethe, Johann Wolfgang von,
1749–1832. 3. Songs, German—19th century—History and criticism. 4. Songs
with piano—19th century—History and criticism. 5. Music and literature.
I. Title.
ML410.S3W36   1999
782.42168′092—dc21   98-32274
CIP
MN

For
Dietrich Fischer-Dieskau,
In grateful thanks for fifty years
of friendship, joy, and inspiration

Goethe and Schubert! O happy bond,
To Germany's eternal fame!

       —Heinrich Panofka

Contents

Photos follow page 48

Foreword

In October 1814, as the great European powers met in Vienna to discuss peace for a war-torn continent, a seventeen-year-old genius began the transformation of an entire musical genre with his setting of a poem from Goethe's *Faust*. *Gretchen am Spinnrade* marks Schubert's first monumental contribution to the German Lied as well as the beginning of his spiritual relationship with another genius of the era—one of the world's great writers—Johann Wolfgang von Goethe.

Schubert had earlier begun to express his musical gifts in several dozen songs, piano pieces, chamber works, opera, symphonies, and a Mass, but it is in *Gretchen am Spinnrade* that he unleashed the full measure of his powers. The musicality of Goethe's words unlocked Schubert's unique voice, and continued to inspire Schubert for the rest of his life, resulting in some eighty musical settings of Goethe texts. Yet, his most intense relationship with Goethe's works came early in Schubert's compositional life. Between 1814 and 1815, he wrote more than one-third of his Goethe songs, which then became the foundation for his exploration of other poets' words.

Although Goethe never publicly acknowledged Schubert's music, Schubert clearly felt the importance of Goethe's poetry. In a diary entry for June 1816, Schubert mentioned performing *Rastlose Liebe* to an enthusiastic audience and commented that "Goethe's musical poet's genius contributed much to the success." Goethe's poetry was also partly responsible for Schubert's fame after his death. *Erlkönig* became Schubert's most popular song in the nineteenth century and inspired other composers to use it as the basis for their creative efforts. Franz Liszt, for example, made a brilliant piano transcription of *Erlkönig*, which he and other performers such as Clara Schumann played to enthusiastic audiences all over Europe. Singer Adolphe Nourrit, the leading tenor at the Paris Opéra, heard Liszt play *Erlkönig* and instantly became a proselytizer for Schubert's music. He even made his own "translations" of Schubert's songs into French, although he did not speak any German! Schubert composed hundreds of songs during his short life of thirty-one years, songs of profound originality and inspiration. The nine-teenth-century German Lied became a major genre in his hands as he probed the mysteries of form and harmony, partners to his effortless, exquisite melodies. A seemingly simple strophic song from 1815, *Nähe des Geliebten* (Nearness of the Beloved), represents a splendid wedding of music and text as the ineffable beauty of Schubert's music heightens the spiritual longing of Goethe's delicate words. Schubert leads the lis-tener into a mystical empathy with the poem, heightening the paradox of the words, "du seist auch noch so ferne, du bist mir nah!" (no matter how far you are from me, you are near me) and the yearning of "O, wärst du da!" (Oh, if only you were here!). Just as a painting or photo-graph can make us more sensitive to the power and beauty of nature, Schubert's music reveals new meaning in Goethe's beautiful words.

Goethe, like Schubert, seemed to dip from an infinite well of ideas, ideas that inspired thousands of song settings, from Wolfgang Ama-deus Mozart's *Das Veilchen* in the eighteenth century to Alexander Zem-linsky's setting of *Wandrers Nachtlied* and Anton Webern's *Gleich und gleich* in the twentieth. And Goethe's presence was also felt by every German-speaking poet who followed him. Much of the wealth of lyric poetry upon which the Lied depended clearly mirrors Goethe's influence.

Goethe's failure to recognize Schubert's musical genius has gener-ated speculation and fierce debate for the last one hundred and seventy-five years. We have only to look at Professor Whitton's bibliography to realize how many scholars have already joined this debate. Anton Webern, in a lecture series of 1932–1933 (published as *The Path to the New Music*), commented, "I want to look at blunders by great minds! . . . Goethe—what did he like? Zelter! Schubert sends him the *Erlkönig*—he doesn't even look at it." We musicians just cannot understand why the great Goethe did not embrace Schubert's music. Yet, we do know that Goethe loved music and immersed himself in it. Perhaps we should simply take Goethe at his word when he wrote to the wife of his pub-lisher, "I am no judge of music, being without knowledge of the means it makes use of . . . I can only speak of the effect it produces upon me, when I let it exercise its powers over me."

Professor Whitton considers a number of provocative possibilities for Goethe's lack of response to Schubert's musical settings of his poetry. He also provides extensive background information about each Goethe poem set to music by Schubert and brings his perspective as a literary scholar to the much argued question of Schubert's literary tastes. By drawing attention to current research on the curricula of nineteenth-century Austrian students through his examination of Schubert's writing style, he concludes that Schubert's literary sensitivities were more highly developed than has been previously realized.

In his chapter on Goethe, Professor Whitton draws a fascinating picture of eighteenth-century German society—the cultural, political, and social context in which Goethe's life unfolds. His lively descriptions of Goethe's romantic pursuits, the inspiration for many of Goethe's finest poems, lend weight to Goethe's much quoted assertion that "everything that became known about me was just fragments of a great confession."

The two-hundred-fiftieth anniversary of Goethe's birth provides a wonderful opportunity to celebrate Goethe's "unseen bond" with Schubert, as Professor Whitton shares his reflections on the rich legacy bequeathed to us by Goethe and Schubert.

> Lorraine Gorrell
> Author, *The Nineteenth-Century German Lied*

Acknowledgments

M y first thanks must go to my professors, Walter Bruford of the Universities of Edinburgh and Cambridge, Eudo Mason of the University of Edinburgh, and to their academic colleague who first introduced me to the joys of poetry set to music, Dr. Hans Eggeling.

These joys were intensified by my long friendship (since 1949) with the musician who, more than any other, has demonstrated that German Lieder consist of music *and* words, Dietrich Fischer-Dieskau.

My thanks go also to Professor Lothar Ehrlich of the Stiftung Weimarer Klassik in Weimar, to Professor Volkmar Hansen of the Goethe Museum in Düsseldorf, and to Dr. Ernst Hilmar of the Internationales Franz Schubert Institut in Vienna, all of whom assisted me greatly during my research work in Germany and Austria.

Thanks are due also to Amadeus Press, Portland, Oregon, for its careful and considerate work.

Finally, my grateful thanks must go to my typist and former secretary, Jean Davison, who has been a model of efficiency and accuracy, and to my wife Marjory, whose sensitivity to German songs and knowledge of German literature and language have been of inestimable value.

About the Text

1. Each Schubert Lied mentioned in the text is accompanied by the appropriate Deutsch number, a number assigned to it in Otto Erich Deutsch's *Franz Schubert: Thematisches Verzeichnis seiner Werke in chronologischer Folge* (Kassel, 1978, 1996), a German version of his original catalog published in English in Cambridge, United Kingdom, in 1950. Thus, *Erlkönig* (D. 328).
2. Chapter five examines every Goethe text set to music by Franz Schubert. The eighty settings are arranged chronologically from 1814 to 1826 and are discussed under four headings: Text, Music, Setting, and Translation or Synopsis. Each entry also includes the date of composition, key, number of measures, and performance time. The chapter begins with a chronological, numbered list for ease of identification.
3. Editions
   The editions of Goethe's works available in Schubert's time were:

   Goethes Schriften (Writings). 8 volumes. (Göschen, Leipzig, 1787–1790). The poems were in volume 8 (1789).
   Goethes Neue Schriften (New Writings). 7 volumes. (Unger, Berlin, 1792–1800). The poems were in volume 7 (1800).
   Goethes Werke (Works). 13 volumes. (Cotta, Tübingen, 1806–1810). The poems were in volume 1 (1806). The 13 volumes of this edition were published again in 1810 in Vienna by Anton Strauss.
   Goethes Werke. 20 volumes. (Cotta, Stuttgart-Tübingen, 1815–1819). The poems were in volumes 1 and 2 (1815).

   Nachlass, shortened form for *Franz Schuberts nachgelassene, musikalische Dichtungen für Gesang und Pianoforte* (Posthumous Vocal Works), 50 volumes (Diabelli, Vienna, 1830–1850).
   Neue Gesamtausgabe (New Complete Edition). Edited by W. Aderhold, W. Dürr, and A. Feil. *Franz Schubert: Thematisches Ver-*

zeichnis seiner Werke in chronologischer Folge. (New Schubert Edition, Series 8, Volume 4, Kassel, 1978).

Alte Gesamtausgabe (Old Complete Edition). Edited by E. Mandyczewski and J. Brahms. *Franz Schuberts Werke: Kritisch durchgesehene Gesamtausgabe* (Old Complete Edition, Leipzig, 40 volumes, 1884–1897).

"Peters." *Franz Schubert: Gesänge für eine Singstimme mit Klavier-
begleitung,* by M. Friedlaender. 7 volumes (Peters, Leipzig, 1885–
1887). This is the popular edition of Schubert's Lieder.

"Supplement." A song published in the supplement to the Wiener
Zeitschrift für Kunst, Literatur, Theater und Mode. *Viennese
Journal for Art, Literature, Theater and Fashion.*

Introduction

The 200th anniversary of the birth of the Viennese composer Franz Schubert in 1997, the 170th anniversary of his death in 1998, and the 250th anniversary of the birth of the German poet and dramatist Johann Wolfgang Goethe in 1999 afforded a splendid opportunity to consider the curious bond that links these two men.

Heinrich Panofka, born in Breslau, Germany, in 1807, lived in Vienna from 1825 to 1829 and met Schubert on several occasions. He became a great admirer of the composer's songs and particularly of his settings of Goethe's poems. After settling in Paris as a music journalist and violinist, Panofka wrote one of the first laudatory articles on Schubert in which he mentioned the link that he felt existed between Goethe and Schubert. "Goethe and Schubert!" he wrote, "O happy bond, to Germany's eternal fame!"[1]

For all who love the German Lied, the bond between Goethe and Schubert was indeed a happy one, yet it remained unseen to the world, for the two men never met or even corresponded. This book describes how this happened by tracing the lives and careers of both men.

Goethe, born in 1749 into the Europe of the Age of Enlightenment, was the son of well-to-do parents in Frankfurt-am-Main. When he died in Weimar in 1832 at the age of eighty-two years, he had become the most famous German of his day, celebrated as the author of plays, novels, and works of philosophy. His fame as a poet bound him to Schubert, who was born in Vienna, Austria, in 1797, one of fourteen children of a modest schoolmaster. Comparatively unknown in his lifetime, Schubert became recognized in our day as the master of that genre of vocal music known as the art song, the setting to music of an original poem. Schubert's settings of eighty Goethe texts made him famous and made Goethe's name better known to a world largely unacquainted with German literature. In Germany, Goethe's works became the classical bedrock of school and university studies of German language and culture after his death in 1832. Throughout the nineteenth century and well into the twentieth, his name and his works were objects of veneration.

The late twentieth century witnessed vast changes in political and cultural attitudes. In 1929, the Anglo-American author T. S. Eliot felt impelled to declare that "unlike Dante, Goethe always arouses a strong sentiment of disbelief in what he says."[2] The lasting legacy of Marxism, the growth of groups antipathetic to autocratic and authoritarian government, and, in German-speaking countries in particular after the Second World War, the association in the minds of young people of Adolf Hitler and his Nazi party with dictatorship in all strata of society—the home, school, university, and political life—led to the democratization of culture. For many of those German young people, Goethe in particular, but also many writers of his day and age, became part of what the dissatisfied students of the late 1960s termed the "musty smell of the past." More modern subjects were now to be studied in place of classical literature, subjects such as industrial and commercial technology, computerization, economics, politics, and, if modern languages, then communicative competence rather than literary studies. Although it will be many years before the works of Goethe vanish from study curricula in German-speaking countries, there are today places of learning from which students of German can graduate without having read a word of Goethe. How then is Goethe's name kept alive at the end of the twentieth century?

Goethe's name is known to literally millions of people worldwide who will never have read a word of his works in the original German or in translation, but who will have heard of his name as the author of those poems that Franz Schubert set as Lieder (art songs), and which are known to and admired by most lovers of music, songs such as *An den Mond* (To the Moon), *Erlkönig* (Erl-King), *Der Musensohn* (The Son of the Muses), and *Wandrers Nachtlied* (The Night Song of the Wanderer). Other Goethe works have been set to music by composers from Beethoven and Schumann to Brahms and Wolf, but few have attained the popularity of Schubert's Lieder.

It seems ironic that, just as Goethe's name is no longer so familiar to the world at large as it was, say, a hundred years ago, Schubert's name has grown in familiarity and respect during these years. At one time he was treated as a little Viennese tunesmith, "fluting away his young days in a grassy solitude," as the British author Richard Capell put it, back in 1928,[3] or as one who had produced some much criticized symphonic works. One of these, the Symphony in C major (D. 944), led that maverick Irish writer and part-time music critic Bernard Shaw to claim in 1888 that "a more exasperatingly brainless composition was never put on paper."[4] That "heavenly length" of Schubert's instrumental works, so praised by his contemporary Robert Schumann, was also much criticized by others. As the twentieth century advanced, it became clear from the writings of the music establishment and the attitude of audiences that the little Viennese composer had entered into *his* European pantheon and was being discussed in the same critical breath as his illustrious contemporaries Haydn and Beethoven.[5]

The first chapter of the present volume traces the development of German song in the eighteenth century from its beginnings as folk song to its metamorphosis into what we now call art song. Chapter two discusses Goethe's interest in and involvement with the music and the musicians of his time, and shows that, rather than being the "genuinely, profoundly un-musical" man posited by critic Hans Keller, Goethe had well-developed musical tastes and sensibilities.[6] Chapter three suggests that Schubert, rather than being the rustic scribbler of music, setting whatever poem was laid before him, was surprisingly well read in the literature of his time, having moved in intellectual circles that kept him in touch with European cultural developments. Chapter four describes the efforts made by friends to acquaint Goethe with Schubert's Lieder, and Schubert with Goethe's poems, and, later, with Goethe personally. In chapter five the work of the poet and the musician are studied; each Lied set by Schubert to a Goethe poem is discussed singly, while the background to both poem and song are presented.

There were enormous differences in age, in social position, but, above all, in the traditions in which Goethe and Schubert were brought up. No person is independent of the times in which he or she lives. Thus, this volume begins with a look at the literary, musical, and societal traditions of the ages of Goethe and Schubert.

PART ONE

CHAPTER ONE

The German Lied before Franz Schubert

Walter Bruford, an authority on the culture and society of eighteenth-century Germany, began his study of the period with a quotation from the Scottish philosopher David Hume: "Germany is undoubtedly a very fine country full of industrious honest people, and were it united, it would be the greatest power that ever was in the world."[1] It was then a country of disparate units, some three hundred in all, "each jealous of its time-honored privileges and little affected by any memories of a common inheritance," Bruford continued. Among that number were some great and powerful states. Frederick the Great ruled the northern kingdom of Prussia from 1740 to 1786, laying there the foundation stone of the most influential German-speaking country of the nineteenth century. He was succeeded by Frederick William II. In the south, the husband of the matriarchal Maria Theresa, the Archduchess of Austria, was crowned king of the German Empire as Francis I in 1745, to be succeeded by Maria Theresa's son, the liberal Joseph II who reigned from 1765 to 1790.

To the west of this potentially powerful political area lay two more traditionally powerful countries whose political, literary, and musical influences were to weigh heavy on their eastern neighbors: France and Great Britain. Louis XIV's long reign lasted from 1643 to 1715 and the cultural hegemony that it established continued under Louis XV and Louis XVI, who reigned from 1715 to 1793. Throughout this period, France was challenged by its major competitor for imperial glory, Great Britain. Britain's literary reputation stood as high as France's. Writers such as Milton, Shakespeare, Dryden, and Pope vied with Corneille, Racine, Molière, and Voltaire as European literary icons. Even when German princes from Hanover, George I to George IV, occupied the British throne from 1714 to 1830, French rather than British influence dominated the German-speaking regions during that cultural period in the eighteenth century known as the Age of Enlightenment.

23

French language, French manners, and French literature all influenced the aristocratic, therefore the dominant, stratum of German society. French writers had few, if any, rivals among the German writers of the time. Music culture was similarly dominated by foreign influences, only here, not solely by French. Since the Renaissance, Italian opera had become increasingly popular. Indeed, it had found a home outside Italy in the seventeenth century, in Vienna, where Antonio Bertoli was the first director of the new opera house built in 1659 on Vienna's Burgplatz.

Without question, the genius of Italian opera lay in the opportunities it afforded to display the voice as a musical instrument, with trills and virtuoso treatment of none-too-important words. These were of secondary importance anyway, and they remained so in much Italian opera well into the nineteenth century, where the many soprano "mad scenes" displayed mainly extended runs, trills, and ornamentations of single phrases or words. Although the Italian works of composers such as Claudio Monteverdi or Christoph Willibald von Gluck received general acclaim in the quarters for which they were written, at the same time an appreciation was evolving of what was termed the *melodia germanica,* an awareness of a new type of music that was being written by and for a new social grouping, the German middle classes.

Although the French middle classes made their opposition to aristocratic dictatorship most clearly felt and heard in the 1790s, there was a growing dislike among the German middle classes of the many foreign importations in language, literature, and music. Where the upper classes found their pleasure in the ornate ornamentations of Italian opera performed for the courts, the middle classes found theirs in what to them seemed to be the more virtuous, even more moral, world of music-making, in the home.

This undeniably patriotic, even nationalistic, aversion to the *opera seria,* popularized in France and Italy, and often based on the Greek and Roman classical heritage, but also to the lighter, less intellectual *opera buffa,* encouraged the development of this *melodia germanica.* Initially *melodia germanica* consisted of simple but attractive melodies to old German texts. Later it became the basis of the new art form, the Singspiel (literally, "song play"), a work of spoken dialogue with interpolated songs.[2]

One composer held what might be called the middle ground: Gluck, a German of Bohemian stock, who had accepted the Italian conventions of the day in his first operas, profusely ornamented da capo arias and interpolated recitatives. He then revolted against what was felt to be the "tyranny of the singer," and his later operas, particularly *Orfeo ed Euri-*

dice (1762), and the true music drama *Alceste* (1767), although both set to Italian libretti, sought a simplicity of style.

Gluck's preface to his *Alceste* contained passages that helped to alter the musical climate. He wrote there that he aimed "to restrict the music to its true purpose of serving to give expression to the poetry."[3] This was a call for simplicity and clarity in music drama by underlining the importance of the words. Such a call had been made by a less distinguished composer to make a place in musical society for German song. Johannes Sigismund Scholze, known as Sperontes, produced his four-part *Singing Muse by the Pleisse* (1736). (The Pleisse is a small river near Leipzig in eastern Germany.) These songs were the first attempt "to provide vocal expression for the emotions bound up with the poems."[4] Sperontes took well-known instrumental pieces and set poems to their existing melodies. However imperfect his collection was, it ended what Hermann Kretzschmar had called the age without song in Germany and was the first popular competition to the imported Italian operas and cantatas.

That Sperontes had taken existing melodies and had set poems (mainly his own) to them did not meet with unanimous agreement. Other composers of the period felt that he had gone down the wrong path. They believed that it was the poet who should supply the impetus, and that the music should simply illustrate the words. In 1757, C. F. Endter wrote in his *Songs for Amusement and Pastime*: "I regard it as an inviolable law that the musical expression must be as compatible as possible with the sentiments of the poem which is to be set to music."[5] Whatever the composition, the German Lied was obviously going to be a vehicle for the amateur, with simple words set to simple music. It would be performed in the home among a circle of like-minded friends, where the singer would accompany herself or himself. Behind the pleasant picture there was a strong moral and patriotic purpose. This was music for ordinary Germans performed in their language. It might have been nationalistic, but one has to remember the resentment aroused by the presence in the larger towns and at the courts of pretentious, Frenchified dandies who would prefer to speak French (or Italian), and not only in front of the servants. For such people, the Lied would be the ultimate in rusticity. For ordinary Germans, these Lieder represented what they most appreciated—naturalness. The Lied was an unpretentious art form whose simple texts and music brought peace and delight.

One of the finest exponents of this new art form, rather curiously, was a member of a family more illustrious in other, less simple musical forms. Johann Sebastian Bach, born in Eisenach, Saxony, in 1685, served many masters during his sixty-five years, including nine years at the court in Weimar where Goethe was later to live for fifty-seven years. Bach's twenty-seven years at the Thomas Church in Leipzig, from 1723 to his death in 1750, are the most notable. His enormous output contained, surprisingly, only five art songs. These are to be found in Anna Magdalena Bach's *Notenbüchlein* (Little Music Book, 1725).

Bach's second son, Carl Philipp Emanuel, was much more prominent in the genre. In 1758 his odes, psalms, and Lieder, some three hundred altogether, were among the first of the true art songs accompanied on the clavier.[6] J. H. Füssli declared that these songs had given the Lied the "quality of an important object" of the times, and Mozart said of this Bach: "He is the parent and we are the children." Bach, Mozart felt, had given depth of meaning to music, both instrumental and vocal, by loosening the bonds of tradition and convention.[7]

C. P. E. Bach's Lieder are among the first to show the transition from folk song to art song. The folk song embraced cradle songs, Christmas carols, and work songs, all handed down orally over hundreds of years. When these songs had more than one stanza, each was sung to the same melody. If more than one singer participated, the resulting harmony would be simple.

When the new music, the *melodia germanica,* appeared on the scene, it was as if the folk song had been refined, yet it did not lose its essential elements: simplicity, tunefulness, and naturalness. Among the first theoreticians to set out the tenets of the new genre were Karl Ramler and Christian G. Krause. In the preface to their *Odes with Melodies* (1753, 1755), they wrote: "The Lieder are to be pretty, fine, simple, not so poetical that a beautiful singer cannot understand them, but also not so light and frothy that an intelligent person cannot read them."[8]

This was one of the most important collections from what came later to be known as the First Berlin School of Lieder. (It will be noted for future reference that the word *Lied* was here understood as a poem to be read as well as a song to be sung.) It was followed by many collections, testifying to the popularity of the new genre. Arnold Feil, a leading German scholar of the Lied, has calculated that some nine hundred collections of Lieder appeared in the eighteenth century: thirty-seven to 1750, about two hundred to 1775, and then more than six hundred in the concluding years.[9] Even those collections, however popular, or perhaps because they were so popular, did not represent great art. Indeed, the adjective used most often by the composers to describe them was "playful" or "merry." They remind a present-day reader or listener of the pretty porcelain Dresden shepherdesses being produced at this time in Meissen, Saxony. Reading these collections in German, one is struck by the similarity to the Anacreontic poems of Friedrich von Hagedorn,

J. W. L. Gleim, or Johann Peter Uz of this period, poems fashioned in the bucolic, cheerful style of the sixth-century B.C. Greek poet, Anacreon. Hamish Ritchie wrote of Hagedorn's poems: "They were never intended to be immortal contributions to the high art of mankind," and he quotes the poet's lines: "I dedicate these trifles / To an age rich in poetry. / They are not meant to be immortal."[10]

We now move from this transitional stage in the development of the German Lied into an age where Germany's greatest composers were living and working. What did they contribute to the development of the art song?

THE NEW GERMAN POETRY

Literature in Germany up to the year 1770 was greatly influenced by foreign writers. Since most of these belonged to nations that spoke Romance languages (French, Italian, Spanish), they were described by Germans as *Welsch,* a word derived ultimately from the Celtic tribe of the Volcae, but used for centuries in Germany to indicate (in a somewhat derogatory fashion) a non-German speaker.

In the 1770s a countermovement to the prevailing cult for foreign manners began in Germany. One can argue about where the first signs appeared; it might have been the love of folk poetry that led poets and novelists to begin to write what looked like folk poetry—four-lined stanzas, usually rhyming ABAB or AABB, with three stresses to each line.

If this movement were to be accepted as the origin of the new poetry, then credit must be given to a literary group in eastern Germany called the Göttingen Grove Circle. Ludwig Hölty was a leading member, and his colleague Friedrich Leopold Stolberg wrote ecstatically in the new patriotic spirit: "I am a German." A much more important and celebrated writer of patriotic odes, Friedrich Gottlieb Klopstock, was also the author of an equally typical Germanic effusion: "I am a German maiden / my eyes are blue, my glance is gentle. / I have a heart / which is noble and proud and good." This was set to music by C. P. E. Bach and published in 1774.

The main impetus of this anti-Welsch movement was to come ironically from yet another foreign country, the misty part of the northern isles of Caledonia, from Scotland. In 1762, the Scot James Macpherson from Inverness published the *Poems of Ossian* purporting to be translations of an ancient Gaelic bard, a type of the Rousseauistic "noble savage." Hugh Blair, a professor at the University of Edinburgh, wrote a critique of Macpherson's translations in his *Dissertation* (1763), comparing

ι with Homer because it was "the poetry of the heart." Interest-
nough, Blair's thesis continued by asserting that Ossian's age was
ιt age when, "as long as two arts (music and poetry) remained
united, music enlivened and animated poetry, and poetry gave force
and expression to music."[11] Macpherson's translations proved to be a
potent symbol for poets of all European nations until his final unmask-
ing as a fraud at the end of the nineteenth century. The similar effect of
his work on Goethe and Schubert is another link in the unseen bond
between the two men.

A second important influence on the new German poetry that
became known as the Literary Revival also hailed from across the English Channel: Bishop Thomas Percy's publication of ancient English and
Scottish folk songs and ballads. These *Reliques of Ancient English Poetry*
(1765) proved to the German theoreticians writing on the new style that,
to renew itself, a national literature must be fed from its roots. The
poems of Macpherson and Percy came, they thought, from the soil of the
respective countries and were therefore true poetry.

The leading advocate of folk poetry and a man who was to prove to
be of immense importance for the later development of poetry and song
was an east Prussian, Johann Gottfried Herder. His early writings, for
example, his *Fragmente über die neuere deutsche Literatur* (Recent German
Literature, 1766–1767), had helped to support the new patriotic line. In
1772 his prize-winning *Über den Ursprung der Sprache* (Treatise on the
Origin of Language), written during his stay in Strasbourg, combined
two most significant themes: first, that Germany needed original works
of German literature to combat those foreign influences, and second, that
to encourage young writers to write German works, works of the past
that described the old German manners and customs, that is, folk poetry,
must be rediscovered. Herder encouraged his younger friend Johann
Wolfgang Goethe, then twenty-one, to set out as "one of the very first
field workers in German folklore" to collect a set of twelve folk songs.[12]

Herder's collection of folk songs was published in 1778–1779 as
Stimmen der Völker (Voices of the Peoples in Songs), his reaction to the
prevailing spirit of the times. Folk poetry, he claimed, may well be
naive, incorrect, even primitive, but it is true poetry, depicting real experiences. Although Herder always wrote of his folk poems as *Volkslieder*,
he nowhere provides any melodies for the poems. Even when he writes
of a poem as being "melodious," he seems to be referring only to the
musicality of the verse. This is an interesting point to be borne in mind
when we look at Goethe's poems, which have been praised for being
able to communicate their meaning through their music.[13]

Collections of folk poetry to music had appeared in Germany before

Herder's; few, if any, possessed that naturalness, the ring of truth that Herder sought. The first collection to approach his ideal was J. A. P. Schulz's *Lieder im Volkston* (Lieder in the Manner of Folk Songs) in three parts, published in 1782, 1785, and 1790. Schulz claimed in his preface to the second edition of the first book (in 1785) that he had chosen the poems only from the best poets who had written for the type of melody he had in mind. Many of his poems came from the Göttingen group mentioned above: Claudius, Hölty, Voss, and G. A. Bürger.[14] Schulz's settings are clearly intended to fulfil the contemporary purpose of accompanying music to "touch the heart." Just as clearly, he realized that the words of the poem had to play as great a part in the whole to achieve the maximum emotional response, a belief that had dominated the musical psychology of the early eighteenth century. The song composer, Schulz wrote, has to be an "observer of human passions"; like Gluck, he was distressed by the trivial nature of the *style galant* of the day. Schulz insisted, too, that each song should possess "the appearance of familiarity" so that it would have the general characteristics of the familiar folk song melody, but would not be a folk song (nor would it have been culled from the past, as Macpherson's Ossian poems had been). This was, as Schulz wrote, "the whole secret of the folk song": it was familiar, yet new, and it was the very novelty of his collection that made it so popular.[15]

The success of these songs was in more than just their novelty. They were part of a new but steady move away from the sometimes vacuous libretti of Italian operas and cantatas to the more natural, German-language folk song. A parallel move from the obsession with Welsch manners and customs to a patriotic revival of native cultural manners brought, in the case of Goethe and other German poets in the 1770s, a higher level of literary writing in all branches of the art, particularly from the Storm and Stress (Sturm und Drang) movement. Song composers had therefore a much greater field of poetic texts to survey, and one would have imagined that the greatest and most inventive German composers would have been only too ready and willing to avail themselves of these enticing new opportunities.

THE VOCAL WORKS OF HAYDN, MOZART, AND BEETHOVEN

The vocal works of arguably the three greatest composers of the late eighteenth century, Haydn, Mozart, and Beethoven, remain rooted in the tradition that regarded song-writing as an inferior art to instrumental composition, opera, church music, or cantatas. Songs were regarded by them and by many other contemporaneous composers as still the province of amateur music-making, an evening's entertainment for family or friends round the piano. Christian F. D. Schubart, director of the Stuttgart Court Opera, described the situation thus: "The daughter plays them (the songs) on the piano and sings to them; the brother takes up the flute or the violin, and the father plays the bass. What a pleasant family concert for winter evenings."[16] This picture is one we shall encounter on many future occasions, not least in the family circles of Goethe and Schubert.

Franz Joseph Haydn

Franz Joseph Haydn came, as so many Austrian musicians have come, from the eastern part of the country. He spent most of his life in the service of the Esterházy family where he was the archetypal court composer of mainly instrumental music, not all of which would be heard or appreciated by the dining guests.

Most of Haydn's early vocal works were re-workings of pieces "which he had performed in Esterháza according to the capabilities of what was available there and were suited to the abilities of the singers, the taste of the listeners and the technical possibilities of the stage," so that these works were, in the main, Italian arias in the prevailing style.[17] Only much later, in 1781, did the composer, now forty-nine, publish with the Artaria firm in Vienna a set of twelve Lieder to which were added another twelve in 1784. These twenty-four songs bear all the hallmarks of their origin: "rhythmically and harmonically simple songs of the Singspiel type, folksy and free of coloraturas."[18] If the singer were included, the pianist could improvise the music for the right hand. The second twelve Lieder separate the vocal line and the accompanist's right hand (Hob. XXVIa: 1–24). Few, if any, of the twenty-four songs have enriched the Lieder singer's repertoire.

In 1790 Haydn visited Great Britain for the first time. He made friends with a surgeon, John Hunter, and his poetess wife, Anne. Her six canzonets were set to music by Haydn and published in London in 1794. These reached a much higher level of competence and interest, as did a second set in 1795. Many of these abandon the normal strophic settings of folk songs (in which the same melody is used for each verse) and are, in fact, through-composed where the music tries to follow the poet's changing thoughts and emotions. The *Sailor's Song* and the beautiful setting of Shakespeare's *She Never Told Her Love* from *Twelfth Night*, act 2, scene 4, seem to look forward thirty years. Yet, of all these songs, the most famous to this day must be Haydn's *God Save Emperor Franz*. Haydn had been inspired by the British national anthem *God Save the King*, and his melody gave first the Austrians and then the Germans the melody for their national anthem. The Austrian anthem was first played in Vienna for Emperor Franz's birthday on 12 February 1797.[19]

Wolfgang Amadeus Mozart

Few Lieder of Wolfgang Amadeus Mozart have attained such eminence. As was true for Haydn, the Lied was of secondary importance for Mozart, something to be composed in leisure hours between more important commissions. Franz Schubert has for a long time been seen as more naive and uneducated than Mozart, yet no sign of the great eighteenth-century German writers was found in Mozart's library on his death—no Herder or Klopstock, no Goethe or Schiller. One has to conclude that he was not very interested in German poetry as such and that his best Lieder are probably those short arias placed in his operas, such as Cherubino's in *The Marriage of Figaro* or Papageno's in *The Magic Flute.*

Mozart, too, was a child of his times and well aware of the movements around him. Between 1768 and his death in 1791 he wrote thirty-three songs with a keyboard accompaniment. Twenty-five of these follow the older strophic pattern where, irrespective of the meaning of the words of the poem, the composer employs the same music, sometimes with unintentional comic effect. Jaunty music is set to serious words and vice-versa. The earliest songs have, like Haydn's, accompaniments that merely double the vocal line or, sometimes, have no top line at all.

Two Mozart songs at least can bear comparison with the greatest Lieder. On 8 June 1785, the year in which Mozart wrote and dedicated to his "father, guide, and friend" Haydn his six String Quartets (K. 387, 421, 428, 458, 464, and 465), he set to music Goethe's poem *Das Veilchen* (The Violet, K. 476). This poem had appeared in a collection of German Lieder for the keyboard (edited between 1778 and 1782 by J. A. Steffan), under the name of J. W. L. Gleim. Mozart had performed before an audience including the fourteen-year-old Goethe in Frankfurt in 1763, but it has always been asserted that he did not know that this poem was written by Goethe (in 1773–1774) and that he set it merely because its dainty rococo story attracted him.[20] Whatever the truth, this tiny song, through-composed and with a tender melody and delicate accompaniment, shows how a genius can be aware of the developments of the age and culture in which he lives without knowing it. Mozart shows here, more clearly than any other composer of the age, how the folk song was metamorphosing into the art song.

The second Mozart song shows a similar, but different development. The composer was busy writing *Don Giovanni* in June 1787, an opera full of the darkest thoughts, although titled a *dramma giocoso*. On 24 June he set to music *Abendempfindung* (Evening Thoughts, K. 523), a German aria by the contemporary poet J. H. Campe. The music carefully paints the evening scene as the poet contemplates life's passing when he, like the evening, will move on to the land of rest. Few operatic ornamentations are here—only a deeply felt awareness of the inevitable outcome of existence—although the final repetition of the last lines, "Oh, it will be the loveliest pearl of all in my crown," might just betray the composer's normal operatic style. Again, we find Mozart, participating, almost by osmosis, in the very birth of the development of the German art song.

Ludwig van Beethoven

The third member of the great triumvirate, Ludwig van Beethoven, made his attitude to song writing very clear. According to J. F. Rochlitz in his *Für Freunde der Tonkunst* (For Friends of Music) (1832), Beethoven said: "But Goethe—he's alive and we should all live along with him. There's no one whose poems can be set so well as his. Only, I don't like writing songs."[21]

Much has been written about Beethoven's less-than-satisfactory writing for the human voice. Many express the deepest sympathy for the sopranos who have to reach the frightening series of top As in the final movement of his Ninth Symphony, Op. 125 ("The Choral"). Only a dedicated Lieder singer (or a brave concert-promoter prepared to take a gamble) would undertake a recital devoted solely to Beethoven's Lieder, since the general view seems to be that the composer, although certainly showing more interest in song writing than his two older colleagues, was nevertheless a not very skilled technician in the genre. Yet a case can be, and has been, made for Beethoven here, and several celebrated Lieder singers have dedicated recordings to him. The supporters of his case, such as Joseph Kerman in his *Beethoven Studies* (1974), remind us that we owe the first true song cycle to Beethoven: *An die ferne Geliebte* (To the Distant Beloved), Op. 98, of 1816, a group of six songs to the poems of a young Jewish doctor in Brno, Aloys Jeitteles. The *Concise Oxford Dictionary of Music* defines a song cycle as a "string of songs of related thought and congruous musical style, thus constituting an entity and being capable of being sung as a series."[22] Thus, here too, and in a field not really his, Beethoven was an innovator, although few composers of stature followed his manner of connecting the various songs by bridge passages. The great nineteenth-century song cycles of Schubert, Schumann, and Mahler offer a series of single songs.

The relationship between Beethoven and Goethe is discussed more fully in chapter two; both men admired the other (although in different ways and for different reasons), but the care and attention that Beethoven paid to his settings of Goethe's poems bear witness to his, at times, almost passionate admiration of the older poet. Indeed, some, such as the distinguished British music critic William Mann, believe that Beethoven's Goethe Lieder have no rival, although Goethe would certainly not have agreed with that assessment.[23]

Beethoven wrote eighty Lieder altogether, some twenty to poems of Goethe. One of these, the jaunty *Marmottenlied* (The Squirrel Song) from Goethe's Singspiel *Jahrmarktsfest zu Plundersweilern* (1773) (Lumberville Fair, in the Goethe biographer, Nicholas Boyle's translation), was written as Op. 52, No. 7, in 1785–1787 for two singers of the electoral prince's theater in Beethoven's birthplace, Bonn. In the same year came his beautiful setting of *Mailied* (May Song), Op. 52, No. 4, then of *Neue Liebe, neues Leben* (New Love, New Life), Op. 75, No. 2, and Mephistopheles' *Song of the Flea* from *Faust I*, Op. 75, No. 3, in 1809. These were followed by *Wonne der Wehmut* (Joy of Sadness) and *Sehnsucht* (Yearning), Op. 83, Nos. 1 and 2. He attempted the great song "Nur wer die Sehnsucht kennt" (Only those who know what yearning is) from Goethe's novel *Wilhelm Meister's Years of Apprenticeship* four times without achieving the success that some other composers did. Beethoven also set the interpolated songs in Goethe's drama *Egmont* (Op. 84) in 1810.

Beethoven's need for (and love of) money is well documented. The Edinburgh publisher George Thomson, a keen follower of Herder's passion for resurrecting and recreating the folk song tradition, had approached Haydn in 1799 to arrange old British folk songs for voice, violin, cello, and piano. He corresponded with Beethoven from the time of the publication of his Third Symphony, Op. 55 ("The Eroica"), in 1803. During the next twenty years the composer arranged 164 of the melodies without understanding a word of the Scottish dialects or, indeed, of the English poems. It would be pleasant to think that the composer, already famed for his instrumental innovations, was attracted by the new musical opportunities afforded by the commission, but the substantial fee offered for the first collection of twenty-five Scottish songs (Op. 108) was the greater attraction. His letters to Thomson are full of arguments about money. Nevertheless, he did not see the task solely as a chore. He wrote: "The Scottish songs show how the slipshod melody can be freely tidied up by means of harmonies."[24] Again, we can see embryonic art songs emerging from the old folk songs, with a true

instrumentalized accompaniment, in which the newly developed pianoforte with its possibilities in harmonics, dynamics, and tone colors
played an ever-increasingly important role.

In 1709 Bartolomeo Cristofori had invented a keyboard instrument
that could produce gradations in volume, also giving the instrument
more resonance and power. Subsequently, John Broadwood's square
pianoforte (the *Hammerklavier*) produced a revolution from 1783 onwards and allowed the piano (and the pianist) to become a true partner
to the voice. Although the songs-around-the-piano scene was to become
a cliché of nineteenth-century domesticity and of what has come to be
termed domestic music (*Hausmusik*) in Germany, the elevation of the
accompanist to the role of a true partner meant that song composers
from this time forward were able to write music for the accompaniment,
which, although part of, was quite clearly different from the music for
the voice. Indeed, many lectures have been held to demonstrate how
the accompaniment to a Lied can illustrate the meaning of the poem
almost as effectively as the vocal line. Felix Mendelssohn's eight sets of
Lieder ohne Worte (Songs without Words) of 1830 to 1845 took this concept perhaps as far as it could go.

THE SECOND BERLIN SCHOOL OF LIEDER

The fall of the Bastille prison in Paris on 14 July 1789 signified the wan-
ing of French aristocratic dominance in Europe. It also allowed writers
in other European countries to use their native languages. This in turn
encouraged composers to set their poems and libretti to music. Mozart's
Die Entführung aus dem Serail (*Il Seraglio*, K. 384, 1782) and *The Magic
Flute* (K. 620, 1791), set to original German libretti, would have given an
impetus to this movement. Herder's and Goethe's interest in the Scottish
odes of Ossian and the more genuine works of Shakespeare also showed
German authors that they could use their country's historical heritage
for their works. There was no need to go back to the Greek and Roman
themes so often chosen by their French contemporaries.

Yet whether the works to be set to music were in French, Italian,
English, or German, the argument about whether the words or the
music were of prime consideration continued unabated. (The Germans
call this the *Wort-Ton* problem.) It might even be thought that the title of
one of the many operas of Schubert's teacher Antonio Salieri encapsu-
lated the problem rather neatly. Salieri had come to Vienna in 1766
where he eventually became Kapellmeister to the Italian Opera, and, in

1786, wrote the opera *Prima la musica e pòi le parole* (First the music and then the words).

The ever-growing treasury of lyric and dramatic poetry in German encouraged the composers of the period to trawl through the published collections and anthologies of poems to find suitable texts for setting to music. They could also make use of the harmonic possibilities of the new pianoforte. Did the flood of new poetry mean that composers were encouraged to rank the word equal to (perhaps even superior to) the music? For an answer, let us turn now to look at three composers who, as Schubert's immediate predecessors, were the major influences on his compositions, and knew and worked with Goethe: Johann Rudolf Zumsteeg, Johann Friedrich Reichardt, and Karl (or Carl) Friedrich Zelter, the leaders of the Second Berlin School of Lieder.

Johann Rudolf Zumsteeg

Johann Rudolf Zumsteeg (1760–1802), born in Baden in southern Germany, was one of the late eighteenth-century composers who was stirred by the literary influence from across the English Channel. Although his fame rests on his many songs, he also composed an opera in the chivalric mode of the ballads of the day. *Die Geisterinsel* (The Isle of Ghosts, 1798) was modeled on Shakespeare's *The Tempest*. Such themes, where the appeal was (still) more to the heart than the head, were the stuff of the many ballads then being written, influenced certainly by Bürger's *Lenore* (1773) and even more by Goethe's ballad *Erlkönig* (1782).

Zumsteeg was regarded as only one of the leading exponents of the genre, but, seen in retrospect, he stood above the crowd. Unlike the majority who related the ballad in simple strophic form and with little harmonic deviations, Zumsteeg dared to experiment with the medium, using harmonic subtleties to adorn his settings and emphasize the details of the story. That this procedure also has its drawbacks is clear when we listen to one of Zumsteeg's interminable settings of ballads. His new approach entailed setting the stanzas to differing melodies, or, often, with interpolated recitatives, which, in ballad settings lasting sometimes up to twenty minutes or more, give the impression of a series of largely disconnected episodes. Yet it was his collection of *Kleine Balladen und Lieder* (Little Ballads and Songs), published in seven volumes from 1800 to 1805, that gave the impetus to what is now known as the Romantic Lied. More importantly, it was one of his ballads, *Hagars Klage in der Wüste Bersaba* (Hagars Plaint in the Wilderness of Beersheba), that inspired Schubert to write his first Lied on 30 March 1811 with a very similar title, *Hagars Klage* (D. 5). The 1781 poem by C. A. Schücking had

nineteen stanzas, but Zumsteeg (followed by Schubert) made the poem
seem even longer by creating a series of episodes, with recitatives and
separate melodies.

Zumsteeg's fascination for the ballad form arose in part from his
friendship with Goethe's close friend Schiller, acknowledged in German literature as one of the masters of the epic ballad form. The year in
which Schiller and Goethe wrote many of the greatest ballads for their
Musenalmanache (The Almanacs of the Muses), 1797, is called the "Year
of Ballads." Many elderly Germans can still recite large sections of ballads such as Schiller's *Der Taucher* (The Diver), *Die Bürgschaft* (The
Pledge), *Der Kampf mit dem Drachen* (The Fight with the Dragon), or *Der
Handschuh* (The Glove). The first three of these ballads were set by Schubert as D. 77 (1813–1814), D. 246 (1815), and D. 594 (1817). They were
only three of the forty-four Schiller poems that Schubert set to music.[25]

Johann Friedrich Reichardt

Johann Friedrich Reichardt (1752–1814) was born in Königsberg in East
Prussia, a contemporary of the philosopher Immanuel Kant, who was
born and died in the same city. In his younger days, the composer was
particularly friendly with J. A. P. Schulz, and, like him, was filled with
that patriotic spirit common to young Prussian musicians of the late
eighteenth century and which led to their wishing to "give the art song
the noble naturalness of genuine folk melodies," to quote Hans Joachim
Moser.[26] Schulz was the originator of the *Lieder im Volkston* and had
insisted that only the best poems, that is, poems that were worthwhile
qua poems, should be set to music. Not surprisingly, therefore, we find
from 1786 onwards that Reichardt was well acquainted with the leading
poets of the age. Of modest background, he was far removed from the
type of subservient court composer of earlier years, although he did
become director of music to three Prussian kings. He was prone to tell
people to their faces what he thought of them and, as Schiller wrote to
his wife, Charlotte, in 1789: "It would be difficult to find a more impertinent man . . . no paper in the house is safe with him around . . . and, as
I hear, you have to be very careful when speaking to him."[27]

Reichardt was highly thought of, both as composer and pianist.
Goethe was so attracted by the composer at first that he invited Reichardt to spend nearly a fortnight with him in Weimar in 1789; as a result,
Reichardt was the first musician to set a considerable number of Goethe's poems, nearly 130. Having composed his first Singspiel *Hänschen
und Gretchen* in 1772, followed by four more, and then four full operas,
he felt able to suggest to Goethe that, given the poet's great interest in

and knowledge of James Macpherson's Ossian poems, which had fig-
ured so largely in Goethe's enormously popular novel *Die Leiden des
jungen Werther* (The Sorrows of Young Werther, 1774), they should
together compose an opera on the subject. In the troubled political climate of 1789–1790 in which backward looks were not fashionable, nothing came of the proposal. Reichardt wrote the music for Goethe's Singspiele *Claudine von Villa Bella* (1789) and *Erwin und Elmire* (1790), and
for his Swiss-based *Jery und Bätely* (1801).

Goethe aside, Reichardt remained one of the most influential pre-
Schubert composers of art songs. One of his many song collections,
Lieder geselliger Freude (Songs of Joy in Companionship), written in 1796
and 1797, catered to as many different types of song-lovers as one could
wish for—male and female solos and choirs, with or without accompaniments. It could be taken as typical of his fierce desire to make music
available to and, perhaps more importantly, educationally effective in
those sections of the community normally untouched by the more intellectual type of art song. Twentieth-century scholars, living what they
believe to be a busy, crowded life, commonly look back in amazement at
what musicians, writers, and painters of past ages could produce in
sometimes relatively short life spans. Such a man was Reichardt. One
can cite operas, Singspiele, music for the stage and for the church, his
work as piano and violin virtuoso, as Kapellmeister, editor, and publisher, not forgetting his post-1790 activities as an active supporter of
the ideals of the French Revolution. These played no small part in his
relationships with Schiller and Goethe. When Reichardt died in 1814,
he left behind some 1500 songs, settings of 125 poets in all. Many of these
still appear in modern anthologies of Lieder and have been recorded by
great singers, particularly his nearly 130 settings of Goethe's poems.

The key to Reichardt's work was his desire to achieve continuity in
change. His impressive technical virtuosity could perhaps have led to
Beethoven-like innovations, but his northern German prudence limited
his innovations to an awareness of poetic genius and a bolder use of
harmonic changes, so that the Lied became a true partnership between
voice and accompaniment. In his *Schreiben über die Berlinische Musik*
(Writings on Berlin's Music) of 1775, Reichardt wrote that "there was
no art so closely related to Nature as song." Furthermore, like other
musicians of the period, he believed that the "true, noble purpose of
music is well known," namely, that "the man who touches my heart,
arouses and soothes the passions, and who will delight me by thoughts
pleasing to the ear and which involve my intelligence, will fully serve
that purpose."[28] Although his music too should "penetrate to the heart,"
as C. P. E. Bach's should, his dislike of the trivial music of the *style galant*

is plain to see, not just because it is trivial, but, again, because it is foreign. The new poetry of the Storm and Stress movement had shown the
way. Every patriotic German composer, he wrote in his essay *Über die
Deutsche Comische Oper* (On the German Comic Opera, 1774), must wish
"that the time will come when we, too, might raise ourselves proudly
aloft as German poetry has just recently done."[29] Reichardt's interest in
the more natural poetry of the Storm and Stress movement had encouraged the rise of the Singspiel as a combination of German words and
music. This, in turn, enthused Goethe enough to make him write the
libretti that Reichardt then set to music. Reichardt's collections of *Odes
and Lieder* (1779–1781) contain many examples of songs from Goethe's
Singspiele.

What becomes very clear from a study of Reichardt's life and work
is that he is anything but a stiff, conservative, subservient musician who
believed that his task was simply to supply pleasantly simple music to
intellectually superior poetic words. In volume one of his *Musikalisches
Kunstmagazin* (1782), Reichardt showed that he was looking for a true
marriage of minds: "That concise, convoluted language sweeping
broadly on can, it seems to me, only be expressed in harmonic ties,
arresting resolutions, progressions by means of dissonances and the
like."[30] These would not seem to be the words of a man who, as Max
Friedlaender claimed in 1916, believed that "only the externals of the
poetic text should be reproduced in the music—the poem should only
be *illustrated* by the music."[31] Friedlaender's words were written at a
time when it was fashionable to show that Goethe's ignoring of Schubert
was primarily due to the machinations of Reichardt, and then of Zelter.

Karl Friedrich Zelter

Karl Friedrich Zelter (1758–1832) was born in Berlin and came from a
markedly un-intellectual background. He was a mason, a builder, who
only later became a musician, but then rose dizzily to become director of
the influential Academy of Vocal Music in Berlin. Some would trace his
brusque, often rude manner back to his unfashionable roots and would
apply Goethe's statement that "it was the authoritarians who hinder
progress" to support the thesis that Zelter's long association with
Goethe, from the late 1790s to their deaths in 1832, helped to close the
older man's mind to any experiments in music generally, and to contemporary music and therefore to Franz Schubert's in particular.

Zelter, like Zumsteg and Reichardt before him, was a patriotic German who abhorred the foreign influences in the musical culture of his
country. Coming of age in the 1780s, he was well aware of the patriotic

force of the literary revival of the 1770s and believed early that it was the poetic word, and Goethe's, above all, which was restoring the cultural independence of Germany. He bitterly attacked those composers who regarded a poem "as a mere document, as a sort of lark-spit on which to turn a melody." The melody must be directed to the main word of the poem if the poem is to remain what it was.[32] This type of remark and Zelter's preference (on the whole) for the strophic song over the through-composed song have led commentators on the Lied to stamp him as "conservative," but he, too, composed many non-strophic Lieder that can be heard on several modern recordings. His later support for a revival of the music of Johann Sebastian Bach did not endear him to the advocates of contemporary music.

For many southern Germans and Austrians, Zelter remains the archetypal northern German with all the characteristics of the race: thorough, efficient, and hard-working on the one hand, inartistic, unimaginative, and sometimes brutal on the other. Goethe wrote to Duke Karl August in 1805 about Zelter: "If hard work, or efficiency were ever to be lost to the world, we could restore it through him."[33] During their long correspondence, the poet veered between admiration for, and impatience with, the composer. For this reason it is easy to see why lovers and advocates of Schubert's music have little time for the man who, they would claim, prevented Goethe from sampling his Lieder.

Zelter first brought himself to Goethe's notice in 1795 when he set the poet's reworking of *Ich denke dein* (I think of you), a poem by Friederike Brun; Goethe said of his setting that he had never thought music could be so beautiful. Zelter set sixty-eight Goethe poems altogether. Few nowadays would place him in the first flight of Lieder composers; his love of church music is too clearly seen in his stiff, choralelike melodies and in his work with secular choirs. He was responsible for inventing what is still a feature of amateur singing in Germany, the *Liedertafel* (literally, the "song table"), that custom of (usually) men singing in four-part harmony in taverns. Yet there are good judges of German Lieder who would defend Zelter, reminding us of our attitudes to contemporary music and wondering how we would have reacted had we been living in Zelter's day and age and been confronted with a Beethoven Fifth Symphony, or, having been brought up on simple melodic folk songs, come to terms with a Schubert *Erlkönig*.

Later in the nineteenth century, Johannes Brahms proclaimed that the strophic song was the highest form of the Lied. A song like Zelter's subtly varied strophic setting of Goethe's *Um Mitternacht* (At Midnight) would fit without shame into any Lieder recital and might prove that the Berlin composer could craft a beautiful melody and a fine accompaniment. Many of his songs, such as Goethe's *Gleich und gleich* (Like and Like), display delightful comic and rhythmical touches along with clever harmonic deviations that show that he was indeed an accomplished musician.

When Zelter died, shortly after Goethe, in 1832, their mutual friend Friedrich Rochlitz, the editor of the music periodical *Allgemeine musikalische Zeitung*, wrote:[34]

> In his Lieder, Zelter wanted nothing else but to place the truly significant and beautiful poem in the center of the ruling emotion within him, and to express that in music; but, at the same time, he wanted to imitate, as far as possible, the form in which the poet had expressed himself, or, at least, to preserve that as best he could; he wanted to do this honestly and sensibly and would not cease until he had attained that goal.

We now turn to see how these and other musicians' views and works affected Johann Wolfgang von Goethe's perception of, and attitude to, music.

CHAPTER TWO

Goethe, Music, and Musicians

A nyone who has read through the huge correspondence (in German) between Goethe and the composer Karl Friedrich Zelter could never doubt Goethe's love of, interest in, and need for music. No one would assert that Goethe was a musician, but to write, as Hans Keller did, that he was "genuinely, profoundly *un*-musical" seems quite ludicrous.[1] For Goethe, words and music were on the same plane. He wrote once: "Were language not indisputably the highest (art) that we have, then I should place music still higher than language and right at the top."[2] He possessed a musicality that many, who were not trained as musicians, share.

> If one understands by musicality, the ability to enjoy music and to make it part of one's life, to incorporate its essence and its intellectual achievements by thinking and commenting on it, to be open to its historical and scientific requirements and to its formal qualities—all that is a quite different form of musicality,

was the opinion of one writer.[3]

For Goethe, music was synonymous with pleasurable emotions. After one of his serious illnesses in 1801, he wrote to Reichardt on 5 February that "the first major longing that I had after my illness was for music."[4] Friedrich Blume quoted this letter in his *Goethe und die Musik* to support his belief that Goethe had a deep relationship to music.[5]

In this chapter we will consider Goethe's knowledge of and interest in music generally and in song-setting in particular. We will also examine his connections with various composers, including Haydn, Mozart, and Beethoven, and his friendships with others, such as Johann Reichardt and Karl Zelter.

The eighteenth century was generally known in Europe as the Age of Enlightenment. Although this century held much promise for all peoples in its pursuit of noble and worthwhile goals, it was also a century of constant warring that brought much misery to many ordinary families. From Louis XIV's death in 1715, Europe was almost constantly in a state of war: the War of the Spanish Succession (1701–1713), the War of the Polish Succession (1733–1738), the War of the Austrian Succession (1740–1748), and the Seven Years' War (1756–1763).

In the midst of these turbulent periods of bloody warfare, on 28 August 1749 at twelve midday precisely, after his eighteen-year-old mother had been three days in labor, a sickly child, Johann Wolfgang Goethe, was born black after a difficult birth.[6] Goethe's house in central Germany, although severely damaged in the Second World War, is still standing in the street called Hirschgraben. The house has been refurbished and is a tourist mecca without equal for visitors to Frankfurt.

In those days, Frankfurt, with a population of thirty-six thousand, was one of fifty-one free cities in a geographical area called Germany, but which had no semblance of unity. Scores of princes, counts, and prelates ruled their tiny, self-contained territories of some two hundred thousand citizens in total. Even then, Frankfurt had something of the European significance that it bears today. Not only was it the venue of the coronation of the new Holy Roman Emperor Joseph II in 1765, it was also the banking center of Europe, which financed many important commercial transactions of the times, mainly, alas, the wars mentioned above. Yet there was another and more pleasant side to the coin, as described by Eda Sagarra: "Music was a feature of everyday life at court, as well as a vital element on all great occasions." Many actors at the theaters in those courts were employed as opera singers, "hence the origin of the Singspiel, forerunner of the operetta with its spoken dialogue and arias with musical accompaniment."[7] Sagarra cited particularly how the Elector of Mainz shared a troupe of actors with the nearby city of Frankfurt.

Goethe's Frankfurt in 1749 illustrates Walter Bruford's bald assertion that "*the* German art is music."[8] Although the city could hardly be called a musical metropolis, the presence of composer Georg Philipp Telemann and the orchestras that he led in Frankfurt till 1721 had brought many to his concerts. Few well-to-do families failed to have their children instructed in playing an instrument or in singing. Nor would they fail to encourage them to attend, not only the many domestic concerts, but also those grand occasions when great musical virtuosi visited Frankfurt.[9]

In his autobiography *Dichtung und Wahrheit* (Poetry and Truth), published in various volumes between 1811 and 1833, Goethe recounts the musical experiences of his financially comfortable childhood.[10] In Book One he tells how his mother accompanied his old teacher of Italian, Domenico Giovinazzi, in Italian arias and duets on the clavier. Thus young Wolfgang was encouraged to learn by heart the Italian words of the Abbé Metastasio's aria *Solitario bosco ombroso* before he even understood them. This Italian experience, and his listening with great enjoyment to the chorales and organ music during his Sunday church visits, fired the boy's musical imagination and led him later to compose an Italian libretto *La sposa rapita* (The Stolen Bride), which he destroyed when he was seventeen.

Goethe's relationship with his strict, upright father, Johann Caspar Goethe, was often a strained one. In Book Eight of his autobiography, he could not resist a slightly malicious comment on his father's musical pretensions: "He tuned his lute longer than he played it." His mother, Katharina Elisabeth, was always genuinely, even passionately, fond of music; she boasted in a charming letter to her son on 19 May 1801 that she "plays not badly for a seventy year old."[11] The little poem that Goethe wrote at this time described his parents' character very accurately: "From Father comes my stature lithe / And the rules that Life entails. / From Mother came my nature blithe / And the joy in telling tales."[12]

Although obviously music-making at that level remained amateurish, Goethe, from his earliest years, was keenly aware of the effect that music could produce. He had learned the basics of music from his piano teacher Johann Andreas Bismann, starting in 1765. A young Jena musician, David Veit, after visiting Goethe in Weimar in 1795, reported to his sister that Goethe played the clavier "not too badly."[13] Goethe's other musical interest, the cello, also accompanied the poet throughout his life.

The nature of Goethe's father led to many disagreements with his son, yet both supported Frederick the Great's Prussia when the Seven Years' War broke out in 1756. The rest of the family championed Austria and were not too downcast when Maria Theresa's French allies occupied Frankfurt in 1759, nor, in retrospect, was Goethe, for the French civilian governor of Frankfurt, the count François Thoranc, billeted in the Goethe house, proved himself to be a highly civilized man. He brought the young boy not only practice in the French language, but also free entrée to the French music and plays being performed in the newly opened theater. These early acquaintanceships with the Italian and French cultures and the music of their languages were to prove important for the poet in later life.

Although Goethe lived to the ripe age of eighty-two, his family felt the hand of death as did so many in those days. After he was born in 1749 and his sister Cornelia in 1750, the other Goethe children—Hermann Jakob (1752–1759), Katharina Elisabeth (1754–1756), Johann Maria (1757–1759), and Georg Adolf (1760–1761)—all died of smallpox, measles, or dysentery. Wealth was obviously no protection. When critics of Goethe's musical taste deride his preference for "cheerful music" and his famed "avoidance of tragedy" in his dramas, they should remember those tragic personal circumstances of his early youth. His beloved sister Cornelia died at the age of twenty-seven, while Goethe was often seriously ill during his long life. Such an illness, a type of tuberculosis that had damaged a lung, forced him to abandon his studies in Leipzig and return home to Frankfurt on his nineteenth birthday in 1768.

Johann Sebastian Bach, who died in 1750, the year after Goethe's birth, looms large in any discussion of Goethe's interest in music and musicians. At a time when the German composer's music had become unfashionable, Goethe continued to listen to and to appreciate Bach's works. Bach had worked as composer, organist, and cantor at the Thomas Church in Leipzig from 1723 to his death there in 1750. His fame was fading when the sixteen-year-old Goethe went, at his father's insistence, to study law at the University of Leipzig.

The city of Leipzig, with roughly the same population as Frankfurt (some thirty thousand), had gained the sobriquet "Little Paris," as one of the major centers of the then-modish French *style galant.* Goethe, wealthier than most of the students, was able to take full advantage of Leipzig's fashionable theaters and concert halls, where the new Singspiele were beginning to be produced. The composer Johann Adam Hiller is credited with having introduced the genre into his Concerts for Music Lovers in Leipzig between 1763 and 1778, having modeled them on the celebrated *concerts spirituels* in Paris.

The young Goethe's music-making in 1766 with a daughter of the famous Leipzig music publisher Johann Gottlieb Immanuel Breitkopf gives us a glimpse of the man of years to come, the poet who always thought in terms of poetry and music. Years later Goethe wrote in a letter of 27 August 1820 to Carl von Schlözer about what a musical setting does to a poem: "A new poem is created by this, something which must surprise the poet himself."[14] The young student had begun to write poems in the then-prevailing Anacreontic style, recalling the verses of the sixth-century B.C. Greek poet Anacreon. Twenty of those were copied down by the publisher's brother and published in 1770 as *New*

Lieder Set to Melodies by Bernhard Theodor Breitkopf. Alas, Breitkopf was no Mozart and the settings remain a juvenile curiosity, particularly since the publication bore only the composer's and not the poet's name. Nevertheless, those were the only Goethe settings to be published for the next twenty years.

Goethe's short-lived love affair with Anna Catharina Schönkopf (known as "Käthchen"), the daughter of one of his favorite innkeepers, and his meeting with a singer who was to play an important role in his future life, were of much more interest and importance. Käthchen was one of the first of many women for and to whom Goethe wrote poems. The singer was Corona Schröter, one of Leipzig's best-known Singspiel sopranos, whom Goethe came to know very well. She was to earn undying fame by being the first to set his ballad *Erlkönig* (Erl-King) to music.

In Book Seven of his autobiography, Goethe wrote that those early poetic attempts set him on a path that led to his turning whatever hand fate dealt him, be it pleasing or painful, into a poem so that "everything that became known about me was just fragments of a great confession." This familiar quotation will be particularly relevant when we examine what Goethe's poems meant for Franz Schubert.

Goethe returned to Frankfurt in 1768 and remained for three years. During that period music was very important to him. The French Opéra Comique was certainly the city's dominant musical force. Goethe attended many performances at the Opéra and, in Book Eight of his autobiography, he wrote warmly of the work of its director, Theobald Marchand.

Frankfurt held little attraction for Goethe after his fairly riotous student life in Leipzig. When, in 1769, his father suggested that he should study for a doctorate in law at the University of Strasbourg in Alsace, the young man was delighted. Strasbourg, with a population of some forty thousand, had been ruled by France since 1679, but a patriotic German movement had been steadily gaining ground there. After his arrival in March 1770, Goethe soon became a leading member of the university's German student circle.

By far Goethe's most important friend at the university was Johann Gottfried Herder, a well-known writer, who had come to Strasbourg for treatment of an eye complaint. Like Goethe, Herder was impressed by the German character of this ostensibly French town. He had written widely on the importance of German language and literature for his nation and had been inspired to dream of rendering a similar service to his national culture. This inspiration came from Scottish writer James

Macpherson's *Ossian* translations and from Bishop Percy's publication of the old Scottish and English ballads.

At twenty-one, Goethe had become something of a man about town, and it was in this guise that he paid a visit with a friend, F. L. Weyland, on 15 October 1770 to Pastor Jakob Brion in the little village of Sesenheim (also Sessenheim), some distance from Strasbourg. Goethe's version of what took place, recounted in Book Eleven of *Poetry and Truth*, has been shown to be embellished—more poetry than truth, indeed—but the love affair with the eighteen-year-old daughter, Friederike Elisabeth Brion, is fairly well documented. As was often to happen in Goethe's life, his feelings there seemed to be sincere, and they were certainly reciprocated, possibly sexually as well.

Before the climax of that affair, Goethe had been asked by Herder in 1771 to undertake a task that appealed enormously to him, one that would change not only his poetic style, but also his life. Goethe had been studying the cello and attending many concerts in Strasbourg, and was therefore very ready, as a poet, to agree with Herder's suggestion that they should emulate Macpherson and Percy and collect some of the old German folk songs of Alsace. In this way, they would discover what they both felt to be the soul of a country—the *Volkslied*, the folk song, that unique combination of words and music. The task fascinated the young student. He returned with twelve Lieder, taken, as he wrote when he sent them to Herder, "from the throats of the oldest dearies" and containing "the old melodies as God created them."[15] Three of these Lieder appeared later in Herder's publication of European folk songs, *Volkslieder* (1778–1779). This was to form an important element in that renaissance of German literature, the Storm and Stress movement of the 1770s. All Goethe's poems from this period, including his work on the "original" *Faust* (the *Urfaust*), were influenced by this introduction to the German folk song and his consequent opposition to the *style galant* and other foreign influences. This attitude could only be emphasized by his liaison with a simple German country girl like Friederike. The resultant poetry, simpler, more direct, and, at times erotic, shaped future poetry in the German language. Since its form proved to be eminently suitable for setting to music, it was to become a link in that unseen bond between Goethe and Schubert. One of the most celebrated examples would be the Ossianic poem *Willkommen und Abschied* (Hail and Farewell, 1775), which immortalized Goethe's visit to and departure from Friederike.

After further meetings with Friederike in 1771, Goethe abruptly left the girl and Sesenheim on 9 August 1771. Although it is unlikely that, as some rumors had it, he abandoned her with an illegitimate child, he car-

ried the guilt around with him for many years to come. He had pro-
ceeded to the title of Doctor of Law, not by the more academically stren-
uous path of degree examinations, but by licentiate, which only
required public disputation of some legal theses. He had, of course,
spent much more time on his writings than on his studies—poems,
essays, *Faust*, and plays such as *Götz von Berlichingen* (1771).

WETZLAR AND *WERTHER*

Qualified now as a lawyer, and, again at his father's insistence, Goethe
took in May 1772 a post in the little town of Wetzlar, some thirty miles
north of Frankfurt, to work in the imperial legal system. Here again the
Goethean heart ruled the head. The outcome was a poetic work, but,
this time, one that was to make his name famous all over Europe.

In June 1772, Goethe met Johann Christian Kestner, who had been
engaged for four years to a pretty eighteen-year-old, Charlotte (Lotte)
Buff. When Goethe presumed too far in his obvious attraction to (and
for) Lotte and kissed her, her fiancé showed his displeasure, and Goethe's embryonic "affair" ended in August. What appeared at first sight
to have been a fairly insignificant event became the seed-bed for the
novel that shook and shocked Europe: *Die Leiden des jungen Werther*
(1774).

As was Goethe's habit when events became too much for him, he
immediately left Wetzlar. This habit earned him the nickname of the
Wanderer, which, curiously enough, he was later to share with Franz
Schubert. He wrote self-pityingly to Kestner on 15 April 1773, after hearing that Kestner and Lotte had finally married on 11 April, and that his
beloved sister Cornelia had also been married. As he had earlier learned
that a Wetzlar friend, Karl Wilhelm Jerusalem, had committed suicide
because of his despairing love for the wife of a friend, Goethe poured his
self-pity into the novel which, as he wrote in Book Thirteen of *Poetry
and Truth*, "allowed no differentiation between poetry and truth."[16]

Literary criticism is not our concern here; what is interesting about
the *Werther* novel is the role that music plays in its development and the
reverberations that it caused in the music world. An epistolary novel,
Werther explores, like so much music of the eighteenth century, the language of the heart. "I turn into myself and find a world," Werther writes
on 22 May.[17] When he is falling in love with Lotte, their mutual love of
dancing brings them together, literally and metaphorically, so that,
when the passionate lover is alone, he can "drum out a contredanse"
on his ill-tuned piano. He is delighted when Lotte performs German

dances with him and is in seventh heaven when it comes to waltzing and "we rolled around one another like the spheres," until Lotte admits to him, in the letter of 16 June 1771, that she is almost engaged to Albert. Later, on 16 July, Werther writes about Lotte playing the piano: "She has a melody which she plays on the piano with the touch of an angel, so simple and so brilliant." Werther-Goethe tells (and not for the last time) of the effect that music has on him: "No word of the old magical power of music seems unlikely to me. How a simple song moves me."

When it is not music that is moving Werther-Goethe, then it is Macpherson's *Ossian* translations. "Ossian has replaced Homer in my heart," he writes on 12 October 1772, as the clouds of despair begin to gather around him. When he makes one of his last visits to Lotte, she hands him his translation of Ossian's odes, and he reads *Kolmas Klage* (Colma's Plaint) to her at some length. (Schubert set this ode to music on 22 June 1815.)

Werther and *Ossian* were later to prove so important to Schubert and the Romantics of the early nineteenth century. *Werther* was translated into English in 1779, and there were more than seven editions available by 1800. Goethe was later moved to learn that Napoleon would not travel anywhere without it and claimed to have read the French translation seven times. In chapter 15 of Mary Shelley's novel *Frankenstein or The Modern Prometheus*, Frankenstein's nameless monster, miraculously able to read, describes Werther as "a more divine being than I had believed or imagined."[18]

The sentiments of the novel obviously appealed to nineteenth-century composers, too. No fewer than seven operas bear the name "Werther" in the title, the most famous perhaps being Jules Massenet's four-acter *Werther* of 1892. Yet famous though Goethe became, it was not the type of fame that German culture, striving to be recognized as independent, was seeking. This novel barred many contemporary composers from considering Goethe's other works as suitable for musical setting. In religious circles such as the Austrian Catholic communities, *Werther* was regarded as immoral, and even the *Hamburgische Nachrichten* newspaper of 21 March 1775 thundered out: "Dear God! What times have you allowed us to suffer!" and condemned the tacit adultery and Werther's suicide as blasphemy.[19] Goethe realized only too well how self-destructive his novel had become. His image as the Wanderer, the isolated one, had been reinforced.

POETRY AND MUSIC IN FRANKFURT

Returning to Frankfurt, Goethe began in the Lent season of 1775 to attend a series of card parties and balls at the home of the Schönemanns, an affluent banking family in Offenbach, not far from Frankfurt. There he met and immediately fell in love with the Schönemanns' sixteen-year-old daughter, Anna Elisabeth, whom he called "Lili." They were engaged in April, very shortly after meeting. Not only beautiful, but vivacious and cultured, Lili was the most intelligent young woman that Goethe had met to date. His remark to Frédéric Soret on 5 March 1830 demonstrates what he thought of her: "I was never so near to real happiness as in the period of that love for Lili . . . she was indeed the first woman that I deeply and truly loved. And I can say that she was also the last . . . and yet I lost her."[20] The similarity to Franz Schubert's experience will be seen to be striking, although many, and not just among female readers, would say that here was one woman who gave Goethe a taste of his own medicine.

Goethe met the composer Johann André at the Schönemanns' musical evenings. Their friendship proved to be more productive than Goethe's previous relationship with Theobald Marchand and the French Opéra Comique. The two men admired the excellent piano playing of Lili Schönemann and shared an interest in setting German poetry to music. André's setting of Bürger's ballad *Lenore* is no masterpiece, but Goethe's enthusiasm for it and his setting of *Das Veilchen* (The Violet, 1774) were probably the cause of his decision to have André write the music for his Singspiel *Erwin und Elmire* (1775), which was influenced by his reading of Oliver Goldsmith's *Vicar of Wakefield* (1766). A respected nineteenth-century critic, Ferdinand Hiller, wrote about Goethe's "lyrical pearls" in this Singspiel that were "far beyond the best texts ever offered to theater composers." One of those pearls was, in fact, *Das Veilchen*.[21] The piece had little success at its Frankfurt première, yet it had no fewer than twenty-four performances in the National Theater in Berlin. (André's setting of another Goethe Singspiel *Claudine von Villa Bella* was less successful.) André was soon superseded in Goethe's musical affections by the young composer Philipp Kayser.

Poetry and music dominated Goethe's years in Frankfurt. His experiences in Strasbourg had given him more confidence in his national musical heritage. He wrote later in one of the alternative passages for his autobiography, "for as soon as we begin to talk about the revelation of the inner self, of its transmission, then poetry, made perfect by music, will be the surest interpreter."[22] These were certainly the years of some of his greatest and, to use Thrasybulos Georgiades' word, most *musika-*

bel (that is, able to be set to music because of their intrinsic musicality) poems. These included the poems in *Faust*, along with *An Schwager Kronos, Der Wandrer, Mailied, Neue Liebe, neues Leben, Heidenröslein, Das Veilchen, Auf dem See, Ganymed*, and *Prometheus*—all of which were "most suitable for setting to music."[23] Many of the poems mirrored his short-lived affair with Lili Schönemann. He wrote *Claudine von Villa Bella*, the most charming of his Singspiel libretti, in 1774–1775, just before leaving for Weimar and after breaking off his engagement to Lili Schönemann in Frankfurt, in September 1775. His later poetic masterpiece *Faust*, "which came to me at the same time as *Werther*," he said to his amanuensis, Johann Peter Eckermann, on 10 February 1829, obviously mirrors his whole life experience at that time.[24]

Goethe's acceptance of the offer to be tutor and companion to the eighteen-year-old future Duke Karl August of Saxe-Weimar-Eisenach in his capital Weimar is an example of what Shakespeare referred to in act 4, scene 3 of *Julius Caesar* as "a tide in the affairs of men / Which, taken at the flood, leads on to fortune." Goethe was to remain and grow old in Weimar for the next fifty-seven years, but he arrived there as a tempestuous twenty-six year old, who was described by an acquaintance in Weimar as "the most handsome, liveliest, most original, most glowing, most impetuous, yet, at the same time, the most gentle, most seductive, in short, for a woman's heart, the most dangerous man she had met in her whole life."[25] This description was sent in a letter to a certain Charlotte von Stein in Weimar on 19 January 1775, a curious introduction to a man who was to play a central role in her life and she in his.

When Goethe arrived in Weimar on 7 November 1775, the city was still a good example of what was called particularism. Like all political systems, particularism had its good and its bad points; bad in that it led to an inward-looking provincialism, good in that, because these small states were largely independent, they had to create their social and cultural structures including army, legal, court, educational, theatrical, and musical establishments. To this day, cities such as Hamburg, Cologne, Frankfurt, Stuttgart, and Munich can boast opera houses and concert halls that are the envy of many capital cities.

This was not, of course, the situation in little Weimar in 1775. It numbered a mere six thousand or so inhabitants, had few connections with the outside world (even the mail-coach could not reach it), and had few claims to fame. Lukas Cranach the Elder (1472–1553) died there, and three of the Bach family had lived there. Johann Sebastian's sons Wilhelm Friedemann and Carl Philipp Emanuel were born in the town in

1710 and 1714, respectively, but only the father has a bust to his name in the square in present-day Weimar.

Any remembrances of Sebastian Bach had vanished in the blaze of 1774 when the ducal palace, the Wilhelmsburg, and Bach's St. Martin's church were both destroyed. Goethe found that Bach's successor as musical director, Ernst Wolf, while a competent musician, had no interest in literature. In his thirty years in Weimar, Wolf did not set a single poem by Goethe; his volume *Lieder of Germany's Favorite Poets* of 1782 ignored Goethe completely. This was not just due to his musical taste, nor indeed to Goethe's immoral reputation, but to the, at times, embarrassingly wild behavior of the young duke and his new courtier. Their nocturnal rides through and parties in the woods round Weimar became the stuff of Weimar scandal and legend.

Years later, in 1818, the poet wrote to a friend, C. E. Schubarth, that he had been told that a group of poems written then were among the "sweetest" that he had ever written.[26] One of these, titled *Warum gabst du uns die tiefen Blicke?* (Why Did You Lend Us Such an Insight . . . into Our Future?), written in April 1776, contains the line "You dropped moderation into my hot blood," which we know in retrospect was the result of his friendship with Charlotte Ernestina von Stein (née von Schardt, 1742–1827). Charlotte von Stein, who had been (unhappily) married to a Baron von Stein, seven years her senior, for eleven years, had suffered seven painful pregnancies and had lost four children. Although we know what she meant to Goethe—some 1800 of his letters are extant— her feelings for him are less obvious, since she had all her 1500 letters to him returned and destroyed shortly before her death in 1827, at the age of eighty-four. Although the depth of their friendship has been endlessly probed but never fully revealed, clearly she calmed Goethe's wildness and, for the next eleven years, supported him in his work for the duke.

While Charlotte von Stein was perhaps the major cause of Goethe's change of behavior, Karl August's mother, Dowager Duchess Anna Amalia, a niece of Frederick the Great, was responsible for encouraging Goethe to further his theatrical and musical interests. Throughout her life, she was more than just a dilettante musician. She was the type of musician that the court lacked, one who, as a skilled pianist, was more interested in making music than analyzing it. She too set Goethe's *Erwin und Elmire* to music, as well as some of his poems. "One did not just make music; aesthetic questions were also discussed, and one sought to relate music to the general intellectual life of the time," wrote Hermann Abert.[27] Paintings of these meetings can be seen today in the duchess' fine house in Tiefurt, near Weimar. Goethe can be seen in these paintings for he often joined in their discussions. As far as we know he never played music with the group, but he did have the opportunity, both there, and with the music-loving family of the Steins, to further his interest in music.

Charlotte played flute and piano, her husband flute, her elder brother cello, and her younger brother the "Mozart" instrument, the glass harmonica. The music played and enjoyed was largely that of Bach's sons, Haydn, and Mozart—harmonic, melodic, and ordered music that blended with Goethe's new quieter life of duty and responsibility and that brought him peace and consolation. He wrote to Charlotte on 22 February 1779: "My soul is slowly freeing itself from the bonds of protocols and documents. There is a quartet playing in the green room nearby. I sit and gently call the distant figures over to me."[28] Quartet music seemed to give Goethe as much pleasure as any form of music. Later, he wrote to his musician friend Karl Friedrich Zelter on 9 November 1829: "One listens to four intelligent people conversing with one another and we feel that we can gain something from their discourse and get to know the characteristics of their instruments."[29]

Yet, as one might expect from a shaper of words and an experienced raconteur, it was the human voice that most fascinated Goethe. In 1776, he traveled to nearby Leipzig to engage the soprano Corona Schröter for the Weimar court. Schröter's presence in Weimar raised the level of theatrical and musical discernment considerably; here was a high-class actress and singer who turned out to be something of a composer as well. Goethe tried his charms again on her when she arrived, but their relationship was to remain strictly professional there. They acted together in Goethe's play *Iphigenie auf Tauris*. Goethe had also written a little Singspiel, *Die Fischerin* (The Fisherwoman), in 1781 and persuaded Schröter to play the leading role. Not only did she do that very well, she also composed the music for the song with which the play (curiously) opens: *Erlkönig*. Writing to composer Philipp Kayser on 29 December 1779, Goethe had stipulated that the song should have a "melody which one can assume the singer had learned by heart and is now recalling in a certain situation. Such songs can, and ought to, have their own definite and complete melodies which are distinct and memorable."[30] Schröter's melody was a very simple one. One wonders how Goethe and his audience would have reacted to Schubert's 1815 setting?

In 1782, the year in which Goethe had been ennobled as "von Goethe" (on 19 April), his friend Herder wrote: "So he is now permanent privy councilor, president of the chamber, president of the war office, inspector of works down to road-building, director of mines" and many other offices.[31] The poet's cultural sanity was probably preserved by two factors. The first was that close, though ambiguous relationship with Charlotte von Stein. Hundreds of letters passed between them, although their houses in Weimar are only a few minutes from each other. Many poems of this time testify to Goethe's unceasing burning passion for the older, married woman.[32] Second only to that diversion was Goethe's equally close involvement with the Weimar court theater as its director.

THE ITALIAN JOURNEY, 1786–1788

Before becoming director of the Weimar court theater in 1791, Goethe embarked on another experience that was to change his life yet again. Tired of his excessive administrative duties in Weimar—"I feel I have wings that are not being used," he had written as far back as 1780[33]— possibly also frustrated by his unresolved relationship with Charlotte von Stein, he left tiny provincial Weimar on 24 July 1786, ostensibly to take the waters in Karlsbad. Having made preparations for an absence of eight months, he was able to arrive in Karlsbad under the assumed name of merchant Johann Philipp Möller. Then, without giving notice of his departure to any one in Weimar, he left for the land of his dreams. Later he wrote of his Italian journey, "At three in the morning, I stole out of Karlsbad because they would not have let me go otherwise."[34]

Goethe's father, who died on 25 May 1782, had been passionately fond of Italy and the Italian language. The desire to "go south" was in Goethe from earliest childhood and seems still to be in every German, who would probably subscribe to Goethe's emotions when he finally reached Italy. "Auch ich in Arkadien" (I am in Arcadia, too), he wrote and used later as the subtitle of his account.

Goethe often described himself as one to whom objects seen were most important, and he claimed that he was attracted mainly by the beauty of classical Italian architecture. This remark is often used to support the thesis that Goethe was, therefore, "unmusical." However, his many comments on music heard during that stay from 1786 to 1788 lead one to believe that it, too, formed a never-to-be-forgotten part of his great experience.

His first music experience was in Vicenza where he saw a performance of an *Il Seraglio* (not by Mozart) on 20 September: "The music was not bad, but was probably by an amateur." A visit to a conservatory by the Church of the Mendicants in Venice on 3 October to hear an oratorio on the subject of King Saul was praised for its music, but not for its "Italianate Latin," which made Goethe laugh.[35] One of his most enjoyable music experiences was on 6 October, listening in the moonlight to the gondoliers singing their melodies to the words of Tasso and Ariosto, the medieval Italian poets. He described the music in some detail: "The melody . . . is something between chorale and recitative; it maintains the same cadence throughout with no fixed time. The modulation is also uniform with a sort of declamation in both tone and tempo." Goethe never forgot this experience. Talking to Eckermann on 3 May 1827 about the songs of Robert Burns, he said: "How many of my songs still live? One or the other will be sung by a pretty girl at the piano, but among our own people, all is quiet," and he thought back to those gondoliers singing passages from Tasso. (By that time, Franz Schubert had composed all eighty settings of Goethe's texts.)

Goethe set off by boat for Rome on 16 October 1786 and arrived on 1 November. During his four months' stay, he enjoyed the benefits of the presence of the small, but artistically active German colony at the Caffè Greco (the Caffè Tedesco, as it became known) near the Piazza di Spagna. The gifted painter, Angelika Kauffmann, a friend of Sir Joshua Reynolds, proved to be a very useful contact, as did Johann Heinrich Meyer, Goethe's future amanuensis in art appreciation.

Goethe's arrival in Naples, then a major city of half a million people, in February 1787 was followed by an ascent of Vesuvius on 2 March. "See Naples and die!" he wrote with heartfelt relief on his return. This type of intellectual tourism prevented him from enjoying quieter pursuits. Those visits, however, can be regarded in another way; after all, he was Goethe and a German. He wrote on 22 March 1787 while still in Naples: "Were I not forced by my German nature more to learn and to do rather than to enjoy," then he could have profited more from the carefree life all around him. (Typically, therefore, it was on the dangerous boat journey back from Sicily to Naples on 8 May 1787 that he wrote his poems *Meeresstille* (Calm Sea) and *Glückliche Fahrt* (Prosperous Voyage), reflecting the sudden becalming of the wind that was drifting the boat towards some dangerous rocks.)

Goethe returned to Rome on 6 June 1787 where he stayed until 24 April 1788. For various reasons not unconnected with matters of the heart, this period proved to be the most productive. He was busy writing the drama *Egmont* in which music was to play an important role. He stipulated two songs for Egmont's beloved Klärchen, the intermezzo and incidental music and the stirring music demanded for the final scene: "Drums, as he (Egmont) goes to the guard and the back-door, the curtain falls, the music begins, and ends the play with a Victory Symphony." The play was finished on 5 September 1787. His writing and quiet life were disturbed only once when he was determined to let Angelika Kauffmann (who was not fond of the theater) hear "the effectiveness of our Cimarosa's music," and he engaged singers from the opera to give a festival for her.[36] Unfortunately, the arrival of so many guests in their fine carriages made the local inhabitants believe that Goethe was a rich milord, a reputation he and his artistic friends were never to lose.

Happy though he was with the excellence of much of the music he heard, Goethe never came to terms with what is still the bane of visiting opera lovers in Italy—the movement and chattering of the audiences. The German group visited a performance in September 1787, and Goethe wrote that only "by a call of 'Quiet!', at first gentle, then louder, and finally imperiously . . . did we bring the whole loudly chattering public to silence."

The arrival in November 1787 of twenty-year-old Philipp Christoph Kayser allowed Goethe to concentrate his thoughts on music again, this time, music for his Singspiele *Scherz, List und Rache, Claudine von Villa Bella,* and *Erwin und Elmire,* as well as for *Egmont.* "You can imagine what a feast that will be!" he had written on 27 October. With this visit in mind, Goethe had been collecting libretti to present *opera buffa* in German in Weimar. He had asked Kayser on 29 December 1779 to write the music for another Singspiel, *Jery und Bätely,* set in Switzerland, and then had set out his demands in a very professional manner. There should be three sorts of vocal music. First, there would be songs that everyone would suppose the singer had learned by heart and could be placed into any situation. Second, there would be arias, where the singer would express the emotions of the moment and, completely lost in it, sing from the bottom of his heart; the melody and the accompaniment were to be handled "very conscientiously." Third comes the "rhythmic dialogue" that gives the whole scene its movement. If the composer is lucky enough to find a main theme, he must bring it out often, giving it nuances by major-minor modulations. And then the dialogue must be "like a smooth golden ring on which arias and songs sit like precious stones"[37] for, as he wrote in his *Italian Journey* on 10 January 1788, "when a Singspiel is good, reading it is not enough; the music must be added in order to express the whole idea that the poet had in mind." Thus, Goethe no doubt always heard or imagined music when he wrote poetic words. A composer and superlative pianist, Philipp Kayser shared many of the Werther-like Goethean characteristics. Since Goethe believed firmly then that the operatic librettist should always yield pride of place to the composer, he had high hopes that Kayser would be the man to clothe his libretti in music. He was to be sadly disappointed. Kayser failed to provide the music requested and faded from the scene. If only Goethe had found a truly gifted composer.

A controversy has always existed about the degree to which an artist's life, and in particular, his love life, should be taken into account when discussing his work. Goethe is the writer par excellence in this controversy, since many of his poems, termed derogatorily "occasional poems," are more or less intimately connected with his many love affairs. One has to live in a barred and bolted academic study not to accept that fact. The relationship with Charlotte von Stein in Weimar had clearly cooled, which may well have been one of the reasons for the flight to Italy. Goethe was only thirty-eight, and few of his descriptions of operas or ballets in the *Italian Journey* fail to mention the actresses' or singers' faces or figures. We know little of the major sexual episode that occurred in Rome in January 1788. It concerned a Faustina Antonini (née Giovanni), a twenty-four-year-old mother of a three-year-old boy, and she seems to have been only too willing to provide Goethe with what he was seeking. These assignations, which he called "agreeable promenades" in a letter to Duke Karl August on 16 February 1788, were his attempt to rid himself of what, on another occasion, he had called "the damned second pillow."[38] The episode is immortalized in the poet's *Roman Elegies*, particularly in No. 5 where the poet runs his hand up and down the back of his sleeping partner: "I see with a feeling eye, feel with a seeing hand," and then he taps out the hexameters as he composes poetry, although he might have been thinking of music as well. Just after that episode, he asked Kayser (on 9 February) to set his erotic poem *Cupido, loser, eigensinniger Knabe!* (Cupid, You Wanton, Self-willed Boy!) to music, describing it as "his favorite" poem.

Another of Goethe's greatest music experiences in Italy came shortly afterwards. "Kayser's presence raised and expanded our love of music," he had written in November 1787, and it was Kayser who accompanied Goethe to the Sistine Chapel on 1 March 1788. There they heard "an old motet by a Spaniard Morales" (Cristóbal Morales, 1500–1553), which reminded Goethe of the collection of Benedetto Marcello's psalms that they had in the house. Goethe dated the first fifty correctly from 1724 (six volumes to 1727) and praised that composer's "intelligence, artistic knowledge, and moderation." On 7 March he was in San Carlo, where they heard a Requiem Mass with two sopranos, "the strangest work that one could hear," and without organ or other accompaniment. (How Goethe disliked the organ. "It doesn't go with the human voice," he wrote, "and it is so powerful. How charming it is, on the other hand, to be in the Sistine Chapel, where the voices are on their own.") He did, however, much appreciate the taste and dignity of the services.

On Sunday, 14 March, Kayser and Goethe heard a Palestrina motet and, two days later, parts of the Holy Week music: "We followed it with the greatest ease and, since we sang it so often with the piano, were able to form a provisional idea of it." Goethe's Lutheran father had managed to stifle any religious feelings young Wolfgang might have had, and he was clearly quite happy to see the end of Holy Week.[39] It was the music that had attracted him so much. The celebrated *Miserere* of Gregorio Allegri was "unbelievably beautiful," as was the choir's "Populus meus, quid feci tibi?" (My people, what have I done to you?). Kayser was ordered to bring back to Germany all the music that was "transportable."

Goethe left Rome on 24 April 1788 to return to Weimar after paying a last visit to the statue of Marcus Aurelius. Later he would write that the statue, seen under a full moon, reminded him of the statue of the Commendatore in Mozart's *Don Giovanni*. The Wanderer identified with Ovid, who, banished from Rome, wrote: "I recall the night when I relinquished much of what was dear to me." Ovid would return to Rome; Goethe never did.

THE INFLUENCE OF SCHILLER AND REICHARDT

Goethe arrived back in Weimar on 18 June 1788 and within a month his life had changed again. In the "English garden" he had helped to create, a lovely park by the river Ilm, stood his little garden house. This two-storied cottage had become a refuge from his heavy administrative duties and from the visitors to his long, formal house on the Frauenplan square in the middle of the city. He was approached one day in the park by a twenty-three-year-old woman, Johanna Christiane Sophia Vulpius, with a request for aid for her brother August who hoped to become a writer. Christiane, who made artificial flowers in a shop, was certainly less grand than Charlotte von Stein, but Goethe's experiences in Rome had given him a taste for sexual excitement and, within a few weeks, Christiane was visiting him clandestinely in the garden house. She lived in the town, but was able to steal over the stone bridge above the Ilm unseen at night, through the park and into the little cottage. This strange liaison, much criticized by the Weimar court ladies, was to last until 1806 when Goethe finally married Christiane. Two erotic poems in particular, *Der Besuch* (The Visit) and *Morgenklagen* (Morning Complaint), often omitted from nineteenth-century editions of the poems, give vivid pictures of their assignations. Thus, Weimar now became a changed town for the poet. Charlotte had never forgiven Goethe his abrupt departure for Rome; the duke, a general in the Prussian army, was often absent on duty, and the dowager duchess had gone to Italy.

In these changed circumstances fortune brought the poet together, in 1788, with the man who was to share his European fame. Johann Christoph Friedrich Schiller, author of many of Germany's most famous ballads, became best known for his plays which then served as libretti for well-known nineteenth-century operas: *Kabale und Liebe* in 1784 (Verdi's *Luisa Miller*, 1849), *Don Carlos* in 1787 (Verdi, 1867), *Maria Stuart* in 1800 (Donizetti's *Maria Stuarda*, 1835), *Die Jungfrau von Orleans* in 1801 (Verdi's *Giovanna d'Arco*, 1845), and *Wilhelm Tell* in 1804 (Rossini's *Guillaume Tell*, 1829). The reason for their success as libretti lay, of course, in the power of the plots rather than in the "musicality" of the language. Till Schiller died in 1805, he and Goethe were among the leading literary figures in Europe. Speaking to Eckermann on 12 May 1825, Goethe said that the public had been arguing for the last twenty years about who was the greater; "Schiller or I. They should be happy that there were two fellows that they could argue about," he chuckled.

By this time, Goethe was engaged in the many intellectual pursuits that were eventually to earn him Thomas Carlyle's sobriquet, "the Universal Man": plays, novels, poems, painting, medical research, and archaeology added to his many administrative responsibilities. What room was left for music? Enough, it seemed. Goethe's questing mind and his genuine, deeply felt interest in (and need for) music had been strengthened by his Italian experiences. Kayser had certainly disappointed Goethe, but was promptly replaced by a man who had set some of Goethe's poems in his *Odes and Lieder* in 1780, Johann Friedrich Reichardt. Reichardt was one of those composers who had set out to combine the naturalness of the folk song with the more demanding aspects of the art song. His setting of Goethe's Singspiel *Claudine von Villa Bella* in 1789 introduced him to Goethe. This gave the poet the opportunity to still his hunger and have a truly professional musician's advice and help, albeit at some distance from Weimar—and a prolific musician to boot. In 1790, Reichardt provided settings for *Erwin und Elmire* and *Jery und Bätely*, as well as incidental music for *Götz von Berlichingen*. In 1791, he wrote music for other works of Goethe: *Clavigo, Lila, Tasso, Egmont*, and for the poems and songs in *Faust I*.

Whether his literary friend Schiller felt put out by this new attraction or whether Reichardt really was the "impertinent man" Schiller had written about earlier, both men eventually fell out with the composer and could not forgive him his Jacobin sympathies. Their ire was displayed particularly in some seventy-six of the sharply critical distichs written for Schiller's *Musenalmanach* (The Almanac of the Muses) in 1797. These were named *Xenien* (Xenia), in the original Greek meaning, "small presents given to a guest after a meal." Here they became viciously rude comments about people who had written against the two Weimar authors.

Reichardt set nearly 140 Goethe poems to music, many of which enjoyed great success in the nineteenth century, particularly the choral settings of 1789 that could be sung by (usually) men in four-part harmony at the *Liedertafeln* ("glee clubs") in taverns. Writers often report that Goethe admired Reichardt because he was also conservative, preferred strophic songs, and insisted that the poet's words were to be given preference over the composer's music. Nevertheless, an examination of Reichardt's songs (nearly 1500 settings of 125 poets) seems to prove that, on the contrary, he took the Lied "not only towards greater openness and spontaneity, but also in the technically opposed direction of ever greater fluidity and integration of melody and accompaniment."[40] In addition, Reichardt clearly saw in Goethe's nature poetry of the Storm and Stress movement almost perfect examples of that naturalness that he and earlier composers had found in the folk songs. Goethe's poems had found the perfect composer, as this comment from the *Gothaer Theaterkalender auf das Jahr 1799* shows:

> Goethe's poetic genius and Reichardt's musical geniality are found together as closely as possible, and Goethe just seems to have been the ideal partner for this artist who is as great in his simple, moving way as is Goethe's language which moves the heart.[41]

Richard Benz thought that Goethe had lost "the best composer that he had found for his poems and Singspiele" when the poet and Reichardt parted company.[42]

The French Revolution in 1789 did not have the immediate effect on Europe that some history books suggest. As in 1914 and again in 1939, the European populace was fairly certain that order would soon be restored. The Goethe family in Weimar was certainly much more concerned with the birth of their first child, Julius August Walther, on Christmas Day 1789. Christiane von Goethe was to give birth to three more children, all of whom survived only a few days or weeks: Carolina, born 21 November 1793, died 14 December; Karl, born 30 October 1795, died 18 November; and Kathinka, born 16 December 1802, died 19 December. One child was stillborn on 14 December 1791.

Goethe may have avoided tragedy in his dramatic works, but he could not avoid it in his personal life or in his heart. The letters between him and Christiane show their love for each other; her letter of 13 May

1793, for example, to Goethe when he was absent at the famous siege of Mainz, expresses her sorrow at not being able to enjoy their lovemaking hours together. His pain at the loss of their son Karl was shown in a letter to Schiller on 21 November 1795: "You do not know what to do in such cases, whether it is better to give yourself up quite naturally to grief, or restore yourself by the help that culture offers you." Goethe usually turned to the latter.[43]

The birth of August, as the child was called at home, did not seem to have given the Wanderer much rest, for his friend Knebel wrote in January 1790 that Goethe was "yearning once more for his Italy." What the poet was looking forward to most of all was hearing the Holy Week music in Venice. "I have to hear the singers of the conservatoria and see the Doge in his solemn procession," he wrote.[44] Goethe left Weimar again on 10 March 1790, but the visit was not a success, and he admitted to the duke: "I must by the way confess in confidence, that this journey has delivered a fatal blow to my love for Italy."[45] (That, in the same letter, he should mention his love for "the little creature in swaddling clothes," whom he had left behind in Weimar, gives a picture of a very different Goethe from the isolated philosophical writer, dwelling in Olympian heights, that so many reverential scholars have attempted to portray over the years.) The Italy of 1790 was now much less Arcadian than that of 1786. Goethe had found more practical preoccupations.

One of Goethe's pre-occupations at this time was the newly founded Weimar court theater. He had acted there from time to time, but had been appointed director in 1791 and had had to struggle at first to woo the public away from the excessively sentimental plays of, say, August Wilhelm Iffland or August von Kotzebue, the latter a native of Weimar. Goethe's endeavors to raise the level of public taste were reasonably successful. He demonstrated as clearly as at any time in his life his love and understanding of music. Keenly aware, as all theater directors have to be, that the public's taste has to be both pandered to and (if possible) improved, Goethe cleverly mixed the entertainment offered. Yet, when he laid down his office, he could look back on a remarkable display of musical taste and discernment; 104 operas and thirty-one Singspiele had been given in the twenty-six seasons that he arranged or directed. There had been eighty-two performances of *Die Zauberflöte* (The Magic Flute), sixty-eight of *Don Giovanni*, forty of *Il Seraglio*, thirty-three of *Così fan tutte*, twenty-eight of *La clemenza di Tito*, and nineteen of *Le nozze di Figaro* (The Marriage of Figaro)—270 productions of works of Mozart. It was a rare recognition of his love for a composer who, ironically, was to halt Goethe's ambitions as a writer of Singspiele. In an entry in his *Italian Journey* for November 1787, when looking back at one of his Singspiele, *Scherz, List und Rache* (Jest, Cunning and Revenge), he admitted:

> All our efforts to make our work simple and limited went for nothing when Mozart came on the scene. The *Entführung aus dem Serail* quashed everything else, and our so carefully produced play was never heard of again in the theater.

In April 1817, Goethe decided to relinquish the directorship of the court theater. For thirty-six years, it had been a source of enjoyment and education. Two-thirds of the programs gave the public the light entertainment it wanted; the other third had attempted to bring it the best of great theater and music.[46] Goethe's *Rules for Actors,* lectures given in the theater from 1803 onwards, attempted to show the players how to enunciate clearly, how to declaim, and how to breathe. Many singing coaches in Germany have confirmed their value, for it was "spoken opera" that Goethe had in mind. A young actor, Philipp Wolf, remembered: "He was constantly appealing to the analogy of music in his instruction. The cast was trained to speak its lines in just the same way as an opera is rehearsed with the *fortes* and *pianos*, crescendos and diminuendos carefully observed"[47]—and all that with a baton in his hand.

Another of Goethe's practical pre-occupations was his enforced attendance with the duke, from August to October 1792, at the disastrous campaign of the Prussian and Austrian princes against the French forces, which ended in defeat at Valmy in the September. Goethe's participation in this campaign may have given the later "young bloods" of Germany and Austria a perception of the poet, which he described to Eckermann on 4 January 1824 thus: "Now, because I hated revolutions, they called me 'a friend of the status quo'." This view of Goethe as a staid conservative has persisted and has played no small part in the condemnation of his (supposed) attitude towards contemporary cultural developments. Goethe knew that life had to change; only, he wanted it to change gradually and in a civilized manner, not rapidly and brutally. He desired "evolution" and not "revolution."

MUSICAL IMAGERY IN *WILHELM MEISTER*

Such a development was seen in a work that Schiller called "the truth of life": *Wilhelm Meister's Years of Apprenticeship* (1795–1796).[48] The aspect of this long novel, which we now consider, is often neglected, namely, the place of music in Wilhelm's evolutionary process. From the earliest stages to the final (Mozartian) conclusion, we see how Goethe employs musical imagery, first to demonstrate Wilhelm's artistic sensitivity, and, second, to bond Wilhelm to important personages in the story.

One must say that many have disagreed with the glowing tributes found in Schiller's letters.[49] Ronald Gray's (sharply) critical introduction to Goethe cites Samuel Butler wondering whether the book was a hoax, and Henry James consigning it to "the class of the great unreadables."[50] The heavy, didactic symbolism begins with the main character's name: Wilhelm (from William Shakespeare) and Meister (meaning "one who will master life"). Again, literary criticism is not our concern here. For us, *Wilhelm Meister* is yet another work where Goethe's love of music permeates the whole, while serving to deepen and explain the *raison d'être* of the main characters.

Wilhelm's life and career proceed through theatrical and commercial experience, life with a bohemian traveling company, and two particularly unusual characters—the twelve- (or thirteen-) year-old hermaphrodite tight-rope dancer Mignon and the mysterious, old, deranged Harper—to end in seeming fulfillment with the Utopian "Society of the Tower," an organization strongly reminiscent of the Freemasons. (Goethe had been a Freemason in Weimar since 1780.) From this point in his life, Goethe, who was nearing fifty, employed and expatiated on the power of music in his works, essays, and letters. Music in language had always attracted him. The disordered prolixity of works like *Wilhelm Meister* showed that Goethe's greatest gifts lay, and had always lain, in his lyric poetry, with its rhythmical musicality, and usually illustrating nature or romantic love. In these situations in this novel, too, even those situations characterized by Walter Bruford as "intellectualized sex," Goethe sets some of his most beautiful poetry.[51]

Many of the characters display the effect of music on their lives; in chapter eleven of Book Two, Laertes, "neither a great actor nor singer," compares words set to music with words spoken in dramas: "then I am a completely different person than when, in prosaic drama, everything is created for me, and I have first to invent the tempo and the declamation." In chapter fourteen of Book Four, Serlo, who organizes weekly concerts, is said to love music very much: "He maintained that, without this love, an actor could never obtain a precise meaning of, and feeling for, his own art," and Goethe, offering once again a "fragment of a great confession," writes in chapter one of Book Five: "Serlo, without being skilled in music himself or playing an instrument, knew how to cherish its great value and sought this pleasure, which can be compared to no other, as often as possible."

Wilhelm's music experiences are most striking and most illuminating for our discussion. In chapter four of Book Two, he meets up with little Mignon, a waif of striking appearance, her "brownish features hardly recognizable through the make-up," and then, not long afterwards, in chapter eleven, with the strange Harper, almost bald with great blue eyes and a long, white beard, clad in a dark brown garment. He began to "prelude" on his harp. All were delighted, but Wilhelm wanted a song:

> The instrument should only accompany the voice; for melodies, runs, and passages without words and meaning seem to me like butterflies or brightly colored birds which flutter in the air before our eyes, and which we should love to catch for ourselves, while a song, on the other hand, lifts itself up to Heaven and incites our better self to accompany it.

Eventually, the old man first slid his fingers over the strings, then attacked them more firmly and sang the first song in the novel: "Was hör' ich draussen vor dem Tor?" (What do I hear outside the gate?). The applause had scarcely ended when Philine, a risqué female, asks the old man if he knows the melody to *The Shepherd Was Dressing for the Dance*, and he accompanies her in a song that Wilhelm "cannot describe to his readers because they might find it tasteless or even quite indecent!"

As the evening progresses, Wilhelm becomes quite drunk and tries to escape Philine's pressing attentions. Bad-tempered and out of sorts, he decides to look for the old Harper to soothe his nerves. In chapter thirteen he finally traces him to an unsavory inn, where, up in the attic, he hears "heart-rending, plaintive sounds, accompanied by a sad, anxious song." Wilhelm creeps to the door, and, "since the good old man was reciting a sort of imaginary poem, repeating a few verses, part singing, part reciting," Wilhelm could eventually just make out the words, "Wer nie sein Brot mit Tränen ass" (He who never ate his bread with tears). The old man could scarcely finish the song for tears nor could Wilhelm listen to it without weeping. Deeply moved, he told the old man how lucky he was to be able to occupy himself so pleasantly in his loneliness. The Harper looked down at the strings of his harp, gently "preluded," and began to sing "Wer sich der Einsamkeit ergibt" (Whoever chooses solitude). His pain, he says, will only leave him in the grave. Wilhelm, as yet quite unaware of the old man's true circumstances, feels kinship with the remark of this "strange person." The author likens the song to one sung by a group, a choir perhaps, where each verse becomes "new and individual, as if it had been invented just in that moment," which is what Goethe always felt when listening to choral music.

Chapter one of Book Three begins with Wilhelm hearing music in front of his door; opening it, he finds Mignon with a zither, singing of her native Italy: "Kennst du das Land, wo die Zitronen blühen?" (Do you know the land where the lemon trees blossom?). We shall look later at the manner in which this song was performed, accepted, and understood (or, as some think, not understood) by Schubert. Sufficient for the moment is that its role in the novel is to prove to Wilhelm that Mignon is Italian and that she is longing for her "father" to take her back home. Wilhelm has not yet put two and two together. (Only later does he discover that Mignon is the child of the incestuous union of the Harper and his sister.)

Throughout the novel, Goethe shows his knowledge of practical work in the theater, and, of more interest to this discussion, he often compares the work of a playwright or actor unsympathetically with that of the composer. In chapter two of Book Four, he writes that actors often do their work "mechanically," each concentrating on his or her part, whereas composers think of the whole orchestra:

> How tireless they are, getting all their instruments in time with one another, how precisely they keep time, how delicately they manage to express the strength and weakness of each note! . . . Each one has to play in the spirit and meaning of the composer.

It may be that Goethe was expressing here dissatisfaction with his theater, but it is nevertheless of note that he, supposedly with no interest in music, should use the model of musicians to posit the ideal situation. One is therefore not surprised to learn that he used a baton when rehearsing his Weimar troupe of actors.[52]

The fourth great poem comes unintroduced in chapter eleven of Book Four. Wilhelm has been attacked and wounded by armed bandits, and has been overcome by the looks of a young lady who sympathized with his plight. This "noble Amazon," as he calls her, haunts him and "he fell into a state of dreamy longing"; as if in tune with his emotions (a recurring situation) comes the song that Mignon and the Harper sing just then as an "irregular duet with the deepest expressiveness": "Nur wer die Sehnsucht kennt" (Only those who know what yearning is).[53] A very different type of longing is expressed by the sexy Philine in chapter ten of Book Five, when she sings of love: "Singet nicht in Trauertönen" (Don't sing a sad song); of course, we know that Goethe always said he preferred cheerful music. Philine's lines about "night being half of life / and the loveliest part, too" might remind us that Goethe was in the early stages of his liaison with Christiane Vulpius. (Goethe asked here for a "very pretty and pleasing melody," which Reichardt, Schumann, and Wolf, but, strangely, not Schubert, all provided.)

Fires were very common occurrences in the eighteenth and nineteenth centuries, and Goethe was to see his theater burned down in 1825. The fire in this novel comes after a performance of *Hamlet* in chapter fourteen of Book Five. Wilhelm fears that the old man has perished in the blaze and searches all over for him, eventually hearing sobbing nearby. He recognized the Harper by the sad song that he immediately started singing: "The song, which he could understand well, contained comfort for an unhappy man near to madness." Alas, Wilhelm heard only the last verse: "An die Türen will ich schleichen" (I shall steal up to the doors).

Just as Mignon and the Harper's duet was directed towards Wilhelm's situation, so too the poem (not a song) that Mignon recites to Wilhelm as he sets out on his journey northwards at the end of Book Five, chapter sixteen is directed to another woman, namely, Aurelie: "Heiss mich nicht reden, heiss mich schweigen" (Don't ask me to speak, ask me to be silent). Goethe writes that Mignon has often recited the poem before; it is, in fact, Wilhelm's introduction to Mignon in the first draft of the novel *Wilhelm Meister's Theatrical Mission,* and it seems at this stage unconnected to the plot. Book Six, which follows, the *Confessions of a Beautiful Soul,* also seems to be unconnected, a diversion from the plot, although we know that its theme faithfully represents Goethe's belief that we must live this life and shape it with our hands; the self-pity of Mignon and the Harper, their "madness through discordant relationships," as Goethe described it, was not his lifestyle, he claimed. Students of his work could only say that this belief came from much experience of such relationships. What was Goethe's style is the splendid description of choral singing given in this book. The author describes a choir singing four-part and eight-part songs that gave the listeners a "foretaste of bliss," music which "through clear and practiced organs in harmonic unity spoke to the deepest, best senses in man."

Goethe had also found this harmonic unity in Mozart's *The Magic Flute,* which had had its première in Vienna in 1791 and which had made an enormous impression on Goethe and his circle when it was produced in Weimar.[54] (In 1815 he appointed Friedrich Beuther as his head designer in the theater; their "Egyptian" décor for *The Magic Flute* performances created a sensation.) The "Society of the Tower," which Wilhelm joins in the later books of the novel, is clearly fashioned on the Freemason-like trials of Tamino and Pamina in Mozart's opera. "There you will learn to know yourself," says Jarno to Wilhelm. Its function is seen in chapter two of Book Eight, where Mignon, the very essence of romantic longing, is dressed as an angel with wings, carrying a lily in one hand, a basket in the other. She takes up her zither and sings "a song with an unbelievable grace": "So lasst mich scheinen, bis ich werde" (Let me look like this, until I become like this). The song is a prelude to her death in chapter five and her burial in chapter eight. The two invisible choirs at her exequies sing the Goethean philosophy: "Do not weep by the dead—children, hurry back into life!" Mignon's tragic death and (in chapter ten of Book Eight) the Harper's death after his suicide attempt, seem maudlin beside Wilhelm's confident assertion at the end of the novel that, now engaged to his "beautiful Amazon," Natalie, he can say: "I know that I have attained a happiness which I do not deserve and which I would not exchange for anything in the world." This philosophy brought Goethe into conflict later with the Romantic spirit of Byronic *Weltschmerz*, the literary pessimism in Europe following the post–French Revolution authoritarian despotism that pitted life against dreams, day against night, health against sickness: "The Classical [spirit] I call what is healthy, the Romantic what is sick," Goethe said to Eckermann on 2 April 1829. That explains, as well as any statement of his, Goethe's attitude to the new Romantic literature and its music. He was shortly to meet up with a musician who shared his opinions.

FRIENDSHIP WITH KARL FRIEDRICH ZELTER

In a letter dated 19 June 1805, Goethe wrote that he had never had the good fortune to have a real composer beside him in Weimar with whom he might have worked closely. The letter was addressed to Karl Friedrich Zelter, who lived in Berlin and who might just have been the very man for the task. Or would he have been? Many believe that due to Zelter, and in smaller measure to Reichardt, Goethe ignored contemporary composers, in particular, Franz Schubert, a charge that we shall deal with in chapter four. Zelter was a remarkable man by all accounts, even if most good judges of music saw his talents to lie more in organization than composition. Nevertheless, it was his setting of Friederike Brun's *Ich denke dein* (I Think of You) that brought him to Goethe's attention at a party in 1795. Goethe loved the melody, but re-cast the poem (as was his wont) into his *Nähe des Geliebten* (The Nearness of the Beloved), preserving the first line of the original poem. In 1796, Zelter sent Goethe his *12 Lieder, am Klavier zu singen* (Twelve Songs to be Sung at the Clavier), which included some settings of poems from *Wilhelm Meister*. He then asked for permission to set some of Schiller's poems, and, later, in 1799, to set some of Goethe's. Goethe's response of 26 August 1799 set the tone for an interchange of letters, some nine hundred in all, which tell us more about Goethe, music, and musicians than any other set of documents. In that first letter, Goethe was plainly delighted to have met a man of like mind. He wrote:

> For, if my poems move you to melodies, then I can certainly say that your melodies have inspired me to many a poem, and, were we nearer one another, I should certainly feel myself elevated into a lyrical mood more often than now.

That is the crux of the relationship: despite Goethe's growing eminence, and, later, his unassailable position as one of the great literary figures of Europe, he never ceased to envy Zelter's busy life among the Berlin intellectuals in constant touch with theatrical, musical, but also social and political events. He always wished that he too lived in a large city.[55] One of the most delightful aspects of their friendship was Goethe's reiterated thanks for the turnips that Zelter never failed to send him from Berlin, receiving news of Goethe's beautiful little garden outside his garden house in return.

Zelter's main value was to keep Goethe up to date with what was happening in the wider world, and not just in the musical world, particularly after Schiller's death in 1805. The early years of their friendship and correspondence were those critical years of Napoleonic dominance in Europe. Zelter, in the Prussian capital, was near to the action, as it were, and reported regularly on the political situation. This was his attraction for Goethe; Zelter was what Scots call a "man o' pairts," not just a musician, but a man of many interests who had his feet planted firmly on the ground and who lived in the real world, unlike some German intellectuals. If, as Max Friedlaender suggested, his compositions rarely rose above "the ordinary,"[56] then another eminent critic, Hermann Abert, claimed that Zelter was anything but "conservative": "Not only did he underline the connection to the genuine Volkslied more strongly than any of his contemporaries . . . (he) was particularly important for the development of the free forms of the Lied," that is, he was interested in more than just the strophic form.[57] This must be stressed, because when music critics write loosely, as many do, about Goethe's being un-musical, they normally justify the charge by their claim that Goethe only liked strophic Lieder, and they cite Zelter's Lieder as having been his model.[58]

Goethe had been planning a continuation of Mozart's *The Magic Flute* for some time and had written to the Viennese composer Paul Wranitzky on 24 January 1796 that he was attempting to write "a new and complicated" work.[59] He thought that he would fulfil this intention by writing a second part to *The Magic Flute*. The dramatis personae are well known, the actors are used to playing the characters, and, since we have the first piece to hand, we can heighten the situations and circumstances without exaggeration and give such a piece a good deal of life and interest.

Alas, nothing came of this, but one of his first approaches to Zelter (on 29 May 1801) was for music to the first scenes of this second part of the opera, which were now ready. (He managed to write eight scenes in all.) Oskar Seidlin wrote that what Goethe dreamed of with this second part "was the combination of intoxicating popular entertainment and the highest poetry," but nothing came of that either.[60]

Goethe's next request (on 30 July 1804) was for Zelter to set various songs in his drama *Götz von Berlichingen;* the detailed request was for a setting lasting eight minutes. Then, on 8 August 1804, a request came for music for the wedding of the young couple in the play, Maria and Franz von Sickingen. Zelter's letter of 25 August 1805 informed Goethe that the version of *Götz* with his music had just been performed in Berlin. Goethe asked plaintively for a program note, emphasizing how isolated he was in Weimar.

This isolation was increased when Schiller, never a well man, died on 9 May 1805. He had had a long and fruitful relationship with Goethe, but one that never reached the level of intimacy of Zelter's relationship with Goethe. Zelter was one of the very few whom Goethe addressed with the intimate "du" form, which he did for the first time in a letter of 3 December 1812.

With Schiller's death, Goethe lost, as he wrote to Zelter on 1 June 1805, "half of my being": "I thought I had lost myself, and now I lose a friend and, in him, half of my being. . . . So now I see every day immediately before me and do what I have to do without thinking of anything further." This was followed by a request to Zelter to set "a suitable symphony" for Schiller's poem *Das Lied von der Glocke* (The Song of the Bell), with a final fugue on the Latin "Vivos voco. Mortuos plango. Fulgura frango" (I call the living. I mourn the dead. I shatter the lightning), which stands under the German title of the poem, to be accompanied by the imitation of the sound of a bell.

Indeed, it seemed as if intimations of mortality bound the two men ever closer together. Zelter in particular was to suffer many tragic personal losses to which Goethe responded with obvious heartfelt sympathy. Zelter's wife and child died on 18 March 1806, his mother on 21 April, while his sister had died only two months previously. Goethe wrote to him on 26 June: "I often think of you and your circumstances.

You have a difficult furrow to plow." Goethe's life at the time held its tragedies. His favorite, Dowager Duchess Amalia, died on 10 April 1807, and then his beloved mother on 13 September 1808. Such intimacies make us realize how much Goethe would appreciate Zelter's pre-occupation with setting his poems, and how much more would have been achieved had they lived nearer one another. Praise for these settings occurs regularly in the correspondence.

Commenting later on Zelter's proposed settings of poems from *West-östlicher Divan* (West-Eastern Divan, 1819), his collection of poems on Eastern themes, Goethe wrote on 30 January 1820: "May they inspire you once again and encourage you to clothe these naked poetic beings with a musical abundance and lead them into the world"; then again, from Karlsbad on 11 May 1820: "I feel that your compositions are identical with my poems, the music, just like an in-flowing gas, takes the balloon into the air. With other composers, I first have to see how they perceived the poem and what they have made out of it," and he is constantly grateful to Zelter for, as he saw it, bringing out the full meaning of the poem. When one reads these letters, one is made very aware of how Goethe must have thought of settings for the poems as he wrote them. "Lieder" always had a dual meaning for him.

Great world events were soon to dominate both men's lives. After hearing the thunder of cannons sounding from the nearby town of Jena on 14 October 1806, Goethe experienced for the second time in his life an invasion by French troops after the Battle of Jena. Apart from its importance for Weimar and the defeated Prussians, the invasion brought one decisive change to Goethe's life. When two French *tirailleurs* broke into his house and threatened to kill him, Christiane stood in front of them and called on some Weimar men for help in driving them out of the house. Goethe's admiration at her bravery, and his memory of her loving care during his many serious illnesses in previous years, led him to ask her to marry him, to recognize "the little friend who had done so much for me and had lived these hours of trial with me, fully and lawfully as my own," as he wrote in his diary on that day. They were married on 19 October 1806, having lived together for eighteen years; Goethe was fifty-seven, Christiane forty-one. Later, Goethe's nineteenth-century biographer, Albert Bielschowsky, would add primly: "Certainly Christiane made his position easier by her modest discretion in the correct acceptance of her inadequate social and intellectual status."[61]

Despite his marriage, Goethe's heart was soon stolen again, this time by the eighteen-year-old foster-daughter of a bookshop owner in

Jena, Minchen (Minna) Herzlieb, in the very next year, 1807. The impossibility of any further interest in her led, first, to a cycle of sonnets in 1807–1808 in which "the 'I' of the sonnets is the 'I' of the aging and famous man,"[62] and then, second, to the long novel *Die Wahlverwandtschaften* (Elective Affinities), published in 1809. That novel's insistence on the indissolubility of marriage and the need to "resign oneself" to a moral code caused, as one would expect, no little discussion among the cognoscenti of Weimar. Goethe's later comment to Eckermann on 14 March 1830 that "he had only written love poems when he was in love," would also have interested them, could they have heard it.

Yet Goethe's life with Christiane did not exclude her from social gatherings altogether. In 1801–1802 Goethe had formed a little social group of selected couples that met on Wednesday evenings to enjoy "good singing and good food." The good company was certainly more important than the good music, but, in 1807, he formed a domestic music group, because he felt the need for more music in his life. He had written to Zelter on 27 February 1804: "This winter I have heard hardly any music and feel I have lost a lovely part of the joys of life." Since Christiane was part of the group, the meetings were held in her room in the house on the Frauenplan square, and the little group, which Goethe used to join as second bass from time to time, soon became a valuable addition to Weimar's cultural life. Goethe's beloved sacred music formed a large part of the repertoire, but Reichardt, Zelter, and the main musical director, Karl Eberwein, also wrote music for the group. On 27 July 1807, Zelter was asked for songs for four to six singers; he could not find many, so he arranged some of Haydn's that had been published two years before in Leipzig. Goethe was also very keen on guitar accompaniments, an instrument much in vogue at the time (as Schubert was to discover too). All the descriptions of this delightful little amateur group stressed the pure pleasure that it gave and received from their meetings. Music thus helped to dispel in some little way the war clouds that hung so thickly over Thuringia in those years. Napoleon's Caesarism dominated Europe, and when Goethe met the dictator in Erfurt near Weimar on 2 October 1808, he was flattered to hear that Napoleon had "studied *Werther* through and through." Johannes Falk reported on 14 October 1808 that Goethe felt he had seen through this man who "will trample down anyone who gets in his way, will get rid of him, even if it were his own son."[63]

The war had naturally strengthened that patriotic feeling among Germans and, in organizations like Zelter's glee club in a Berlin inn, many of the songs sung would be calls for brotherhood, with appropriate slamming of beer mugs on the table. As Goethe wrote to Zelter on 17

May 1815: "What cannot be sung together is really not a song at all, just as a monologue is not a drama." His *Bundeslied* and *Tischlied*, also set by Schubert (see song nos. 27 and 20, respectively), are interesting examples of the genre. Not too surprisingly, Goethe believed that dictators like Napoleon would prefer a different type of music. He said once to Chancellor von Müller on 24 June 1806: "Napoleon, who was a tyrant, is said to have liked gentle music, and I, presumably because I am not a tyrant, love noisy, lively, cheerful music. People always long for what they are not!"[64] He was to meet Napoleon on two further occasions in Weimar and never lost his admiration for a man, who, although "a tyrant," had, in Goethe's opinion, saved Europe from the worst excesses of the French Revolution. "That was a real guy!" he said admiringly to Eckermann on 11 March 1828.

BEETHOVEN AND GOETHE

After Schiller's death in 1805, Goethe undertook more regular visits to the then-popular Bohemian spas, Karlsbad (now Karlovy Vary), Marienbad, and Teplitz (Teplice), to take the restorative waters. In many of his letters to Zelter he had asked his opinion of modern composers. Goethe felt that many of them were hypochondriacs who believed that "even joyous music can make you sad!" So many of them were setting poems to music "which leads us heavy-footed Germans out of this world, which we shall be soon leaving in any case!" (22 January 1808). Goethe, now in his late fifties, had tried very hard to understand the modern modes; many of these younger composers sent him their music and settings of his poems. One of these, Ludwig van Beethoven, born in Bonn in 1770, and resident in Vienna since 1792, had been fascinated by Goethe's works since his youth. When he was twenty, he had set songs from one of Goethe's Singspiele and longed for recognition from the great man. On 8 August 1809, he asked the publishing firm of Breitkopf and Härtel in Leipzig to send him the complete works of Goethe and Schiller, which he then quotes regularly in his correspondence.[65] In a letter of 6 June 1810, he offered the firm ten numbers, an overture and entr'acte music to Goethe's play *Egmont*, and a setting of "Kennst du das Land" from *Wilhelm Meister. The Song of the Flea* from *Faust I*, which Goethe had finished in 1806, is next mentioned, on 21 August 1810.

Beethoven had sought the help of Elisabeth (Bettina) Brentano as intermediary, since she had met Goethe in Frankfurt. In his letter to Goethe of 12 April 1811 he obviously believed that she had given Goethe a favorable impression of the fiery, but now almost completely deaf composer. At last, Beethoven plucked up enough courage to write to a man whom he had called "the nation's most precious jewel." In that letter of 12 April 1811, he also promised Goethe that the poet would shortly be receiving from the Leipzig publishers his music to *Egmont*, "that glorious Egmont . . . which I have felt and reproduced in music as intensely as I felt when I read it." Goethe's answer from Karlsbad on 25 June 1811 invited him to come to Weimar.[66]

Although Goethe's eventual meeting with Beethoven in the Bohemian spa Teplitz has become legendary, it is actually anecdotal, since it is largely based on the much exaggerated reports of Bettina (now married in 1811 to the friend of her brother Clemens, Achim von Arnim, one of the leaders of the Heidelberg Romantic school). Bettina published her (supposed) correspondence with Goethe in 1835, quoting frequently from three letters by Beethoven. Only one of these (that of 10 February 1811) is now believed to be genuine.[67] Goethe had heard performances of Beethoven's piano sonatas in May 1811 in Weimar by Baron Oliva: "That encompasses everything," he is reported to have said, "but it loses itself always in elementary things, yet there are also endless beauties in the details."[68]

Beethoven and Goethe first met in Teplitz on 19 July 1812, where Goethe was taking a six weeks' cure. Many of Europe's aristocracy were there, including the empress of Austria, but Goethe was the cynosure of all eyes. G. H. Lewes, Goethe's nineteenth-century biographer and his first British biographer, put the now accepted story into circulation for English-speaking musicologists—how Beethoven described how he and Goethe were walking together in Teplitz when the "whole imperial family" came towards them. "We saw them coming from a distance and Goethe separated from me to stand aside; say what I would, I could not make him advance another step." Lewes then continues in italics: *"I pressed my hat down upon my head, buttoned up my great coat, and walked with folded arms through the thickest of the throng."* Lewes was quick to remark that this proved that "Goethe was a man of the world, a man of courtesies, and a minister."[69] Alas, the whole story is built upon one of those doubtful letters that Beethoven is said to have written to Bettina von Arnim in 1812.

The most-quoted Goethean comment on Beethoven likewise points up the deaf composer's temper and vulgarity. After meeting Beethoven on 19 July 1812, Goethe wrote to his wife Christiane: "I have never seen an artist more collected, more energetic, more intense. I can well understand how strange he must seem to (the rest of) the world."[70] Then to Zelter from Karlsbad on 2 September 1812: "His talent amazed me; only, he is a quite untamed person who is, of course, not wrong to find the

world detestable, but he certainly does not make it more enjoyable, neither for them nor for himself by such behavior." Beethoven's negative
comment about Goethe is also well known. His letter to his publishers
from Franzensbrunn on 8 August 1812 finishes: "Goethe delights far too
much in the court atmosphere, far more than is becoming to a poet."[71]
These comments do not suggest that Beethoven sensed a "fellow musician" in Goethe. Rather, they show that Goethe recognized the unkempt
artist possessed the stuff of greatness and that Beethoven's deafness was
the real cause of the composer's antisocial behavior. Goethe finished his
letter of 2 September 1812 to Zelter: "He is much to be pardoned and
pitied, however, for he has lost his hearing, and that perhaps damages
his social persona more than his musical. He who is in any case laconic,
becomes doubly so through this deficiency."

One wonders whether Goethe was identifying with Beethoven here.
Some of the best works of both men had been criticized and neglected,
after all. Goethe's liaison with Christiane was a running sore in Weimar's body politic, while Beethoven's antisocial behavior was legendary
in Vienna. Finally, despite Goethe's literary eminence, he was, like Beethoven, essentially a bourgeois artist living in a society ruled by aristo-
crats.[72] Yet Goethe never ceased to admire his great contemporary.

WEST-ÖSTLICHER DIVAN

Goethe's distancing of himself from the up-and-coming Romantic
school of artists is often regarded as one reason for his attitude towards
the music of his day as well. The Romantics' tendency towards what he
called the "bizarre, grotesque and caricature-like" elements in their
works had not prevented him from welcoming the publication of the
collection of folk songs titled *Des Knaben Wunderhorn* (The Youth's
Magic Horn, 1806) by Clemens von Brentano and Achim von Arnim
(the celebrated Bettina's husband). The collection, which was dedicated
to him, reminded Goethe of his efforts in Strasbourg in 1771, but maybe
also of the seeming evaporation of his lyrical powers. In his review of
the collection, he wrote that this volume should be placed on a composer's piano "to allow the poems contained therein to be given their
full rights," either by painting them with their "well-known, traditional
tunes" or "by fitting them with tunes which suited them," showing once
more how essential he felt music was to bring out the full glory and
meaning of a poem.[73]

T. J. Reed writes of Goethe's lyrical powers in the years after Schiller's death: "Age does not favor lyrical writing; old men are less likely to

fall in love, to feel each new spring as a revelation, or in general to suffer the sharp emotions that stimulate lyric." Well, maybe, but he did go on to write of Goethe: "Yet there were stirrings."[74]

On 23 February 1814, Goethe had sent Zelter a distich: "Now I wouldn't know what special things you still have / I have enough still! I still have ideas and love!" In the summer of that year, after the political skies had cleared in the wake of the French occupation of Frankfurt, and during a return visit to his home town, he had met Marianne von Willemer (née Jung), the thirty-year-old wife of one of his banker friends. An instant attraction blossomed into a serious love affair, and poetry poured from both partners in that and the next year, 1815. Von Willemer and Goethe took the part of the fourteenth-century Persian lovers Hafiz-Hatem and Suleika, whose passionate love affair had recently (1812–1813) been made known through the translation of Hafiz's poems by the Viennese orientalist, Joseph von Hammer-Purgstall. The poems were published in 1819 under Goethe's name as *Westöstlicher Divan*, a "divan" being a collection or anthology of poems. For Goethe, this was "a new, eternal youth," reminding him again of his time in Italy. He wrote: "You should not be worried, happy old man / Though your hair is white, love you still can!" (In fact, his fine hair was still brown.)

In 1814 Goethe began to make regular journeys to the little town of Berka, a few miles from Weimar, to visit an old friend, the baths inspector Johann Heinrich Schütz. Goethe would rest, while his friend played Bach, Handel, and Mozart on his "very tuneful Viennese piano." Schütz had a fine collection of Bach scores, a rarity in those days. Years later, on 8–9 June 1827, Zelter reminded Goethe in a letter: "You once said: 'I get into bed and let our mayoral organist [Schütz] in Berka play *Sebastiana*'," and Goethe answered: "I told myself it was as if the eternal harmony were talking to itself, just as must have taken place in God's breast shortly before the Creation." Zelter had once said that Bach's "basic element was solitude," and the eighteenth-century peace of these rare moments, the order and harmony of Bach's music, must have contrasted so strongly with the tempestuous, to Goethe, disordered music of a Beethoven; it must have been balm to the soul of a sixty-five year old. That much of the rest of the musical world at that time regarded Bach's music as too rational, too orderly, too mathematical, even too scholarly and dull, accounted for the young Felix Mendelssohn's regard for Goethe when they met in 1821. Mendelssohn and Robert Schumann were to be prime movers in the Bach renaissance of the 1830s.

On 8 June 1816, Zelter received a letter from Goethe: "When I tell you, blunt, sore-afflicted son of the earth, that my dear little wife has left us, then you will know what that means." Christiane von Goethe died after a painful illness on 6 June 1816, aged only fifty-one. Goethe wrote in his diary the bleak sentences: "Near end of my wife. Last terrible struggle of her being. She died around midday. Emptiness and deathly silence in, and around me."[75] (It was during those trying days that Josef von Spaun sent Goethe the packet of Schubert Lieder from Vienna.)[76]

Goethe must have felt that it never rains but that it pours when, in April 1817, through an intrigue of the actress Caroline Jagemann, who was known to be Duke Karl August's mistress, he resigned as director of the Weimar court theater. Jagemann had put on a play, *Aubry de Mont-Didier's Dog or the Woods near Bondy,* with a trained dog as the star attraction. When Goethe learned of this "stupid action," it only added to his feeling of isolation after Christiane's death. He retired to his little garden house in the park by the river Ilm, and, in a letter to Zelter of 29 May 1817, quoted the subtitle of his *Italian Journey,* "Auch ich in Arkadien" (I am in Arcadia, too).

When one adds to these personal setbacks the fire that destroyed all the precious Bach and Handel scores of his friend Schütz in Berka on 25–26 April 1816, and which brought Goethe hurrying over to Berka by coach to console his old friend, then one must surely agree that 1816–1817 was not one of Goethe's happiest periods, nor was 1816, curiously enough, Europe's, since poor weather led to a general failing of harvests and much starvation in the countryside. (Goethe's favorite turnips were among the casualties!)

The next year found Goethe installed in his little corner room in Jena, enjoying "peace and quiet." He went on writing, of course, as usual, but it was an event in his family's life that restored him to his old self. His son August had married Ottilie von Pogwisch on 17 July 1817, the year after Christiane's death, and on 9 April 1818, Goethe was able to look forward again, when Ottilie had a child, Walther Wolfgang, on whom Goethe doted. Their second child, Wolfgang Maximilian, was born on 18 September 1820, and the third, a girl, Alma, in 1827. (She died aged only seventeen, in 1844.) Neither boy had children, so the Goethe line died out with their deaths in the 1880s.

Like most grandfathers, Goethe took a great interest in his grand-children's education, particularly where music was concerned, although the little poem that Goethe wrote for Walther, *Cradle Song for the Young Mineralogist,* on 21 April 1818 vividly illustrates Goethe's celebrated mineralogical interests. Goethe had always shown an interest in the education of the young; in May 1783 he had taken in the young Fritz von Stein, Charlotte's son, and had educated him during the next three years. The memory of a thrilling night ride on horseback to Tiefurt just outside Weimar in April 1779, with the seven-year-old Fritz seated in front of him, had given Goethe the idea for *Erlkönig*. In his diaries, conversations, and correspondence, Goethe regularly mentions his grandchildren, who often interrupted his meetings and working hours.[77]

The arrival in Weimar in 1819 of a famous musician compensated in part for Zelter's departure for Vienna that year. Johann Nepomuk Hummel had been a pupil of Haydn and Mozart, and a close friend of Beethoven. He came to Weimar to take over the direction of music in the city, now much more famous, largely because of Goethe's and Schiller's literary eminence. Goethe recognized his exceptional talents immediately. He said to Eckermann on 14 February 1831: "It is strange that of all the talents, the musical one shows itself earliest, so that Mozart in his fifth year, Beethoven in his ninth, and Hummel in his tenth, amazed their contemporaries by their playing and their compositions." But he did not fail to add: "But, of course, a phenomenon such as Mozart remains a miracle which cannot be explained."

On 4 April 1816, Zelter had written to Goethe about another "phenomenon" whom he had encountered, a seven-year-old boy, Felix Mendelssohn-Bartholdy, whose family was well known in literary circles in Berlin. The boy's grandfather, Moses Mendelssohn (1729–1786), had been a celebrated philosopher. The boy's father, Abraham, was very anxious that his brilliant pianist son should play for Goethe. The years between that letter and Felix's eventual appearance in Weimar in 1821 had seen many additions to the Goethe house; one of the interesting ones had been Goethe's purchase of a superb Viennese Streicher piano (similar to the piano lost in the fire in Schütz's house in Berka).[78] One of Hummel's pupils, Karl Hartknoch, had played it for the first time and Hummel improvised for half an hour on it, Soret recalled on 5 November 1822, when he played "with a power and a talent of which it is impossible to give any idea if one has not heard it." The piano still stands in the Juno Room in Goethe's house, dwarfed by the enormous marble *Juno Ludovisi*, a likeness of the Roman emperor's daughter, Antonia Augusta.

Zelter brought Mendelssohn (now twelve) to play for Goethe on 4 November 1821. The boy did all that Goethe could have wished; he played a variation on a theme that Zelter gave him, then a Bach fugue from a score that Goethe often compared to "illuminated mathematical exercises," according to a diary entry of the tenor Eduard Genast of 6 June 1814. Goethe then took out some scores from his collection, and the boy deciphered these, at times, hastily written manuscripts without difficulty, and then finished with one of his piano works. He stayed there with Goethe until the nineteenth, playing to him every afternoon, and eventually becoming a close friend of the family. Ottilie von Goethe, who had dedicated herself to looking after her aging father-in-law, edited a little magazine called *Chaos* and persuaded Mendelssohn to set a poem by Friederike Brun. On Mendelssohn's next visit, in 1822, the seventy-three-year-old Goethe solemnly pronounced his feelings for the boy: "I am Saul and you are my David." His recognition of Mendelssohn's talents opened many doors for the young composer, who never failed to show his gratitude.

Such visits brought Goethe out of his self-imposed isolation. Many celebrated men beat a path to his door, especially scientists and art experts and, of course, his correspondence never ceased. The Weimar edition of his works (1887–1919) contains no fewer than fifty volumes of his letters. Indeed, in the last sixteen years of his life, he wrote as many letters as he had done in the previous sixty-seven. Many of the letters obviously show that the lack of what Goethe called Zelter, "a genuine reliable musical friend" (on 28 September 1821), was one reason for his isolation. As he grew older, he longed to hear the beautiful voice of a singer (preferably female), or the blend of instruments in a quartet. He had once written to Charlotte von Stein in August 1782: "Just as music is nothing without the human voice, so would be my life without your love,"[79] and after hearing the famous coloratura soprano Angelica Catalani sing during a visit to Karlsbad in 1821, he wrote a curious little poem for Zelter on 14 October: "In a room or in a concert hall / There's ne'er too much to hear. / And that is when I first recall / Why we've been given ears."

THE POWER OF MUSIC

Young twentieth-century students of Goethe are often perplexed by the contrast between the two images of Goethe; the one, the severe, patriarchal Olympian, famed throughout the world as philosopher, poet, novelist, scientist, indeed Carlyle's "Universal Man"; the other, a man who, from his first encounter with a girl (Gretchen), when he was fourteen, never ceased to be attractive to and attracted by women. The answer is perhaps a simple one; Goethe, as he said himself, was simply "a man with his contradictions." He was a man with an extraordinary range of intellectual interests, but he was also an emotional, sensual and sensuous man. That his poems so attracted composers, and that he was attracted by their music, is therefore not surprising; musicians, too, are intellectual, but also emotional people who "feel" music and words set to music, and are not only interested in the technicalities of the medium. That surely explains Goethe's next, at first sight, surprising liaison. He still corresponded with his Suleika, Marianne von Willemer, but after a journey to the Bohemian spa of Marienbad in July 1821 (and again in 1823), a new love appeared. He stayed there with the von Levetzow family, whose granddaughter Ulrike was just seventeen. Goethe, now seventy-one, was "in a passionate state," to use Eckermann's words. Fortunately, common sense, mainly, it must be said, on the part of Ulrike, prevailed, and this last "blessed love" of his life subsided, although not before the old man had proposed to her. As always with Goethe, there had to be the "fragment of a confession," this time in the poetic form of the beautiful *Marienbad Elegy* (19 September 1823), in many ways a sad epitaph to the loss of youth.

Shortly before he finished it, there came a concatenation of three of our major themes: poetry, love, and music. On 10 June 1823, a young student, Johann Peter Eckermann, wrote in the first pages of his now famous *Gespräche mit Goethe* (Conversations with Goethe): "He (Goethe) received me most cordially, and the impression of his person, made this day one of the happiest of my life." That visit began a nine-year friendship during which Eckermann visited Goethe regularly, often stayed in his house, and gave the literary world what was deemed to be a verbatim account of his conversations with the Olympian. Alas, his accounts are often blinded by his veneration for Germany's greatest figure, and we of the age of tape recorders are very doubtful of anyone's ability to give a verbatim account without such a record, but we do receive nevertheless fascinating insights into Goethe's personality. Unfortunately for our purposes, Eckermann seems to have been largely unmusical, and his accounts of Goethe's musical interests are few, and, often, clearly incorrect or imprecise.

The evenings of 27 and 28 October 1823, for instance, turned out to be such events, of more importance to us than to Eckermann, it seems. On the 27th, Goethe told him that they were to hear a young Polish pianist, which interested Eckermann far less than the poem Goethe laid before him, the *Marienbad Elegy*. The young man then delicately explained Goethe's "passionate inclination" for Ulrike von Levetzow and found the conclusion of the poem "truly unusual and deeply moving." The next evening, the Polish pianist, Maria Szymanowska, a pupil of the Irish composer John Field, played for Goethe. When he first heard her in Marienbad he had called her performance "unbelievable," and could compare it only to Hummel's, except that when she finished playing "and comes and looks at you, then you don't know whether you should be happy that she has finished!"

The effect of music on Goethe is never seen so clearly as in that year 1823. On 15 August, he had been given a private concert in Marienbad where he had heard Anna Milder-Hauptmann, formerly of the Vienna Opera, and, since 1816, prima donna of the Royal Opera in Berlin. She sang "four little songs which she managed to make great," Goethe wrote to Ottilie on 19 August.[80] This great singer, a pupil of Schubert's teacher, Antonio Salieri, and Beethoven's first Leonore in *Fidelio* in 1804, still moved Goethe to tears when he thought back to the evening in his letter to Zelter on 24 August 1823. (This singer was to become a link in that unseen bond between Goethe and Schubert.)

Maria Szymanowska moved him even more to great poetry; indeed, after hearing her play in Marienbad, he wrote, on 18 August, the beautiful poem *Aussöhnung* (Reconciliation), which begins: "Passion brings grief!" This poem is, however, also a passionate paean to the power of music to calm sorrow and induce the acceptance of fate: "The eye fills with tears and feels in lofty longing / the divine worth of music and of love." The poem then became the third part of the so-called *Trilogy of Passion* of which the elegy to Ulrike von Levetzow was to be the first. (The Polish pianist seems to have been equally attracted to Goethe. Zelter wrote to him on 9 January 1824: "She is madly in love with you and has given me a hundred kisses on the mouth for you!")

Not surprisingly, Goethe wrote to Zelter on 24 August 1823 of "the truly most remarkable thing: the enormous power of music over me in these days." He regretted being able to hear only one opera a week in Weimar (*Don Giovanni* or Cimarosa's *The Secret Marriage*), and added: "but then, one appreciates what it means to be bereft of such a pleasure, which, like all superior pleasures, raises a man out of, and above himself, and, at the same time, out of the world and above it." Could an unmusical person have written that?

Not unsurprisingly, this "passionate" excitement took its toll on the health of the aging poet who, in November, fell seriously ill with a heart condition (pericarditis). "If only the pain would go away from the side of my heart," he complained on 16 November 1823.

Once he had recovered and resumed his normal daily routine of literary work and entertaining his many visitors, Goethe was delighted to find that Handel's *Messiah* was to be produced in Weimar. Like Bach, Handel is not normally associated with the spirit of the 1820s, but Goethe's love of *Messiah* went back to the 1780s, when he prepared it for a production in Weimar. He heard (and produced) it regularly in the following years, on 14 April 1824 in his house, for example, when Eckermann portrayed Goethe "sitting some distance away, listening intently . . . full of admiration for the wonderful work." (Zelter's essay on Handel's *Judas Maccabaeus* was the last music document that Goethe read.)

One of the many literary visitors in later years was one peculiarly relevant to our theme: Wilhelm Müller from Dessau. This young poet was introduced to Goethe on 20 September 1827. He had published a series of poems, including *Die schöne Müllerin* (The Miller's Lovely Daughter) of 1820–1821, and had followed these with *Winterreise* (Winter Journey) of 1823, another curious example of the workings of Fate because, on 30 November 1823, Franz Schubert had written to his friend Franz von Schober: "I have not composed anything since the opera except a few Müllerlieder." These were Schubert's settings of Wilhelm Müller's cycle of poems, *Die schöne Müllerin* (D. 795), in 1823.

In 1825, Schubert was to write to Goethe and send with the letter three of his Lieder, but neither Goethe nor Müller knew anything of the Viennese composer. When the letter arrived, he, or his secretary Friedrich John, noted in the diary: "Packet from Felix, from Berlin, quartets. Packet from Schubart [*sic*] from Vienna. Compositions of my poems." Felix Mendelssohn received an answer, but Schubert did not.

Felix Mendelssohn and Zelter remained Goethe's musical confidants from now on. They were an interesting pairing: Mendelssohn had been Zelter's pupil, an infant prodigy, son of wealthy and cultured Jewish parents in Berlin, who had given him the taste for literature that he was to share with his almost exact contemporary and friend Robert Schumann. Both are often listed as Classical Romantics and both were influenced by Weber and by Schubert. Mendelssohn used to play to Goethe examples of music from the Bachs to Beethoven. He wrote to his parents on 25 May 1830 about Goethe's kindness to him, how they would sit and talk for an hour or so, and how Goethe would show him his engravings or talk about Victor Hugo's play *Hernani* or Lamartine's elegies. When he played to him, the old man would sit in a corner "like a thundering Jove," his eyes glittering with pleasure. He did not want to hear any Beethoven, but, when Mendelssohn played him the first movement of Symphony No. 5 in C Minor, Goethe was strangely moved. First of all, he said: "That doesn't move me at all. It just amazes (me); it's grandiose." Then he growled a little bit more, and, after a long time, he said: "That is very great, absolutely wonderful, you would be afraid that the house would fall in—and then, when they all play it together!"[81]

Mendelssohn remained faithful to Goethe after his death in 1832, setting many of his poems and part of *Faust I*. Goethe would certainly have seen him as the "keeper of his seal." Writing to Zelter on 3 June 1830, Goethe praised Mendelssohn for reminding him of the music of the past and for introducing him to the music of the present and the future, to the "great, new technicians." Zelter, on the other hand, was what Germans call one of the "old brigade." For Goethe, he was the upholder of the old virtues: order, decency, hard work, and the Protestant ethic. His many Lieder are very varied; a setting like *Um Mitternacht*, with its attractive dark melody and cleverly varied harmonies, would live in any recital. His method of setting was simple:[82]

> When I want to set a poem, I try first of all to penetrate the meaning of the words and bring the situation alive for me. Then, I read it aloud until I know it off by heart, and then, by reciting it again and again, the melody comes by itself.

A very critical comment on Zelter was made by the musician Christian Lobe when he visited Goethe in July 1820 and tried to convince him that Zelter's music was old-fashioned. Lobe granted that this was not noticeable in Zelter's vocal melodies, which were very much in the folk song mode, but in the accompaniments: "Zelter's are rarely anything more than the necessary filling-out of the harmony, and the extension and the balancing of the rhythmic flow. The newer composers, in their better works, have raised [the accompaniments] to the level of a partner (in the emotions)." Lobe then had to show Goethe what he meant by playing the accompaniment of a Zelter Lied following with what reads like Beethoven's setting of Klärchen's song from *Egmont*. "Fine," said Goethe, but he admitted that the experiment had not convinced him and added: "This is the dangerous demon for you younger people. You create new ideals quickly—but how about their realization?" He was certain that what Lobe had said must have occurred to every composer already, "but if the musical work can bear the realization of this principle, and whether other disadvantages for the enjoyment of the music will not arise from it, that is another question."[83] Goethe was seventy-one at the time of this visit, but hardly in his dotage. As he said once to a friend: "Each of us would have been quite a different person had we been born ten years earlier or later!"[84]

By the 1820s, Weimar was unrecognizable as the little town of six thousand or so that Goethe had entered in 1775. Statesmen and literary men and women of all sorts and conditions came to visit the town and its leading citizen. Goethe's conversations with Eckermann and Soret mention every distinguished person of the age who either visited him or with whom he corresponded. In his later years, the poet's visits to other places were strictly limited and he never visited Vienna. When he was in Karlsbad or Marienbad, he received many invitations to visit the Austrian capital, but nothing came of them. Several famous Austrians came to visit him in Weimar. In October 1826, Franz Grillparzer, the dramatist and a member of Schubert's circle of friends, spent some time with Goethe, but he never mentioned Schubert's name. The Austrian administration had imposed a severe censorship on the traffic of literature and music, one of the results of which had been that the works of the German classics—Lessing, Goethe, and Schiller—had been more difficult to come by. The Austrians had therefore turned to their indigenous literature. Goethe had met the Austrian chancellor, Prince Metternich, on his visits to Karlsbad in 1818 and 1819, for he had had to write to him on 30 July 1817 to beg permission to have his works published in Austria.

Reading between the lines of Goethe's observations on Austria, one has the impression that the poet was in no hurry to visit the country. Germans have traditionally held ambiguous views about their southern neighbor. Goethe had always supported the Prussian cause against Austria in the various eighteenth-century wars, and his close friendship with the Berlin musicians Reichardt, Zelter, and Mendelssohn, in particular, must have influenced his thinking. Certainly, Zelter's report in his long letter to Goethe about his visit to Vienna from 20 July to 9 August 1819 was unlikely to raise Austrians in Goethe's estimation. Zelter had written of the Austrian's attitude to life: "He will live and enjoy every minute—and that's that!" and of a performance of Mozart's opera *La clemenza di Tito* that it had a cast of "female singers only (four in number) who could all be grandmothers—though they were all in good form." The fact that the Austrian aristocracy spoke Italian and French rather than German annoyed the down-to-earth Prussian who felt, too, that the music in the famous Burgtheater in Vienna could not match that in Weimar.[85]

Goethe did not need to travel far to enjoy music now, for his fame had ensured that the leading musicians of the day would wish to perform for him. Anna Milder-Hauptmann's private concert in 1823 at the house of Dr. Heidler in Marienbad has already been mentioned. Two other equally celebrated sopranos were also to perform for Goethe: Henriette Sontag and Wilhelmine Schröder-Devrient. Sontag, born in Koblenz, was the solo soprano in the first performance of Beethoven's Ninth Symphony ("The Choral") on 7 May 1824 in Vienna (at which, incidentally, Franz Schubert was present). Her appearance in Rossini's *L'Italiana in Algeri* in Berlin on 3 August 1825 caused a "Sontag fever" just as Rossini had caused a "Rossini craze" in Vienna in the 1820s. She sang in Goethe's house on 4 September 1826: "Demoiselle Sontag sang beyond compare," was the old man's comment. What he praised particularly in her singing, was that, in contrast to the sheer brilliance of the Italian coloraturas, Sontag's interpretations of Lieder (where she was accompanied by Hummel), seemed to Goethe to be more intense, a perceptive critical remark.

On 24 April 1830, Goethe entertained Wilhelmine Schröder-Devrient. Born in Hamburg, she too excelled in the great dramatic roles such as Leonore in Beethoven's *Fidelio* and Pamina in Mozart's *The Magic Flute*, and was to be Wagner's Venus in his first *Tannhäuser* in 1845 in Dresden. She had sung at an important concert in Vienna on 7 March 1821, at which Johann Michael Vogl had performed Schubert's newly published *Erlkönig*. This setting, near the end of Goethe's long life, provided what might have been the true bond to Schubert. The soprano sang Schubert's setting to Goethe; he kissed her on the forehead and said: "I have heard this composition once before, when it didn't say anything to me at all, but, performed like that, then the whole becomes a visible picture."[86] (This was reported by the singer Eduard Genast who had been sure that Goethe disliked "through-composed" Lieder.) Was this perhaps the sign that Goethe was beginning, if not to accept the new type of song, then at least to see that it was the work of those "great, new technicians" whom Mendelssohn had mentioned?[87]

Goethe's views on the two types of Lieder are, in fact, ambiguous. Some comments are quoted to show that he always preferred the song style of his youth, strophic songs where the music simply decorated the words. In a letter to August Wilhelm Schlegel of 18 June 1798, he wrote of Zelter's Lieder: "What is original about his compositions is that, as far as I can judge, there is never just one bright idea, but *a radical reproduction of the poetic intentions*" (italics added).[88]

What he did not like was what Germans called "word-painting in music": "To paint notes by notes: to thunder, rage, splash and smack about is detestable," Goethe wrote to Zelter on 2 May 1820. This was, of course, closely linked with what he regarded as the worst feature of through-composition. In his *Annals* of 1801, Goethe wrote about a singer Wilhelm Ehlers. He had managed to show the singer how reprehensible all this so-called through-composition of Lieder was, "whereby the general lyrical character (of the poem) is sacrificed, and a false involvement with detail is demanded and achieved."[89] On the other hand, Adalbert Schöpke was told on 16 February 1816: "To imitate thunder in music is not art, but the musician who can create in me the sensation that I am hearing thunder, would be much to be treasured."[90]

Goethe hated noise, above all, at all times, which is why he disliked the organ and preferred intimate chamber music to concerts with large orchestras. This dislike is not peculiar to him, but, when one considers the far cry from a folk song such as *Heidenröslein* to a heaven-storming song such as Schubert's setting of Goethe's *Prometheus*, it helps to understand the difficulties of a man living at a musical crossroads.

Far from being a "genuinely, profoundly *un*-musical" man, as Keller claimed, Goethe had as wide a range of musical interests, sympathies, and experiences as the average non-musician. Like most continental musicians of his age, Keller, an ex-Viennese instrumentalist, made a very clear distinction between *Musiker* (musician) and *Musikliebhaber* (lover of music). This distinction is not valid in other countries whose citizens do not enjoy the musical education of the Viennese. Goethe who, after all, knew more than just the bare basics of music, who learned more than one instrument and even tried his hand at composing, was musical in a different sense. Even so, his passionate interest in the technicalities of music, part of his insatiable curiosity, has also to be credited to him.

Goethe's *Theory of Sound*, planned in 1790–1791 with Reichardt and written with Zelter in 1810, hung on his bedroom wall, until the refurbishment of his rooms in the 1990s. This document was part of his study of science; he wrote a complementary *Theory of Colors*, which brought him into conflict with the supporters of Isaac Newton. It was typical of the man that he regarded music as an important and integral part of human nature. He spent many hours of his correspondence with Zelter and others arguing about what he took to be a fundamental human emotion, the difference between the major and minor modes. John Reed's examination of Schubert's music includes the sentence: "Schubert's instinctive awareness of the emotional colour of individual keys is an essential part of his genius for finding the best musical form for an individual text."[91] Goethe realized this intuitively as well, and the magical move from the major into the minor in Schubert's music would have been understood by Goethe as a move into a different emotional state. His *Theory of Sound* showed similarities to his *Theory of Colors*. He claimed there that the colors yellow-orange-vermilion represented "activity and movement," while blue-purple-crimson showed "longing and peace." On 22 June 1808 he wrote to Zelter that it would not be wrong to compare a picture with a "great" effect to a musical work in the major, a picture with a "gentle" effect to a musical work in the minor. Would Schubert have disagreed?

Reading the Goethe-Zelter correspondence of April to July 1808 where they argue their case so vehemently, one is invigorated. As one would expect, the professional musician argued the "theoretical" case, the amateur music lover the "human" case. Goethe believed that, for a large percentage of the human race, it was the effect of a piece of music that mattered, not the analytical components of the work. "What is a string and all the mechanical make-up against the ear of the musician?" he wrote. Zelter clearly disagreed, as most professional musicians and musicologists would have, but he gave in to the great man and to Goethe's derogatory remark about "theoretical know-alls of music." This was also why Goethe laid so much stress on the importance of rhythm in music. His poetry is dominated by rhythm; he makes Wilhelm Meister in the *Years of Wandering* hear music while he is out on his solitary walks:

> Inside one a secret genius seems to whisper something rhythmical to me so that, when I am out walking, I always move in time and think I hear gentle notes of music which accompany a song which presents itself to me in one pleasant way or another.[92]

Rhythm is basic to the language of poetry and of music, and it is no coincidence that the greatest interpreters of Schubert's Goethe Lieder are those who have a sovereign command of rhythm. Writing about Dietrich Fischer-Dieskau, the famous accompanist Gerald Moore stated: "(Rhythm) is the lifeblood of music and he is the master of it."[93] T. S. Eliot, not the greatest admirer of Goethe, noted this element in his poetry: "I know that a poem or a passage of a poem may tend to realize itself first as a particular rhythm before it reaches expression in words, and this rhythm may bring to birth the idea and the image."[94] That is what made Goethe's poems so suitable for setting to music.

When Goethe celebrated his seventy-fifth birthday in 1824, many of his friends and acquaintances were dead, and his letters to Zelter and others, and his conversations with Eckermann (or Soret), Chancellor Müller, and so on, betrayed the loneliness and sense of isolation that he was beginning to feel.[95] The birth of granddaughter Alma on 29 October 1827 compensated in part for the death of a woman who had meant so much to him in his early years in Weimar: Charlotte von Stein who died, lonelier than Goethe, on 6 January 1827 at the age of eighty-four. She had celebrated with the rest of Weimar's leading citizens the fiftieth anniversary of Goethe's arrival in Weimar in November 1775, although that anniversary lost some of its glory after the monument to his endeavors to bring music and theater to Weimar, the court theater, had burned down on 21 March 1825. Goethe felt then that he had lost part of his life. "The scene of almost thirty years of loving toil lies in ashes." He stayed in bed all day, reported Eckermann on 22 March 1825.

Goethe then engrossed himself in what he now called his "main business," the second part of his *Faust*, which he completed (and sealed) in 1831. He always regretted that Part I, famous now throughout Europe, had never been set to music. He always believed too that only one man was worthy of the task. "Mozart should have composed Faust," he said to Eckermann on 12 February 1829, for it would have been composed in the style of *Don Giovanni*. The Frenchman Hector Berlioz tried to approach Goethe with his *Huit Scènes de Faust* but was rejected by both Goethe and Zelter. Yet Goethe still tried to come to terms with the "moderns." Eckermann reported that Goethe spoke quite knowledgeably on 7 October 1828 about Rossini's opera *Moses in Egypt* (1818) performed in Weimar that month, but could not understand how his guests could like the music and detest the story. For Goethe, the libretto and the music of an opera had to go hand in hand. That was the whole point of opera. During his Italian journey, Goethe had claimed to Philipp Kayser on 14 August 1787 that it was the one thing he had learned in Italy: "to subordinate the poetry to the music." What if Goethe had found an equally gifted composer to prove to him that the German Lied also consisted of two equal parts?

Goethe experienced the virtuoso art of Niccolò Paganini on 20 October 1829, but found little pleasure in a display that, he wrote to Zelter on 9 November 1829, was "a pillar of flame and clouds," very different from his beloved Bach. On 11 March 1829, his young friend Felix Mendelssohn rediscovered Bach for the nineteenth century, when he conducted the first performance for almost a hundred years of the *St. Matthew Passion*. Zelter's report gave Goethe enormous pleasure: "I seem to hear the sea roaring from the distance," he wrote on 28 March 1829, as he thought back to those blissful hours with Johann Schütz in Berka. But Mendelssohn's Bach was very different from Goethe's Bach. Goethe's was a Bach for the hours of solitude, a Bach without trumpets.

One of the last musicians to visit Goethe was a young girl who was later to play her part in the development of the German Lied and the spreading of knowledge of Goethe's poetry. On 5 October 1831, a twelve-year-old Clara Wieck was brought by a proud father to play to the grand old man of Weimar. She played some new Parisian compositions that pleased Goethe greatly, and had Goethe but known, he was listening to a musician who, with her husband, Robert Schumann, was to continue the work of Franz Schubert in Vienna in making Goethe's name known throughout the world.

Having looked at the poet's experience of music and musicians, it is time now to turn to Schubert's acquaintance with poetry and poets.

CHAPTER THREE

Schubert, Poetry, and Poets

Views on Schubert's literary taste will always be varied, from those who will never cease to claim that he regularly chose poems by "second-class authors,"[1] or the Schochows' belief that he "regarded poetry less from an intellectual than from an emotional standpoint,"[2] to Walther Dürr's confirmation of our opinion that Schubert's choice of texts shows a "literary-aesthetic quintessence."[3] Like Goethe, Schubert had little time for those poseurs who considered themselves "aesthetic" or "cultured," and, as Eduard von Bauernfeld once suggested, Schubert would certainly have said "Amen!" to Goethe's witty little distich: "I would rather get worse, / than get bored!"[4]

The well-worn discussion about the extent and the standard of Schubert's literary and aesthetic taste was spectacularly revived by the results of the researches of David Gramit and Ilija Dürhammer.[5] Most earlier (foreign) commentators had settled for the weary cliché that "if a great deal of the verse in Schubert's songbooks is naive and poor, the reason is in part to be found in the fact that German literature simply had not the provision to supply the child of genius." (Richard Capell's comments go on to exclude Goethe from the charge.)[6] Knowledge of German literature among Anglo-Saxon intellectuals is not widespread, unfortunately, and particularly not among musicians who, if they have a knowledge of any foreign language, then it is usually French, or, if they are products of elite schools, perhaps Greek or Latin. They always have to rely on poor translations, which make the reader cringe and doubt the quality of German poetry. An imperfect knowledge of German and the quality of some of the English translations have led many non-German-speaking foreign critics to underestimate the worth of some of the German poetry that Schubert chose to set to music, and led them in consequence to underestimate Schubert's literary taste. People who know German would agree that Schubert set poems that awak-ened a musical response within him. A suitable poem evoked a wonderful response. Like Goethe, he sensed the musicality of words, whether they were, to use Thrasybulos Georgiades' word, *musikabel*, that is, able to be set to music because of their intrinsic musicality. Many British critics have dismissed Wilhelm Müller's poems in *Die schöne Müllerin* and *Winterreise* as "romantic tushery." Studies such as Susan Youens' have helped to dispel that notion.[7]

In this chapter we will attempt to show that Schubert retained a lively literary interest all his life; he was open to the new movement in poetry and philosophy and was able to write poetry and prose in good High German, acceptable to educated readers. The picture given in many foreign countries of a shy, retiring musical genius, rejected by women and living his thirty-one years in dire poverty, has, of course, some truth in it, but only some. Descriptions of the composer in Rudolf Hans Bartsch's 1912 novel *Schwammerl*, in Emil Berté's *Das Dreimäderlhaus* (1916), and its American version *Blossom Time* by Sigmund Romberg (1921), and *Lilac Time* by G. H. Clutsam (1923) in Britain, were wide of the truth and gave rise to some of the misunderstandings.

Franz Peter Schubert was born at half past one on the afternoon of 31 January 1797. His father, Franz Theodor Florian Schubert (1763–1830), was thirty-three, his mother, Maria Elisabeth Katharina (née Vietz, 1756–1812), was forty. Both parents were immigrants to Vienna.

Schubert's father had left school at sixteen and completed a year's study at training college to qualify as an assistant schoolmaster. As was the custom in eighteenth-century Europe, he had had a sound grounding in Greek and Latin and was later to study philosophy for a semester at the University of Vienna. At age twenty he left Moravia in 1782–1783 and obtained a modest position as a teacher beside his brother at the Carmelite School in Vienna. Shortly afterwards, he met Elisabeth Vietz, a domestic servant from Silesia in southern Austria. They fell in love and took what was a rather bold decision for people living in a strict Catholic country in those days, when they elected (in 1784) to live together in what is now Badgasse, 20, which still lies two streets behind the lovely parish church in the Lichtental district of northwest Vienna (now Vienna IX). Lichtental had a population of some seven thousand. Vietz, then twenty-eight, soon became pregnant. A hurried marriage took place on 17 January 1785, and their first child, Ignaz, was born eight weeks later on 8 March 1785. Since Elisabeth Schubert's father had had to leave Silesia in some disgrace, the birth of Ignaz so soon after his parents married, left his parents with a guilt complex that was to affect their many future children.

Father Schubert, a fairly typical German schoolmaster of the times, was a strict disciplinarian, pious, upright, pedantic, and moral. He was, nevertheless, obviously not averse to his marital pleasures. Elisabeth Schubert bore him fourteen children in sixteen years (1785–1801), before she died, aged fifty-six, in 1812. Schubert was the twelfth child, but only four of the previous eleven children had survived more than a few months. Ignaz was eleven, Josef three (although he died on 18 October 1798), Ferdinand two, and Karl one. As was typical for the era, the children of the lower and poorer orders were not the only ones who died young; we recall the deaths in the comfortably-off Goethe family. Apart from the normal reasons, such as poor and unsanitary accommodations, lack of good food, and endemic diseases, it seems that Elisabeth Schubert also bore within her an infection transmitted from the weaving business of her family. This tragic family history, and the father's continuing insistence on concealing his correct age and the birth date of his first child, were to play a significant role in Schubert's relations with his father, and, as a result, in his life.

Schubert was born in a tiny kitchen alcove of a one-room flat in the Himmelpfortgrund district of Vienna. The house, located on what has become Nussdorferstrasse 54, nowadays a wide, main street, was refurbished in the 1990s, and many of the interesting family relics removed. In Schubert's time, some three thousand people lived in the district in eighty-six houses. Sixteen families lived in the Schuberts' building alone. In 1801, the family moved over the road to Säulengasse 3, where the father had a new schoolroom. This house, where Schubert was to compose *Erlkönig* and many other Lieder, is now the Schubert Garage. The contrast with the opulence of the Goethe home in the Hirschgraben in Frankfurt is striking and makes one appreciate the gulf between the two boys' appreciations of what life might hold for them.

Like Goethe, Schubert was born in a tumultuous period in world history. Not only was the political status quo disturbed, but there were revolutions in the social, literary, and musical hierarchies as well. The general antipathy to the dominance of the French eighteenth-century aristocracy had continued, which meant that first reactions to the French Revolution of 1789 were favorable. The execution of Louis XVI and Marie Antoinette in 1793, however, and the consequent Reign of Terror, followed by the declaration of war against Prussia and Austria, betokened a loss of sympathy for France. Napoleon was twenty-eight in 1797 and was soon determined to become ruler of Europe. Francis II was the Holy Roman Emperor; George III was fifty-nine and had been king of Britain and Ireland for thirty-seven years. Frederick the Great of Prussia had died in 1786. His successor, Frederick William II, had died in 1797 and been succeeded by Frederick William III, whose troops under Marshal Blücher were to play an important role in Napoleon's defeat at the Battle of Waterloo on 18 June 1815.

It is at least arguable that Europe has never since boasted such a constellation of luminaries in the literary and musical firmaments. In Germany, Goethe was forty-eight, Schiller thirty-eight, Schlegel thirty, Novalis twenty-five, while Heine was born in that year 1797. In England, Wordsworth was twenty-seven, Coleridge twenty-five, Jane Austen twenty-two, Byron nine, Shelley five, and Keats two. In Scotland, whose literature was to play such an important part in Schubert's life, Burns had just died, Scott was twenty-six, and Carlyle two, while Macpherson of the *Ossian* odes had died in 1796, aged sixty. In France, Beaumarchais was sixty-five, Saint-Simon thirty-seven, and Chateaubriand twenty-nine. Alfred de Vigny was born in 1797 and Victor Hugo was to be born in 1802.

Vienna, with a population of about a quarter million in 1797, was generally recognized as the music capital of Europe: Haydn was sixty-five—*The Creation* would have its première in 1798—Mozart had died in 1791, aged thirty-five, while Beethoven, at twenty-seven, not yet deaf, was on the point of becoming the lion of Europe. Still to come to Vienna were Carl Maria von Weber, Gioacchino Rossini, Niccolò Paganini, and many, many more. The age was one of cultural grandeur, contrasting strongly with the unbridled political and martial passions of the ruling and military classes.

The Viennese, who often thought of their town as "the mother of genius," were well aware of their musical and cultural status, displayed daily in the Masses heard in their scores of churches throughout the city and in the popular music played and heard in the inns, on the streets, and in the theaters. Like all Austrian schoolmasters, Schubert's father studied music as part of his training, and he ensured that his surviving children would also play and understand music: at eight, Franz could play the violin and participate in the family quartets at home well enough for his father to decide that he should have professional tuition from Michael Holzer, the choirmaster at the Lichtental parish church.

Clearly Schubert was no child prodigy, unlike Mozart, for example, who, at six, could play sonatas and concertos and improvise for hours on end out of his head. Of all the great composers, Schubert was one of the few who was not a virtuoso performer. Rarely is much made of his piano-playing in contemporary documents, which might account for the lack of critical attention paid to his instrumental compositions as they were published. His brother Ignaz, who taught him piano, felt, on the other hand, that Schubert's piano-playing was so superior to his after a very short time that he could no longer teach him anything. Schubert's father wrote, in 1830, that Michael Holzer was left with tears in his eyes, for the young boy seemed to know everything he tried to teach him. From these reports, it is obvious that the Schubert home, though small, was not an uncultured one. (One has to realize, of course, that the majority of those eye-witness reports were published many years, some fifty usually, after the events and have to be treated with a great deal of caution and, at times, even, skepticism.)[8]

Michael Holzer persuaded Schubert's father to take young Franz to the celebrated Italian composer Antonio Salieri, the musical director to Emperor Francis II in Vienna. Schubert had been composing little pieces since he was five and took some of these along to the interview in 1807. The fifty-seven-year-old Salieri was quite impressed, both with the boy's music ability and with his singing, and suggested that he should take one of the examinations for selection as a choirboy in the Imperial Chapel. Schubert's successful application on 30 September 1808 was to introduce him to a much more advanced musical and literary culture.

SEMINARY EDUCATION IN MUSIC AND LITERATURE

The Vienna Boys' Choir has become famous throughout the world, and is the almost-direct connection between our time and Schubert's. Schubert made rapid strides as a treble choirboy in the kaiserlich-königliches Stadtkonvikt (Imperial and Royal City Seminary), founded in 1803 and, before long, was invited by the student musical director, Josef von Spaun, to play second violin and then to become his orchestral assistant at the seminary. Spaun had come from Linz to study law and was to be the first of the three men who determined the direction of Schubert's life.

After Schubert's death in 1828, Franz Liszt, an ardent admirer of Schubert's music, had planned to write his biography, but nothing came of it. In 1857–1858, Ferdinand Luib thought that he would write one and wrote to all those who had known Schubert. Finally, in 1865, Heinrich Kreissle von Hellborn published the first true biography on which future writers have drawn so much.[9] It is from Luib's material that Spaun's remarks (made in 1829) about his first meetings with Schubert are taken: "Above all, it was the wonderful symphonies in G minor of Mozart, and of Beethoven, which made the deepest impression on the young Schubert every time," an impression Schubert recalled to the day of his death.[10] The young boy made an impression first on Salieri and then on the director of the seminary orchestra, Wenzel Ruzicka, who found, as Holzer had found, that there was not much that he could teach the boy.

Schubert's experience of Napoleon was not quite as pleasant as Goethe's had been. The French occupation of Vienna lasted from 13 November 1805 to 13 January 1806 and brought an end to the thousand-year-old Holy Roman Empire. The French returned in 1809, bombarding Vienna on 9 May. A stray shell fell on Schubert's seminary, fortunately causing neither death nor injury. By 1811, Austria, having had to pay the huge levy that Napoleon had laid on it, was brought financially to its knees. The currency was devalued, and faith in the banks and lending institutions vanished, while the new chancellor, Prince Metternich, who was to stay in office until 1848, began to seek ways to restore aristocratic influence in the country. Therese Brunsvik, the woman most likely to have been Beethoven's "Distant Beloved," wrote: "The man who went to bed in March 1811 with the comfortable feeling of being a capitalist, having provided for his wife and children, got up in the morning as a beggar."[11]

Schubert never knew the great days of the Hapsburg empire, so he was one of the first generation of composers to suffer such humiliation when publishers found themselves unable to promote the younger Austrian composers. If, as his letters prove, a composer of the stature of a Beethoven had difficulty with publishers, what chance did an unknown like Schubert have? (On the other hand, we know that, as his expertise developed, many more of his works were published than is often realized.)

Although Schubert was receiving an above-average education as a choirboy in the seminary and was regularly at the top of his class in most academic subjects, he had had a good deal of ground to make up, since his father, albeit somewhat superior in education to many Austrian schoolmasters of his generation, had had little opportunity to acquaint himself with developments in modern Austrian, let alone in German literature.[12]

Fortune now shone on Schubert, as it had on Goethe, for he found in the seminary a group of friends who, first, greatly admired the budding musician, and, second, came from the type of bourgeois background that had the education (and the financial wherewithal) that Schubert so conspicuously lacked. Ferdinand Luib's 1858 material contains contributions from men such as Anton Holzapfel (second violin and cello), a later philosopher turned composer, Benedikt Randhartinger (tympani), Anton Stadler, Josef Kenner, and Michael Rueskäfer, who were to become men of substance in nineteenth-century Austria, and most of whom earned more from their reminiscences of Schubert than Schubert ever earned from his music. Yet, without these good-hearted colleagues, Schubert would never have had the means to find and to study the books, anthologies, and music scores, nor indeed the very paper on which to compose. If, as Stadler reported, Schubert had to neglect the "dry schoolbooks" to practice violin and piano, then the daily full orchestral sessions (two overtures and a symphony) deepened his knowledge of contemporary music.[13]

From 1809 to 1811, Schubert made substantial progress in the seminary, both in his academic studies and in his music. In September 1810, Count Kuefstein received a note suggesting that Franz Schubert should be shown special consideration "since he has such a special talent for music."[14] He was now the outstanding treble in the seminary, playing first violin and often leading the orchestra as well, when Ruzicka could not attend. He was not the shrinking violet, as he is so often portrayed.

Schubert's compositions also were garnering praise. We have his first song, or, at any rate, the first to have survived, written on 30 March 1811. It brings an interesting connection with Goethe's world, for it is clearly based on Zumsteeg's *Hagars Klage in der Wüste Bersaba* (Hagar's Plaint in the Wilderness of Beersheba) of 1792. It is a setting of that same poem by Clemens Schücking but, 370 measures or so in length, Schubert's song *Hagars Klage* (D. 5), has remained something of a trial for singer and audience alike.

In 1811, Schubert's character seemed to undergo a change, the first perhaps, but certainly not the last. The change was surely connected with the general malaise caused by the war situation and the grave economic crises. Young though he was, he was affected by the sense of impending catastrophe, as all young Europeans have been in our century. The malaise deepened when his voice began to break, and when his beloved mother died on 28 May 1812.[15] Fortunately, Josef von Spaun had returned to Vienna from Linz to take up a legal post and he generously offered to take Schubert to the opera. They saw five or six works, including Mozart's *The Magic Flute*, which was as great a hit in Vienna as it was in Goethe's Weimar, but also the two Singspiele *Das Waisenhaus* (The Orphanage) and *Die Schweizerfamilie* (The Swiss Family) by Josef Weigl (1766–1846), a man who had worked with Mozart and was later to deny Schubert what would have been an important betterment to his financial condition. Such contacts stimulated Schubert's imagination; he had been interested in the art of the Singspiel and had begun to compose one, *Der Spiegelritter* (The Knight of the Mirror), after a play by August von Kotzebue in December 1811. Spaun had given him this text and probably also Kotzebue's *Des Teufels Lustschloss* (The Devil's Pleasure Castle). McKay suggested that the German author's irony and parody of romantic works was lost on Schubert, and Goethe was not impressed either, it might be recalled.[16]

The early biographies of Schubert seemed to agree that the academic work in the seminary completely excluded any study of German literature. Recent research, however, has shown that Austrian students would have been aware of some of the great names in German literature. *Institutio ad eloquentiam* was the guiding textbook for Austrian teachers from the beginning of the eighteenth century to 1848. Students were instructed how to develop their "clarity of thought, pleasantness and dignity," and how to follow the prescribed rules in German style and usage.[17] From the few examples of Schubert's German that we possess, it can fairly be claimed that he had been taught how to write a correct High German (the language of educated German speakers), although we know that daily intercourse would be in the native Viennese dialect (as it still is today). Thus, the *Institutio* would not only shape his style, but the examples of good and imaginative German writing would shape his attitude to and knowledge of German prose and poetry.

Quotations from the Greek and Roman classical authors were, naturally for the age, in the majority in this textbook, especially from Cicero and Virgil (the *Aeneid*, in particular). German poetry was represented by excerpts from the leading writers of the Göttingen Grove Circle and from those belonging to the classical age of German poetry, that is, representatives of the schools of poetry known as Rococo, Anacreontic, and the Age of Sentimentality, what we called "the poetry of the heart" that preceded the revolution of the Storm and Stress movement.

In the 1805 edition of the *Institutio*, Friedrich Gottlieb Klopstock, the poet of the twenty-thousand-verse epic *Messias* (1748–1773), took pride of place, since the earnestness of his works would correspond most closely with the ideas of the *Institutio*.[18] In the 1812 edition, which Ilija Dürhammer suggests was probably used by Schubert's teachers, that place was yielded to Gotthold Ephraim Lessing, the Saxon author of the plays *Minna von Barnhelm* (1767) and *Emilia Galotti* (1772). There were fifty-two quotations from Lessing versus sixteen from Klopstock. Three poets from the Göttingen Grove Circle, Ludwig Hölty and Matthias Claudius with three excerpts each, and Friedrich Stolberg with six, were also represented. Bürger's *Lenore* had four excerpts in the book, Friedrich von Matthisson eight, the Swiss poet J. G. von Salis-Seewis seven, while Michael Denis, the Austrian translator of Macpherson's *Ossian* in 1768–1769, had six. An author of fables, Gottlieb Konrad Pfeffel from Alsace, was in second place with twenty-three excerpts, well ahead of Goethe's friend Schiller with thirteen. And Goethe? He was represented by one excerpt only—fairly clear proof of the deleterious effect of his

Werther, but perhaps also because of rumors about his sexual behavior. Schiller, on the other hand, has always been thought of as the true guardian of German morality. Schubert realized this too, setting twenty-seven of Schiller's ballads and poems in 1814 before he discovered Goethe.

The reason for advancing such a detailed account of authors represented in the *Institutio* is that, with one exception, Schubert, up to 1815, set poems only by those writers whose work appeared in that book. (The exception was the Italian verses of Abbé Metastasio, known also as Pietro Trapassi, who died a court poet and an alcoholic in Vienna. He made his name as an opera librettist, but with a difference—he was a true poet. "The result was that every composer in Italy, and many outside, set Metastasio's dramas to music over and over again.")[19] Antonio Salieri, sixty-two in 1812 and resident in Vienna since the 1770s, himself the composer of many operas, had remained resolutely Italian, and he encouraged the young, talented Schubert to try his hand at setting Metastasio's texts to music, for example, his *Misero pargoletto* (D. 42) of 1813, the *Pensa che questo istante* (D. 76) of September 1813, and *Son fra l'onde* (D. 78) of 18 September 1813. We are reminded of the accusations of conservatism leveled against the aging Goethe when Spaun relates how Schubert's "youthful fire and originality" varied so much from the "forms which the gray-headed musician had always respected as the only acceptable ones." Spaun then tells how Salieri strongly disapproved of Schubert's inclination towards the German Lied in which Salieri found "only barbaric words which were not worth the trouble of setting to music."[20] (The British Schubert scholar Richard Capell repeated the Italian's strictures in his 1928 book on Schubert when he called the German language "uncouth and repellent" and suggested that some of Schubert's Lieder should be sung in English translation.)[21]

From 18 June, a week or so after his mother's death in 1812, Schubert visited Salieri twice weekly, and, although much of the time was taken up with compositional exercises, leaving the fifteen-year-old boy little opportunity for exercising his musical ideas, he would never have denied the benefits gained from his distinguished teacher. It may be that these very disciplined sessions, as well as the normal tight seminary discipline, irked the growing boy. His reports began to be less satisfactory, his relations with his father and his church worsened—a typical development in the life of any gifted youngster who is beginning to feel that he has achieved all he can at a particular point in his life. His father's remarriage on 25 April 1813 to Anna Kleyenböck (1783–1860), barely eleven months after the death of Schubert's mother, would certainly have contributed to the personal feeling of rebellion.[22]

Such a rebellious feeling would have been strengthened by the patriotic emotions raised in all Austrians when news came of Napoleon's defeat at the Battle of the Nations in Leipzig in October 1813, the month in which Schubert completed his first symphony (in D, D. 82), and a canon for three male voices *Auf den Sieg der Deutschen* (To the Victory of the Germans, D. 88). At that time, all German speakers, except for the Swiss, were "Germans." Schubert's father shared the patriotic emotions, even celebrating the return to Vienna of Emperor Francis on 16 June 1814 by displaying a banner outside his house with a patriotic verse. He did not share either his son's rebellious emotions or his desire to become a composer. That was an "art form without prospects"; Franz should become a teacher. The upshot was that, after five years' study at the seminary, Franz, at the end of October 1813, went to a teacher's training college, St. Anna's, to qualify him to teach at his father's school, a daunting prospect for a would-be composer.

Schubert left the seminary with a musical and academic education well above the norm. He had a reasonable knowledge of classical and German literature, he had demonstrated his ability to compose both instrumental and vocal music, and he had been fortunate to have heard good opera with his friend Josef von Spaun. What is more important, perhaps, his interest in the German Lied had been awakened by the study and performance of those Lieder introduced by his friends, particularly those of Zumsteeg and Beethoven, in which he said he could wallow for days.

THE LIED IN AUSTRIA

In chapter one we outlined the condition of the German Lied before Schubert. What was the state of the Lied in Austria at that time? To begin with, one should recall Maria Theresa's determination to keep Austria apart from other Germanic nations, an apartness that largely dissuaded Goethe from visiting Vienna. Her enlightened son, Joseph II, was not able to reform as much as he would have liked, and his successor eventually had to bend the knee to Napoleon.

The main Viennese protagonist of the Lied was Joseph Anton Steffan whose collections of German Lieder for the keyboard, published from 1778 to 1782, were of particular significance. The Viennese Lieder school did not provide the theoretical program of the Berlin schools, but since it was based on the vocal productions of Haydn and Mozart, it meant much more to Austrian composers. Most Viennese Lieder are closely related to the developing Singspiel, which had its roots in Italian opera. This gave more room for ornamentation and the use of unusual keys, and it afforded the piano a more important role.[23]

Schubert grew up with this type of Lied in Vienna, but the main influence on his early style was undoubtedly that of Zumsteeg and his *Kleine Balladen und Lieder* (Little Ballads and Songs), published in Leipzig between 1800 and 1805. We noted the first result: his song *Hagars Klage* of 1811. There were other models to follow, such as Goethe's friend Reichardt. Schubert copied out Reichardt's setting of the monologue from Goethe's *Iphigenie* as an exercise in the seminary and he used Reichardt's *Lieder der Liebe und der Einsamkeit* (Songs of Love and Solitude) of 1804 as examples to follow. From 1811 to 1816, his choice of poems was also clearly influenced by his study of Zumsteeg's Lieder, although, interestingly enough, these Lieder were settings of texts by the same poets whom he had encountered in the *Institutio ad eloquentiam*. Common to all of these was Bürger's ballad *Lenore* (1773), which had taken Europe by storm and had greatly influenced the new direction being taken by German poetry. It had led directly to the Goethe-Schiller *Year of Ballads* of 1797, when they, and particularly Schiller, produced the poems so admired by musicians of the Lied. Six of Schubert's thirteen early Lieder (up to 1813) are based on Schiller's ballads, seven on ballads in Zumsteeg's style.

GOETHE

Schubert lived at home in the Säulengasse from 1813 to 1816 while attending the teacher's training course at St. Anna's. There, too, he worked hard at his academic subjects and sailed through the final examination. Outside the college, he had twice-weekly lessons with Salieri, while his involvement with the family quartet and with the local church continued. Although there were major events during these years, including the birth of Anna Schubert's first child, Maria, on 22 January 1814, so soon after his father's remarriage, and the celebration of Napoleon's banishment to Elba in 1815, by far the most important one was Schubert's meeting with the sixteen-year-old Therese Grob, a local girl who sang soprano in Schubert's church choir.

An indication of Schubert's early recognition as a composer was the invitation to write a Mass to celebrate the hundredth anniversary of the founding of the parish church in Lichtental. In 1978, the church produced an interesting little book describing the event.[24] Schubert had already composed a Kyrie movement on 15 April 1813, which bore unmistakable traces of Haydn's Nelson Mass (of 1798). Schubert's Mass in F Major (D. 105) for four solo voices, mixed choir, orchestra, and organ was written between 17 May and 22 July 1814. According to the church's account, the Mass was performed on 16 October, but latest research suggests that this was unlikely and it probably took place on 25 September.[25] Schubert had conducted the work with his proud teacher Salieri in the congregation. The main soloist was Therese Grob. His love for this girl, who, according to Anton Holzapfel, was "no beauty, but with a nice figure, rather plump, and with a round, fresh, childish face," was to be an enduring one.[26]

Although it is not certain that what next took place is directly concerned with the burgeoning love between Franz and Therese, it is certain that it was the beginning of that unseen bond between Schubert and Goethe. Apparently Schubert had read with great interest Part I of Goethe's *Faust*; the poet's *Collected Works* had been published by Cotta's press in Vienna in 1810. The heart-rending soliloquy of the simple German girl Gretchen, who was loved, seduced, abandoned, and deranged by Faust, the aged professor now rejuvenated by the cynical Mephistopheles, and finally driven to drowning her child, for which crime she was sentenced to death, must have moved Schubert deeply, as it indeed moved many people. Gretchen does not sing this soliloquy, but speaks it while at her spinning wheel, musing on her intoxicating meeting with Faust. Schubert set the poem to music on 19 October 1814. His through-composed setting (D. 118), with the monotonous whirring in the accompaniment, representing the spinning wheel, then that wonderful pause when Gretchen thinks of Faust's kiss ("And, oh, his kiss!"), has long been regarded as the turning point in the history of the German Lied. Of course, since the song was not published by Cappi and Diabelli in Vienna until 1821 (then as Op. 2), it is false to pretend, or to claim, that it changed anything in 1814. For us, its relevance is the proof of Schubert's early awareness of, and reaction to, Goethe's poetry.

What was it, however, that Schubert had discovered in Goethe's poetry? Salieri's reported claim about his pupil, "He can do everything; he composes operas, Lieder, quartets, symphonies, and whatever you want!" was probably justified.[27] It seemed as if the young man could compose anything from quartets to symphonies, but to create something so innovatory with the poems of Germany's greatest poet— poems, moreover, not widely read in Vienna then—was an amazing achievement.

We have suggested that Schubert discovered, intuitively perhaps, what Goethe felt about poetry, namely, that musicality, rhythm, and rhyming were the prime elements of great verse and of great songs. A few years after *Gretchen am Spinnrade*, in 1817, Hans Georg Nägeli, a musicologist and music publisher in Zurich, wrote an essay for the *Allgemeine musikalische Zeitung* in Leipzig, titled "Die Liederkunst" (The Art of Lieder). In it, he claimed that a higher form of Lied must be created that would lead to a new epoch, "whose distinguishing feature would be a hitherto unrecognized 'polyrhythm,' so that linguistic, song, and playing rhythms would be merged into a higher artistic whole—a 'polyrhythm' which is as important in vocal music as polyphony is in instrumental music."[28] Thus, a song composer would not just reproduce what the poet had presented to him as a text; he would interpret the poem, alter it in so doing, and create out of the aforementioned elements, a new "polyrhythmical" work of art. Nägeli, who was later to offer to publish some of Schubert's works, must have believed that the young composer had achieved this goal with *Gretchen am Spinnrade* and some of the other post-1814 Lieder (although not all of those were through-composed). We would suggest another way of looking at *Gretchen am Spinnrade:* a great poem and a great musical setting create a higher synthesis, where the whole (the song) is greater than the sum of the parts. The setting justifies Bauernfeld's remark that anyone who understands poets as well as Schubert does must be a poet himself.[29]

Having discovered Goethe and experienced the power of his poetry, Schubert, on 30 November 1814, set another three of his poems, *Nachtgesang* (Night Song, D. 119), *Trost in Tränen* (Consolation in Tears, D. 120), both strophic settings, and on 3 December 1814 *Schäfers Klagelied* (Shepherd's Lament, D. 123). All these poems are found under the heading "Lieder" in Goethe's *Collected Poems*, having been written between 1801 and 1814. Schubert must then have turned back to his copy of *Faust* to write, on 12 December 1814, his *Szene aus Faust* (D. 126), "Wie anders, Gretchen, war dir" (How different you were, Gretchen). The scene where the Evil Spirit mocks the now pregnant Gretchen makes us wonder if Schubert was anticipating the possible consequences of too close a liaison with Therese Grob? It is surely proof positive of what poetry meant then to the seventeen year old. He had not just opened a book of poetry at random and picked out a poem with which to pass the time. These poems spoke personally to him; he shared the sentiments of their creator.

Schubert certainly seems to have been set on fire by this meeting with Goethe's poetry, for the next two years, 1815–1816, were among his most productive, certainly as far as Lieder were concerned. Nearly 250 can be attributed to these two years, more than forty to poems by Goethe. One always has to remember in totaling up Schubert's Goethe settings that many poems were set more than once, and a few were started, but never finished, so count as fragments. One critic has stated correctly: "Goethe's poetry remains, as it were, the point of orientation in the diversity of his Lieder 'oeuvre'."[30] Otherwise, Schubert continued to set poems by those authors with whose poems he had been familiar in the seminary: Matthias Claudius, Ludwig Hölty, Johann Jacobi, Friedrich Klopstock, Theodor Körner, Ludwig Kosegarten, James Macpherson's *Ossian*, Friedrich von Matthisson, J. G. von Salis-Seewis, and Friedrich Schiller.

Stadler recalled that he and Holzapfel used to shut Schubert up in a room with paper and "some volume of poems or other," while they went to church. When they returned, a song would be ready on the paper.[31] That remark "with some volume . . . or other" has led to the charge mentioned earlier that Schubert composed whatever was put in front of him, irrespective of its quality. This certainly would not say much for his intelligence or literary sensitivity. Ilija Dürhammer's massive article effectively denies the truth of some of these careless remarks; she documents much more realistic-sounding comments such as those of Anselm Hüttenbrenner in his reminiscences written for Franz Liszt in 1854. After Hüttenbrenner had praised a new Schubert Lied, the composer would say:[32]

> Yes, that's a good poem; you think of something sensible as soon as you hear it; the melodies stream out, so that it's a real joy. With a poor poem, nothing will come; you torture yourself with it and nothing comes out but dry-as-dust rubbish. I've rejected many poems that were foisted on to me.

Few would deny that Schubert's choice of Goethe poems in 1815 and 1816 contained some of the finest of the Weimar Prince of Poets, and it was significant that Schubert should choose the best of these for the packet that Josef von Spaun elected to send to Goethe with his famous letter of 17 April 1816. The packet contained seventeen Goethe settings: *An Schwager Kronos, Jägers Abendlied, Der König in Thule, Meeres Stille, Schäfers Klagelied, Die Spinnerin, Heidenröslein, Wonne der Wehmut, Wandrers Nachtlied, Erster Verlust, Der Fischer, An Mignon, Geistes-Gruss, Nähe des Geliebten, Gretchen am Spinnrade, Rastlose Liebe,* and *Erlkönig.* Although we shall look at the letter, its circumstances, and consequences more closely in chapter four, it is worth mentioning here that the poems of the first volume are, largely, superior to the poems of the second, which were never sent. Whether that was Spaun's or Schubert's decision is not known.

SCHUBERT'S FRIENDS

Ilija Dürhammer postulated that "Schubert had proven interests in art and literature which is shown by his friends who were almost exclusively artists, particularly poets and painters."[33] Ewan West has pointed out that there were indeed many other prolific composers in Vienna with whom Schubert had no contact whatsoever.[34] He seemed therefore to have preferred the company of non-musicians with whom he could discuss aesthetic matters unrelated to music. Even if, as we know, many of these sessions were to end up in drunken merriment, they certainly dispel any suggestion that Schubert was a solitary, poverty-stricken rustic, creating his immortal compositions in some miserable garret. Since many of his companions were talented poets, it was only natural that Schubert should reward their friendship and good company by setting their poems, many of which tell us a good deal about Schubert and his war-torn, economically stricken Vienna.

Schubert was at home among these writers and painters, because he himself enjoyed writing as well as setting other people's poems to music. Anton Holzapfel recalled the poem that Schubert had written in 1813 or so, during his time at the seminary, based, not so surprisingly, on a Klopstockian theme, namely, the power of the Almighty. Holzapfel was surprised that a boy of sixteen could write verses in a style "barely understood by those in the higher classes of the Gymnasium."[35]

Inhabitants of German-speaking countries have always been accustomed to composing verses for special occasions. In fact, at one time it was almost impossible to leave a German family with whom one had been staying without writing a few dedicatory lines in the family *Stammbuch*, a record of family events and thus much more than an autograph book. Schubert liked writing such verses, for example, the full-blown text for a cantata on his father's name-day on 4 October 1813. (In Catholic countries, a person's name-day was celebrated as well as the actual birthday.) This cantata, *Zur Namensfeier meines Vaters* (D. 80), was written for three male voices with guitar accompaniment and is the only genuine Schubert guitar accompaniment. It begins in heroic Grecian style with a call to Apollo to "descend and inspire our songs."[36]

Again, the closeness of the relationships between these friends meant that occasions of joy and sorrow would often be marked by poems, some of which would be set to music by Schubert. Perhaps because of those occasions of personal confession, as it were, Schubert began a diary to which he committed some of his innermost joys and worries. What is striking about the diary is, again, the contrast between the quality of his formal German, irrespective of the, at times, high-flown, idealistic thoughts expressed, and that old-fashioned image of the unlettered Viennese tune-smith. (It was surprising how many radio and TV programs, books, and articles produced in 1997 for the bicentennial of Schubert's birth felt it necessary still to refute this description. It was obviously deeply rooted.)

One diary entry particularly relevant to our theme is dated 13 June 1816, where Schubert writes of Mozart and Goethe in the same entry: "It was a bright, light, beautiful day which will remain with me throughout my life. The magical notes of Mozart's music still echo as from afar." He had attended a musical occasion at which the violinist Martin Schlesinger had played in Mozart's String Quintet in G Minor (K. 516). Such impressions, Schubert wrote,[37]

show us a light, bright, beautiful distant prospect in the darkness of this life to which we can look forward with confidence. Oh, Mozart, immortal Mozart, oh, how many, oh, how infinitely many such blessed impressions of a brighter, better life have you burned into our souls!

Then he wrote of his contribution: "I played some Beethoven variations, sang Goethe's *Rastlose Liebe* and Schiller's *Amalia*. Unanimous applause for the latter, less for the former. Although I regard my *Rastlose Liebe* as more successful than *Amalia*, one cannot deny that Goethe's musical poetic genius contributed much to the applause." *Rastlose Liebe* (Restless Love, D. 138) and *Amalia* (D. 195) had both been composed on 19 May 1815, and it is interesting how Schubert could describe Goethe's genius as musically poetic, for Josef von Spaun had sent off his packet of Schubert Lieder to Goethe on 17 April 1816, just two months before this concert. Undeterred by the lack of response from Goethe, Schubert turned to him again in September, and set the three Harper's songs from *Wilhelm Meister* as a little song cycle (D. 478).

On 16 June 1816, Schubert wrote a poem for the fiftieth anniversary of the arrival of his teacher Antonio Salieri in Vienna and set it to music (*Beitrag zur fünfzigjährigen Jubelfeier des Herrn von Salieri*, D. 407). It is a nice, touchingly humorous tribute to the old man. That day he commented in his diary on the occasion and its music. It is, of course, probable that an evening arranged in honor of an old man brought up on the mid-eighteenth-century canon of Gluck had not been too complimentary to modern composers, but, nevertheless, it was surprising that Schubert should comment so brusquely that the eccentricity of one of their greatest German musicians which bizarrely combines and confuses the tragic with the comic, the agreeable with the repulsive, the heroic with howlings, the most sacred with clowning, and does not distinguish between them, driving people mad instead of lulling them to love, incites them to laughter instead of raising them up to God.

This entry betrays Schubert's ambiguous attitude towards its subject, Beethoven, but when one recalls Goethe's verdict on Beethoven after that meeting in 1812 in Teplitz, one wonders what he would have thought of Schubert had Spaun enclosed such a comment with his packet of Lieder. He might even have congratulated the young composer on his perspicacity.[38]

One might think of that diary entry as mature criticism of one reasonably experienced composer of another. Whether the quasi-philosophical entries made later on 8 September 1816 could be accepted as profound considerations of Schubert's personal and Vienna's political situation is more open to question. Such writings were, of course, on every hand at this, the height of the Romantic Movement, an age that was to supersede Goethe's and Schiller's dream of a humane classicism, with a revival of unclassic individualism, not unlike, though less negative and turbulent than the Storm and Stress movement of their youth.

August Wilhelm Schlegel had delivered his celebrated lectures Über dramatische Kunst und Literatur (On Dramatic Art and Literature) in Vienna between 1809 and 1811, although he is probably best remembered for his magisterial translations of seventeen of Shakespeare's dramas between 1797 and 1810 that made Shakespeare a truly national poet of the Germans. His brother Friedrich had pronounced in one of his Fragments written for the Athenaeum: "Romantic poetry is a progressive, universal poetry" in which all the arts were to merge. "It embraces everything that is poetic."[39] Schubert would surely have agreed with another description of music adumbrated by one of the Romantics who lived in Jena, a few miles from Goethe's Weimar: Wilhelm Heinrich Wackenroder declared music to be "the land of faith where all our doubts and all our sufferings are lost in a sea of sound." The youngest of the Romantics was Ludwig Tieck, a close friend of Wackenroder and an early admirer of Goethe. He began his poem Glosse (1816): "Love thinks in sweet tones / For thoughts are much too far away / Only in music does she like to beautify all she will."[40] Perhaps the most influential of all the Romantics was Friedrich von Hardenberg (known as Novalis), a student at Jena in Goethe's time, whose Hymnen an die Nacht (Hymns to the Night, 1800), an outpouring of religious grief, made such an enormous impression, particularly as Novalis died "Romantically" young, at the age of twenty-nine. (Schubert set four of the hymns, D. 659–662, in May 1819.) It looks, therefore, as if Schubert was well acquainted with these Romantic ideas. The diary entries of 8 September 1816 were written after a meeting of his like-minded friends whom he saw regularly.

"LOST LOVE"

On 20 August, Schubert had been rejected for a position as music instructor at a teachers' training college in Laibach (now Lubljana), which would have allowed him the wherewithal to marry Therese Grob. Recent research has brought to light the so-called Law on Consent to Marriage, and this work makes clear that Schubert would not have been allowed to marry a woman whom he could not support or properly maintain.[41] In 1815, Emperor Francis I of Austria issued the law which stated, among other things, that those "of the lower orders" would not be permitted to marry unless their income "allowed sufficient maintenance for the feeding of the family." A frightening number of people could not be married without political consent; included among these are musicians. Although Schubert was technically an assistant teacher at the time, he too needed permission. Since members of the aristocracy, property owners, leading civil servants, and most professional classes were not included in the ban, it was held to be a typically anti-democratic measure from the chancellor Metternich, backed by his sinister chief of police, Count Joseph Sedlnitzky. One of the unsurprising consequences of this law in Vienna was the rapid rise in illegitimate births: in 1834, there were ten illegitimate to every twelve legitimate births.

It now seems that this law destroyed Schubert's dream of happiness with Therese and perhaps even soured the remainder of his short life. He was always prone to bouts of depression, from which indeed many Viennese suffered. Ignaz, Schubert's elder brother, wrote bitterly on 14 August 1824: "The latest news is that a mad suicidal craze is raging here, it is as if people knew for certain that, once they were on the other side, they could jump straight into heaven."[42] Hans Fröhlich wondered if the infamous Föhn, that warm debilitating wind that blew in from southern Europe, might not be the cause.[43] The weather was bad in 1816, and the harvests failed, bringing massive unemployment to Vienna and the countryside.

Schubert's diary entries of 8 September began with a quotation: "Man is like a ball played with by Chance and the Passions." He thought that this saying was "extraordinarily true" and went on to use the Shake-spearean image in *As You Like It* of man as an actor playing several roles on the stage, subject to the whims of the audience of the moment. In heaven, however, man will be subject only to the praise or disapproval of the "Universal Stage-Director." Schubert then pronounced as "happy" (or maybe "lucky") the man who finds "a true male friend" and happier the one who finds a true female friend in his "woman" or "wife." Schubert goes on to call marriage a fearful thought for an un-married man in these times; if he does not marry, his alternatives are "misery or gross sensuality," and he accuses the "monarchs of his age" of being blind to these facts of life. Schubert finishes his reflections with a poem whose last lines were to be strangely echoed in Wilhelm Müller's *Die schöne Müllerin* poems (1820). ("The Maid of the Mill," as it is usually translated, is actually "The Miller's Lovely Daughter.") Schubert's poem runs: "Strange questions / do I hear everyone say? / No more to be risked here. / We must just bear it and suffer. / So, good night / till you awake." Müller's poem *Der Müller und der Bach* (The Miller and the Brook) ends: "Good night / good night / till everything awakes." (Mc-Kay writes that "some of this is very jejune stuff," but we agree with her that most entries reflect Schubert's "real personal concerns.")[44]

It is often overlooked that the younger generation of Romantics revered the Goethe of *Werther* and *Wilhelm Meister* as their master. Schu-bert had done the same with his settings of so many Goethe poems in the years 1814–1816, and, although we noted that Goethe dismissed Romantic literature as "what is sick," all his writing up till then on hu-man emotions and experiences had fed the philosophies and the litera-ture of the Romantic Movement.

We must regard Schubert's 1816 diary entries in this light. Hans Fröhlich saw "lost love" as one of the four major themes of Schubert's art, the other three being yearning, wandering, and death.[45] Certainly fifty of Schubert's Lieder concern death.[46] Schubert's "lost love" changed his life. He never forgot Therese, nor she him. Although she married a baker, Johann Bergmann, on 21 November 1820, she kept in her possession a bundle of sixteen Schubert Lieder apparently written for her alone. When she died in 1875, childless, aged seventy-seven, she bequeathed them to a nephew who discovered a title page added by Therese: "Lieder (man-uscripts) by Franz Schubert, which I, solely and alone, possess." One of these songs, *Klage* (Lament), begins: "No longer shall I bear the burden of this pain." Schubert's first setting of this poem, *Der Leidende* (He Who Suffers, D. 432), was in May 1816, and neither the author of the poem, nor the writer of Therese's manuscript, are known. The sentiments could cer-tainly have been Schubert's. In his memoirs of 1854, Anselm Hüttenbrenner wrote how, during a walk, he had once asked Schubert if he disliked the opposite sex. "Oh no," Schubert replied:[47]

> I loved one girl very dearly and she me. She was a teacher's daughter, somewhat younger than I was, and she sang the soprano solos in a Mass which I composed really beautifully and with deep emotion. She was not really very pretty, she had pock-marks in her face; but she was good, (she was) an angel. For three years I hoped to marry her, but I couldn't find a position which would maintain us both. She then married another man, at the wishes of her parents, which hurt me greatly. I still love her and, since then, no other girl has meant as much to me or more. She just wasn't meant for me, I suppose.

From that time on, Schubert's deepest friendships were made with men who shared his musical and literary interests, his sense of fun, and his emotions. Although a paradoxical figure in many ways, now reveling in high spirits in inns and coffee-houses, now sitting ill and dispirited alone, composing songs on texts of blackest despair, Schubert also had the wonderful gift of communication. One of his friends, Johann Mayrhofer, always admitted that his poems only seemed readable to him after Schubert had set them to music. He put his feelings into touching words:

> Tell me, who taught you Lieder, so honeyed and so fine?
> They summon up a heaven from out this troubled time.
> The land was lying mist-clothed, veiled before our eyes,
> You sing, the suns are shining, and Spring around us lies.

Schubert set the poem as *Geheimnis. An Franz Schubert* (Secret. For Franz Schubert, D. 491) in October 1816. Mayrhofer was to become one of the group of intellectuals who helped to shape Schubert's aesthetic growth.[48]

Although a lost love was an important factor in the second half of Schubert's short life of thirty-one years, some compensation was found in the fairly large group of friends who gathered around little Schwammerl in the years after 1816. (*Schwammerl* literally means "little mushroom" in the Viennese dialect and can be translated "tubby." In Schubert's case, it was probably a friendly allusion to the little man's plumpness as he stood only five feet, one inch, or one meter fifty-seven.)

In many ways, this was a first step into adulthood. The age itself was exciting, turbulent, and challenging. The Battle of Waterloo on 18 June 1815 had seen the end of Napoleon's dictatorship, but the democratic ideas and ideals that he had rescued from the mindless excesses of the Reign of Terror after 1793, and which survived his misguided megalomania, had taken root in the hearts of young Europeans growing up between 1815 and 1820. In Austria, those ideals had met with an abrupt shock. In 1809, Emperor Francis I had appointed Metternich as his adviser, and both men were now intent on crushing any revolutionary ideas that Napoleon might have inspired, a suppression that was to last thirty years and eventually bring about the 1848 revolution. A close watch was kept on schools and universities; books, newspapers, and music scores were censored, and youthful groups ("Jacobins" to Metternich) and meetings were strictly controlled.

Friedrich Schlegel's stay in Vienna from 1808 to 1829 had enormous consequences for Austrian culture. Metternich and Chief of Police (from 1817) Sedlnitzky had sought to prevent seditious German literature from reaching Austria. There was a short period of freedom after the French left Vienna on 20 November 1809, when publisher Bernhard Bauer was able to bring out a *Deutscher Parnass,* an anthology of German poetry. It is claimed that half the poets in the anthology were set later by Schubert, who must therefore have been well acquainted with modern German literature. For example, Goethe's *Collected Works* had also reached Vienna in 1810, and when Schlegel founded the *Österreichische Beobachter* it included selections from Goethe's and Schiller's lyric poetry.[49] Ernst Hilmar wrote: "He introduced German literature—(and Schlegel regarded German literature as the quintessence of intellectual life)—to Austria."[50]

Many other distinguished Germans then made their way to Austria: Theodor Körner, from 1811 to his death in the 1813 Leipzig battle; Joseph von Eichendorff stayed a year in 1811 (and is inscribed on the university's honors board); and Clemens von Brentano from 1813 to 1814. Brentano was first married to Goethe's friend, Maximiliane von La Roche, and was the brother of Goethe's slavish admirer Bettina (von Arnim). Brentano and Achim von Arnim, Bettina's husband, had published the highly influential collection of folksongs *Des Knaben Wunderhorn* in 1805–1808. (The strange title is that of the first poem.) Dedicated to, and much praised by Goethe in a review, it is surprising that Schubert, so alive at the time to literary influences, was not moved to set some of the attractive poems, for there were certainly mutual contacts between the Schlegel circle and Schubert's friends. The poets of his 1818–1823 Lieder show a strong leaning towards Schlegel's Romantic-Catholic influence.

In this era of what Hilmar called "the authorities' antipathy to culture,"[51] Schubert began to frequent this circle of like-minded friends in group meetings that were to extend the young, modestly educated composer's literary horizons. We have mentioned his good fortune in having such friends in the seminary, who, although from a vastly superior social milieu, were so impressed by the young composer that they wished to retain his friendship. The names of these young men, most of them older than Schubert, continually recur in O. E. Deutsch's documentation: Josef von Spaun from Linz, Josef Kenner, poet Johann Mayrhofer, Anton von Spaun (Josef's younger brother), Anton Ottenwalt, and Anton Stadler. Another group of friends were mainly from Vienna: Franz von Schober, Franz von Bruchmann, the painter Moritz von Schwind, and Eduard von Bauernfeld.

As one would expect, there was much quasi-philosophical talk among these young men, full of idealistic hopes for a better, future life, free from the horrors of war and the shackles of censorship. As a whole, the Romantic Movement was built up on the word *Sehnsucht*, a "yearning" for a better world, which some, like the early German Romantics in Berlin and Jena around 1800, believed they saw in the folk tale books and fairy tales of the Middle Ages. The later group, centered on Heidelberg, had been more influenced by Napoleon's patriotic and nationalistic fervor, which they adopted. Their yearning was a more practical, political one, for a better Germany. To support this aim, Brentano and Arnim wrote patriotic songs, while Theodor Körner not only wrote such songs, but actually died for his country at Leipzig in October 1813. Schubert had met Körner at a performance of Gluck's *Iphigénie en Tauride* in January 1813 and had been fired by his patriotic fervor, as had his friend Spaun.

The Austrian group's philosophy was summed up by Anton Ottenwalt in a letter of 28 July 1817 to Franz von Schober: "It was in the year of the comet 1811 when we said we want to be called brothers because of our mutual love of goodness." This "love of goodness" sounds very Romantic, typical of impractical young men remote from worldly concerns, but the group was certain that its aims had a practical goal. Anton von Spaun wrote to Schober on 13 August 1816: "We must study the people and all the (past) ages and the best of what was done and said in and by the best of them . . . so that we know what we want and can work for the good of those we love, for our brothers." In an undated letter to Schober, he wrote: "We can topple tyrants, die for the Fatherland . . . we can act and achieve true greatness!"[52]

Their goal was made public with the appearance of a journal *Beyträge zur Bildung für Jünglinge* (Essays on Self-Education for Young Men), a study of "the good, the true, and the beautiful." Classical authors, both ancient and modern, as well as the group's contemporary friends, were represented by texts and poems, which were then discussed in detail at their meetings. In the light of Schubert's passionate involvement with Goethe in 1815 and 1816, it is interesting to note that the great Weimar poet was represented by one quotation only.[53]

No letter or contribution from Schubert exists among all these writings, but his long friendship with the main contributors must have had a great influence on his intellectual development. He found not only poems there that he could set to music, poems that he would never have come across otherwise, but also a source of "self-education," the possession of which gave him confidence to meet and consort with people above his social station.

One of these, and the second man to influence Schubert's life and work, was the distinguished elder baritone, Johann Michael Vogl (1768– 1840), whom Schubert had first heard in Gluck's *Iphigénie en Tauride* in January 1813. Vogl, now forty-nine, had enjoyed an illustrious operatic career, including the role of Don Pizarro in the May 1814 performance of Beethoven's *Fidelio*. He was an imposing figure who had had a good classical education and was a considerable linguist, having translated Epictetus's *Enchiridon* into four languages. (His regard for Walter Scott was to be shared later by both Schubert and Goethe.) Not surprisingly, Vogl found the tiny Schubert an uninspiring sight at their first meeting in early 1817. Schubert had fortunately certain recent compositions behind him that allowed him to meet the singer on his territory. Two songs on classical themes were with him at their meeting: *Memnon* (D. 541) on a poem by Mayrhofer, and *Ganymed* (D. 544) by Goethe. Josef von Spaun wrote later: "When *Memnon* and *Ganymed* were accompanied for him (Vogl), which however he only sang *sotto voce*, he became even more friendly." Although Vogl then left the room, he first patted Schubert on the shoulder, saying, "There is something in you, but you are not enough of an actor, not enough of a charlatan. You squander your fine ideas, without taking them far enough." Later, he expressed his amazement at the profundity and maturity of such a young man.[54]

From 1817 Schubert and Vogl became firm friends. The older man naturally took the honors wherever they performed, but Vogl was ever generous in his praise of the young composer. Vogl was not without his faults. Many singers nowadays curse him for some of the ornamentations that he added to Schubert's scores, but without his support Schubert would not have gained the little public acclaim that he did receive. Dietrich Fischer-Dieskau, who many would claim has done for Schubert's Lieder in the twentieth century what Vogl did for them in the nineteenth, sees Vogl's literary interests as responsible for his wishing to champion a composer whose settings give clear evidence of his understanding of the deeper meaning of the poems.[55] In his diary, Vogl wrote:[56]

Nothing proves the need for a good school of singing more clearly than Schubert's songs. How else can we interpret his truly divine inspirations, his musical clairvoyance and all of which the German language is capable? Many of us could learn, perhaps for the first time, that his world consists of poetry in sound, words in notes, thoughts clothed in music. We could learn that the poems of our greatest poets, transmuted into his musical idiom, become even greater.

Eight more Goethe poems were set in 1817, and another fifty Lieder were written to poems of this group of friends with whom Schubert was not only consorting, but actually living, first of all, with Josef von Spaun, and then, from the fall of 1816 to August 1817, with the family of Franz von Schober. Schober, a year younger than Schubert, was born in Malmö, Sweden, of wealthy parents, and came to Vienna in 1815 to study law. He was the third and, eventually, the major influence in Schubert's life and, alas, his death. Before Schober played that role, however, Schubert received an invitation at a very appropriate time. His father had received a new appointment to a school in the Rossau district, not far from Himmelpfortgrund, and now in the Grünetorgasse, a sidestreet off the Porzellangasse, in the same district (IX) of Vienna. Schubert was unable to share his father's elation, and this led to an angry exchange of words and the realization on both sides that the time of parting was nigh.

Baron Karl von Schönstein, a gifted tenor-baritone to whom Schubert was to dedicate his song cycle *Die schöne Müllerin,* came to Vienna in 1818. He related in his memoirs of 1857 that Schubert was invited by Count Johann Karl Esterházy to tutor his two daughters on his estate in Zseliz, Hungary (the present-day Zeliezovce in Slovakia). By this time, Schubert had composed a considerable number of works: six symphonies, piano works, seven stage-works, and, of course, many Lieder, although few had yet been published. *Am Erlafsee* (On Lake Erlaf, D. 586), was his first song to be published, in January 1818, although there had been some public performances of his music. This invitation from an aristocratic family lifted his spirits enormously. He set off for Hungary in July, twenty-one years old. It was his first time away from Vienna. Had recognition come his way at last?

The Zseliz Esterházys were only distantly related to the family in Eisenstadt in Austria's Burgenland who had been Haydn's employers. There were two daughters, Marie, aged sixteen, and Caroline, aged thirteen. Although both countesses are called "good children" in Schubert's letter of 8 September 1818 to Schober, most critical attention has been directed to the mention of the "very pretty chambermaid," who was often Schubert's "companion."[57] The young woman was Josefine ("Pepi") Pöckelhofer, who has been held responsible for infecting Schubert with venereal disease. It would seem that Schubert, away from home for the first time, suffering the pangs of lost love, succumbed to the undoubted charms of the girl. Schubert's first biographer, Kreissle von Hellborn, and Schubert's friends, mention the affair *sotto voce*. Schönstein, for example, wrote: "A love affair with a maid which Schubert started up shortly after his arrival in the house, soon yielded to a more poetic flame," a reference to an undoubted platonic affection that Schubert entertained for Countess Caroline.[58] Modern writers and less inhibited critics, accustomed to attributing most disorders in artists' lives to sexual problems or incompatibilities, make great play with the Pepi episode. Peter Härtling's imaginative re-creation of Schubert's life describes how Pepi seduced Franz in a barn, and he follows that with an excursus on its possible consequences: the attack of syphilis at the end of 1822. Was Pepi responsible?[59] British biographer Elisabeth Norman McKay exonerates Pepi from this charge and quotes approvingly Spaun's, perhaps innocent, belief that, although he agreed that Schubert felt great affection for his pupil Caroline, he was convinced that "Schubert had no relationship . . . with any other girl."[60]

When Schubert returned from Zseliz on 19 November 1818 after his four months' stay, he made the difficult decision to give up teaching and to live independently after the example of his great Viennese contemporary, Beethoven. Schubert had earned much money in Zseliz and could now move in to the Wipplingerstrasse flat with his friend Mayrhofer who had been supplying him regularly with poems to set to music. (In all, Schubert set forty-seven of Mayrhofer's poems.) Indeed, it is to this period that Georgiades' perceptive remark is most relevant: "(Schubert) was the first to compose no longer for the 'others,' but for himself—for himself and those like him."[61]

We now find Schubert regularly in the company of these better-off, better-educated, better-housed friends. The group round the Spaun brothers and their short-lived journal *Beyträge* had concerned itself with promoting what Anton von Spaun proclaimed as "the divine in man," namely, friendship which, in turn, meant extending the hand to all who were to be united against the "limitless power" of the Austrian censorship. Their ideals made them sound like an Austrian version of the Prussian League of Virtue, which was also striving for a world shaped by the noblest enlightened virtues of the French Revolution.

Schubert's other group of friends was more concerned with aesthetic progress, with art, music, and poetry. They too had been inspired by the fine-sounding democratic and poetical ideals emanating from France, but one soon hears a more idealistic note in their utterances. Franz von Schober's poem *An die Musik* (To Music), which Schubert set in March 1817 (D. 547), contains the key to their philosophy, it has been suggested: "Divine Art, in how many gray hours / have you transported me into a better world?"[62] They are recognizably the brothers of the German Romantic Movement, although the emphasis on virtue seems to link them to the hard-headed Prussian Protestant work ethic rather than to the normally more easy-going Viennese.

The strange point about it all is that the ideals so eagerly embraced by both the German and the Austrian Romantics, which seem at first sight to be fresh, revolutionary thoughts, hark back to the Age of Enlightenment. Goethe and Schiller had enthusiastically trumpeted these ideals in their classical period: in Goethe's *Iphigenie* (1787) and *Tasso* (1790), and in Schiller's *Don Carlos* (1787), where his Marquis von Posa pleads with King Philip of Spain, "Give them freedom of thought." Nor has it escaped notice that the German Romantics' word *Sehnsucht* (yearning) was mirrored in Goethe-Schiller's longing for classical Greece.

Schubert's compositions in 1818 to 1820 reflect this abiding interest in the contemporary poetry of the Romantics, yet it was Goethe who gave him one of his most satisfying moments. On 28 February 1819, the twenty-three-year-old tenor Franz Jäger sang Goethe's *Schäfers Klagelied* (Shepherd's Lament, D. 121) in Vienna, the first public performance of a Schubert Lied. The *Wiener Allgemeine Zeitung* of 4 March called it "a beautiful composition," and Berlin and Leipzig journals followed suit on 22 and 24 March.[63] In that year, Schubert set another five Goethe poems, which heralded his return to the poems of the Weimar giant whom he had neglected in his involvement with the Romantics in 1818. In addition, he was still writing for the theater in the hope that he would be able to make there the name that his songs and instrumental works had as yet failed to make for him. On 19 January 1819, he completed in a few weeks what has turned out to be one of his best Singspiele, *Die Zwillingsbrüder* (The Twin Brothers, D. 647), but, just as Goethe had failed to find a composer for his libretti, so Schubert always failed to find a good librettist for his stage works. It was perhaps easier to find texts for his Lieder, since they did not need to be translated into stage-scenes. One wonders indeed why he never tried to write a libretto to suit his music? He started no fewer than nineteen Singspiele in all, including a setting of Goethe's *Claudine von Villa Bella* in August 1814, but none has gained universal acceptance. McKay, a recognized authority on Schubert's works for the stage, believed that this was caused, at least in part, by the Viennese music publishers' unwillingness to take risks with "new works" by "serious composers." Another reason was one that has always bedeviled the publishing and performance of classical music, namely, the enormous appeal of lighter works, "dances, short piano pieces, and arrangements of popular operas written for amateurs of limited accomplishment."[64]

Yet a far more cogent reason was the extraordinary popularity of the operas of Gioacchino Rossini who, providing thirty-six operas from 1810 to 1829, caused the celebrated Rossini craze in Vienna. (His five months' concert tour in Britain in 1823 brought him in nearly seven thousand pounds sterling.) The craze had begun with his *Tancredi*, given in Italian in 1816, and in German in Vienna in 1818; in 1817 came *L'Italiana in Algeri*, and then, on 29 April 1819, *Otello*, which Schubert went to hear. (In a letter to Anselm Hüttenbrenner of 19 May 1819, he declares that one cannot deny Rossini "extraordinary genius"—and a note of envy creeps in.)

Another visitor, with interests relevant to our study, also went to hear that *Otello*. On 20 July 1819, Goethe's friend Zelter arrived for a three-week stay in Vienna. He wrote a long letter to Goethe describing his stay from 20 July to 18 August before he moved on to Prague and Dresden.[65] He went straight to the Kärntnertor-Theater to see a performance of *Otello*, and he too called the composer "without doubt a man of genius." The performances of three farces on the next night left him helpless: "My chest is still sore from laughing so much," he wrote, but the plays were "below the vulgar."

His general opinion of the Viennese is interesting considering our discussion of the views of Schubert's circle of friends. "You can see why these people are not political," he wrote to Goethe. "They want to live for, and enjoy, every minute—and that's enough. Politics are boring!" On Thursday, it was Rossini again—this time *La gazza ladra* (The Thieving Magpie) in German. The music, Zelter wrote, "is near to Mozart, but he is more daring and profound." He heard Mozart's *La clemenza di Tito* shortly afterwards, but thought that the Weimar production was superior—that, no doubt, was for Goethe's eyes only. The four female singers "could have been grandmothers," but they all sang quite well.

Then came a meeting that makes us ponder. Zelter met Antonio Salieri (now sixty-nine), who felt himself to be "out of date." Zelter vehemently denied that, "for his talent is still flowing and none of his pupils rate above him," but there was no mention of one of his pupils: Franz Schubert. Next, Zelter met Josef Weigl, "a pretty, fattish man of the world," a pupil of Mozart and Haydn, and the man who had been preferred to Schubert for the post of Kapellmeister to the court.

On 29 July, Zelter walked to the palace of Schönbrunn with Salieri who, "because he is so full of melodies, speaks in music." Salieri had written a Requiem Mass for his wife who had died in 1807. Not following her as quickly as he had expected he would, Salieri composed a shorter Mass, saying: "That one's good enough for me!"

Zelter heard that Beethoven was living outside Vienna, but no one could tell him where. The composer was now completely deaf, it seemed, so "it was a waste of time visiting him," Zelter was told. He was also told that Archduke Rudolf was supporting Beethoven with fifteen hundred gulden per year, but, Zelter's informant added, "Really, he's a fool!" On 14 August, Zelter met up with Beethoven on the main road from Mödling outside Vienna. Zelter reported to Goethe: "The unfortunate man is as good as deaf and I could hardly keep back my tears." They embraced each other warmly.

Another curious event took place the day Zelter went to see Wilhelmine Schröder in the play *Merope*. "Her voice is resonant," he wrote, "but her breathing is at fault." Schröder (later Devrient), after appearing as an actress in Vienna from 1819 to 1821, took up singing. She married Karl Devrient in 1823 after her greatest success, as Leonore in Beethoven's *Fidelio* in 1822, for which she was rehearsed by Beethoven. She also sang Schubert's *Erlkönig* to Goethe on 23 April 1830 and is known as the first great European singing-actress. It was strange that Zelter should see her when she was only fifteen.

On 15 August, Zelter met the twenty-seven-year-old Franz Grillparzer whose dramas *Die Ahnfrau* (The Ancestress, 1817) and *Sappho* (1818) were establishing him as Austria's leading dramatist. Grillparzer came to see Goethe in Weimar in 1826, but never mentioned Schubert, although, by that time, they knew each other quite well. Goethe found him a pleasant, agreeable man, but neither Goethe nor Eckermann thought much of *Die Ahnfrau* when it was produced in Weimar. With Grillparzer on that day was the Abbé Stadler, who had been close to Schubert and knew him well enough to compose an organ fugue in his memory after his death in 1828. But again, neither mentioned Schubert. What if Zelter had brought back news of Schubert's wonderful settings of Goethe's poems?

Thus, Zelter's visit passed with the Prussian full of praise for the city, but critical of some of the music. The music in the Burgtheater, for example, was not "as well organized" as that in Weimar, but he did try again to get Goethe to come to Vienna. He would find him a room in Baden (outside Vienna) for a mere twelve gulden per day, he wrote.

So, once again, Fate passed by our two characters. Whether Zelter heard nothing about Schubert is, of course, impossible to prove. Some feel that he kept Schubert's settings from Goethe, either from jealousy, or because he honestly felt that Goethe would have had no time for them. He was of enormous value to Goethe, not at all the humorless pedant often described and derided, but a man who traveled widely, and who could observe (and describe) new musical phenomena accurately and expertly. The usual cliché that "he did not like through-composed songs" and therefore would not have liked Schubert's and was instrumental in keeping them from Goethe, strikes us as being too dogmatic. Granted, it would not be surprising that a man of sixty-one, a much more advanced age in those days than now, might look askance at the work of a new young composer in his field, but Zelter did promote the young Mendelssohn after all, and we have noted how he (and Goethe) admired Rossini's pyrotechnics. We believe therefore that Zelter neither saw nor heard Schubert's Lieder, nor did Goethe.

Had Zelter met Schubert in 1819, he would have met a twenty-two year old who was beginning to believe in his ability, one who with the help of talented and influential friends whom he had made (Michael Vogl, above all) might be about to fulfil the potential that all his friends (at least) had long recognized. He had traveled outside Vienna and had received praise and recognition from many important people. His songs were being sung in homes, at musical gatherings, and in public now, too. The contemporary love of "Variations" had led to Sylvester Paumgartner in Steyr begging him to write variations on the theme of the song *Die Forelle* (The Trout, D. 550) of 1816–1817, which then became the fourth movement of the Piano Quintet (D. 667) of 1819. Although his *Erlkönig* had been offered for sale by his friends, led by Leopold Sonnleithner, at a house concert on 1 December 1820 (when one hundred copies were sold in the evening), it was not until March 1821 that Cappi and Diabelli published it as Op. 1, leading among others to an *Erlkönig* waltz published on 13 August 1821. (Kreissle von Hellborn thought that a "profanation.")[66]

In addition, Schubert was still dreaming of a breakthrough as an operatic composer. The opposition to German opera in pro-Italian Vienna was considerable. The court and the upper classes still spoke Italian and French—even Zelter had to remark on the coarse dialect of the Viennese—and their enthusiasm for Rossini left a native Austrian little chance of success. Schubert's dogged persistence in seeking out librettists also owes something to his ever-increasing interest in literature and drama. When a decent libretto eventually came from a gifted colleague such as Eduard von Bauernfeld, Schubert never managed to finish the opera *Der Graf von Gleichen* (The Count of Gleichen, D. 918), which, incidentally, included a setting of Goethe's *Wonne der Wehmut* (Joy of Sadness, D. 260).[67]

There were now other gray clouds on the horizon. In March 1819, the assassination in Berlin of Goethe's *bête noire*, the arch-conservative, egotistical dramatist August von Kotzebue, by the student Karl Ludwig Sand, led to an increasing surveillance of student and debating groups such as Schubert's. His friend Johann Senn was arrested at a party in his rooms, along with Schubert and a few friends. Senn was then imprisoned on a charge of sedition and eventually deported back to the Tyrol. Schubert escaped without a charge, but the ensuing fear of police intervention temporarily halted the meetings of their literary circle.

A much larger and blacker cloud was soon to descend. Because of the police intervention in Austria after the 1819 incident, Schubert was pleased to get away from Vienna for a time. He set off on a journey to Michael Vogl's native heath in Steyr. The beautiful scenery and the mountain air made Schubert write to Mayrhofer from Linz on 19 August 1819: "I had a wonderful time in Steyr—and will have it again. The countryside is heavenly." When he returned, Mayrhofer and he decided to part, Schubert moving into a room of his own.[68]

It is still not clear what caused the undoubted change in Schubert's character during the next few years. Some blame the continuing strife with his father, which plainly upset both men. Others attribute the change to the stifling police censorship that had caused the friends' journal to close and to limit the number of their meetings. Then the news of Therese Grob's marriage in 1820 might well have turned the knife in the wound again. We know that Schubert had never forgotten her, and the episode with Pepi Pöckelhofer had remained just that. There are most certainly grounds for suspecting that the twenty-two year old, to whom the thought of marriage was now anathema, nevertheless retained (as had his father) a healthy sexual appetite, and that he now began to look around for satisfaction. We feel sure that his father's second marriage in 1813, so soon after his mother's death, caused resentment in the son, although we know he got on well with his stepmother.

Franz von Schober had arrived in Vienna in 1815 to study law, and he immediately became a leading member of Schubert's circle of friends. He was a handsome, debonair man, and, in that retrospective painting *Schubert Evening at Josef von Spaun's* by Moritz von Schwind (1868), in which Vogl is singing to Schubert's accompaniment, Schober is shown paying much more attention to the woman beside him (his future fiancée) than to the music. Schubert liked Schober from their very first meeting; his letters betray a true soul-companionship, an intimacy not unusual in those days. Schubert wrote to Schober on 8 September 1818 calling him "a wonderful fellow" and his feeling for art "the purest, truest that one can imagine."[69]

It would really not be surprising that a young man from a father-dominated, none-too-affluent home should welcome attentions (of any sort) from wealthy, educated, and intelligent young men such as Schober and his friends. When, in addition, their attention not only flattered the young composer, but also extended his intellectual horizon by offering him participation in their philosophical discussions and introducing him to a wider range of poetry and imaginative literature than he had ever known, then this was a certain source of friendship at a time when familial and other closer bonds had been broken. And then, of course, there was the opportunity to write music to their poems, and to have the resultant songs performed, albeit in domestic circumstances.

When Schubert broke with his father after his return from Zseliz in 1818 and moved in with Johann Mayrhofer, he began a peripatetic existence that earned him the Goethean nickname of the Wanderer. He lodged in no fewer than twelve houses, although he returned from time to time to the schoolhouse in the Rossau district, and now and then lived on his own. His most constant companion was Franz von Schober. Josef Kenner, in a letter written for Ferdinand Luib on 22 May 1888, said that Schober "despised women and knew only two kinds, the worthwhile ones who went to bed with him, and the unworthy ones who could not rise to this opportunity."[70] To have become so friendly with such a man, at such a time when his spirits were low, meant that Schubert was open to being led astray.

Schober had been absent from Vienna for a year; the friendship intensified on his return at the end of 1820 (or early in 1821). He had made nothing of his grand artistic projects; he tried playwriting, play-producing, acting, publishing, even lithography, but, as he had no real need to earn money, his efforts were half-hearted, his love of pleasure too great.

Most biographies of Schubert mention his attachment to Schober. The older ones, such as the first, the 1865 biography of Kreissle von Hellborn, make little mention of the negative aspects of the friendship. A musician's biography such as Maurice Brown's (1958) deals with those incidents in two pages, whereas a 1996 biography by Elisabeth McKay has an entire chapter on the relationship entitled "La dolce vita" and another chapter on Schubert's illness and death.[71]

Schober's and Schubert's visits to the various houses of ill-repute in

Vienna cannot be documented. Oblique references are to be found in the letters and diaries of their friends who clearly regretted Schober's influence on the composer. Peter Härtling is more ready to give rein to the imagination. He writes, for example, of Schober's urgings: "Come on to the girls with me, Schubert," and later of Schubert's remarks to Schober, "You seem to me to be like a terrible mixture of (Don) Giovanni and the Commendatore; the fires of Hell already are licking your feet."[72] As fanciful, however, as accounts like these may read, they may not be all that far from the truth.

The tragic results of the true episodes are now widely publicized in the latest biographies and journals. *Schubert durch die Brille* (Schubert through the Spectacles), the journal of the International Franz Schubert Institute, based in the house where Schubert died, in Kettenbrücken-gasse Nos. 6–9, in Vienna IV, has naturally been particularly interested in the topic.[73] Informed opinion now seems to agree that Schubert contracted syphilis not from the sexual intercourse with Pepi Pöckelhofer in Zseliz in 1818 but during those wild years with Schober in Vienna.

It is therefore both ironic and tragic that Schubert's final illness and death should have been caused, however indirectly, by his passionate desire to better himself by mixing with wealthier and better-educated friends. At the time of these visits to brothels with Schober, Schubert had begun to attend meetings with an artistic group which called itself Ludlam's Cave and which began its activities in 1818, meeting in the Schlossergassel near St. Stefan's Cathedral. The group name was taken from a romantic drama by Adam Ohlenschläger (1779–1850). All the members had to have artistic interests, either as actor, singer, poet, composer, or simply "a friend of the arts."[74] In true Romantic fashion, the members (called "bodies") bore assumed names that referred, either by pun or literary inference, to their artistic leaning. (Non-members were "shadows.") Schubert was invited to visit the group as a "shadow" on Christmas Eve 1821, and had yet another brush with the police, when, on his second visit, during Lent, he was playing the piano for dancing. The evening was interrupted by a police commissioner who forbade dancing. Schubert's bitter remark, "They do that to me, because they know how much I like playing for dancing," speaks volumes.[75] Among other literary luminaries who visited the Cave and became members were Friedrich Rückert (in 1818), Carl Maria von Weber (in 1823), Franz Grillparzer (on 4 March 1826), and Ludwig Rellstab (in 1828). These are names that bind Schubert firmly to the literature of the day. (Schubert's name in the Cave was "Volker the minstrel," a medieval name for the musician.)

There was much drinking, smoking, and dancing during the meetings—Weber took great exception to the smoke and the noise—but they also held serious literary and philosophical discussions and readings of celebrated works. Goethe's *Tasso* is mentioned as well as the medieval *Nibelungenlied*, Homer, Shakespeare, Novalis, Jean Paul, and, of course, *Ossian*. The three-hour sessions were greatly enjoyed by Schubert, and we know from various sources that many of the Lieder written then were based on poems of the authors present or taken from books mentioned and discussed. The last meeting took place on 16 April 1826, when the police, who had been suspicious of the group for some time, entered the restaurant during the night and took possession of all its documents and music scores. The next day, many of the artists were visited by the police, including Franz Grillparzer who was, incidentally, a civil servant, as well as a dramatist.

On 30 January 1821 a friend of Schubert, Josef Huber wrote to his fiancée, Rosalie Kranzbichler, describing an evening that Schober's sister, Sophie, had organized in his house. She had invited Schubert and fourteen of his friends to listen to music and enjoy a drink or two. Huber wrote:[76]

> A lot of splendid Schubert Lieder were sung and played by him until after ten in the evening. Afterwards, we had some punch that one of the group had brought, and since it was very good and there was plenty of it, the company, happy in any case, became merrier, so it was three in the morning before we broke up.

This was the first Schubertiade, a social evening devoted to the composer's music, at which only men were present; when women were invited, there was dancing with music provided by Schubert at the piano.[77] The composer rarely danced. In all honesty, he was often the worse for wear after some of these evenings. He wrote once to his elder brother, Ferdinand, that he had been unable to work that day, "since I'm under the weather today because of yesterday's stupidities."[78] When women were present, the behavior was markedly less boisterous. On 17 December 1822 the dramatist Grillparzer recalled an evening where he watched Katharina Fröhlich, his "eternal fiancée," as she sat by the piano listening to Schubert playing. The sight entranced him and moved him to write a poem to her, although he never married her.[79]

Franz von Schober, Schubert's "evil spirit," again showed the positive side of his influence on the composer by starting up a series of literary reading evenings or "book circles" at which he often recited poetry. In a letter from Schubert to Josef von Spaun dated 7 December 1822, Schubert mentions that there were often three meetings a week where, usually, contemporary writers and poets were discussed, read, and quoted. This group had different literary and intellectual interests from those of the earlier groups that Schubert had now and then attended. The strong classical influence, a relic of the Enlightenment's rationalism, gave way now to the choice of more Romantic texts. Although Goethe was represented here by *Faust, Pandora, Tasso,* and his very strange *Novelle,* there was some antipathy to him and a growing lack of reverence. Franz von Bruchmann, in particular, was keen to get rid of what he termed "this Dalai Lama" who had dominated his youth. This may well have accounted for the lack of any Goethe settings by Schubert in 1823.

Other well-known writers mentioned were the dramatist Heinrich von Kleist and Ludwig Tieck, both Germans, indicating that German writers were now being discussed. By this time, of course, Schubert had set some seventy Goethe texts and was thus able to speak with some authority. His introduction to Heinrich Heine's poetry was to bear fruit only much later, at the end of his life, indeed, when he had read Heine's *Reisebilder* (Travel Pictures) in 1828. In a letter to Spaun of 7 December 1822 Schubert revealed that he was sending him three songs of the Harper, *Suleika* and *Geheimes* (both from Goethe's *West-östlicher Divan*) as well as his *Der Musensohn* (The Son of the Muses), *An die Entfernte* (To the Distant Beloved), *Am Flusse* (By the River), and *Willkommen und Abschied* (Hail and Farewell). According to a report in the *Wiener Allgemeine Zeitung* for 13 December 1822, the Harper's and the *West-östlicher Divan* songs were published by Cappi and Diabelli in that month, too.[80]

ILLNESS

Despite all the attention being paid to his work, and the invitations, even demands, to attend various functions, Schubert was at this time rarely well enough to attend many of them. Critical attention has centered for some time on the reasons for his ill health. Although the earlier biographical studies accepted that he was ill, late nineteenth-century prudery prevented them from suggesting a cause. On the death certificate of 1828, the cause was the nebulous "nervous fever," a generic term for *typhus abdominalis,* a plausible cause in Viennese conditions of that day and age. Twentieth-century musicologists such as Otto Erich Deutsch and Maurice Brown went a little further. The latter, for example, wrote, "Certainly the course of the illness suggests that Schubert was suffering from it [venereal disease]," but then moved on quickly to the music. A 1928 article by the Hugo Wolf specialist, Frank Walker, "Schubert's Last

Illness," was a brave attempt to lift the curtain, but it took the investigative biographers of the 1980s and 1990s to uncover the whole story. Of the many studies, perhaps Hans D. Kiemle's article "Woran starb Schubert eigentlich?" (What did Schubert really die of?), and McKay's final chapter are as informative as any.[81]

In 1989 the American professor Maynard Solomon wrote an article titled "Franz Schubert and the Peacocks of Benvenuto Cellini."[82] The article discussed Schubert's alleged "sexual unorthodoxy" and caused a stir. The reference to peacocks was to be found in a note by Eduard von Bauernfeld in his diary in August 1826 to the effect that "Schubert (is) half-sick (he needs 'young peacocks' like Benv. Cellini)."[83] Deutsch pointed out in a footnote that Benvenuto Cellini (1500–1571) used to eat young peacocks as a tasty bite after a meal, but "that had nothing to do with the fact that he was syphilitic" or homosexual. (Interestingly, Goethe had translated Cellini's autobiography and had found great pleasure in the life of a man whom he compared, with evident satisfaction, with the unsentimental, down-to-earth Zelter. It was published in Vienna in 1806.)[84]

From 1989 onwards, there was a regular stream of letters and articles on the subject. This is not the place to enter into a long discussion of the topic, which is only of interest to us in that it shows how close Schubert was to the men who were introducing him to the literature and thought of the times. In many of the letters that passed between the friends, and in their diaries and memoirs, regular reference is made to their sleeping together and their love and admiration for one another.[85] It was all part of their emphasis on that "love of the good," which was personified in the eighteenth-century phrase of J. J. Winckelmann that the feature of Greek classicism was "a noble simplicity and a quiet grandeur." This was also the tenet of nineteenth-century Greek studies, and it had some influence on the Freemason philosophy of Goethe and his friends.

The modern tragedy of AIDS is naturally in the mind of every commentator. The prevalent view, which is also presented here, is that Schubert's fatal illness, syphilis, was caused by his sexual activities in the brothels of Vienna. There has long been a view that the great emphasis on the study of classical Greece, where homosexuality was an accepted feature of upper-class society, much affected upper-class life in Victorian England. Histories of the famous English public schools would bear this out. The historian of arguably England's (if not Britain's) most famous public school writes of the period around 1860 when the classics were almost the only discipline studied: "In general, sex plays a small part in Victorian memoirs, and references such as there are *tend to be veiled* . . . (there is) a strong taint of mischief and worse evil" (italics added).[86]

Such were also the friendships of these reading circles and Schubertiades; the men were heterosexual, and many had wives, fiancées, or girl friends. Schubert's case was slightly different. His tiny, overweight, shy figure added to his inborn inferiority complex and made him seek clandestine liaisons for sexual satisfaction. The consequences were really not unexpected.

Many of these complexes are to be found in a little story written by Schubert that sparked off many of the discussions mentioned above. The story *Mein Traum* (My Dream), written in pencil on 3 July 1822, is clearly autobiographical in the main and has attracted the attention of modern, psychologically orientated commentators. The writer, devoted to his family, is banished by his father for "not tasting the delicious dishes at a feast." He then wanders away to far-off regions until news of his mother's death reaches him. A temporary reconciliation with the father follows, but it only leads to another altercation and another banishment. A return to his mother's grave sees him finally reconciled with his father.[87] (A long article in *Schubert durch die Brille* discussed all the psychoanalytical dream theories.)[88]

We are inclined to treat the story as a not untypical product of a disappointed, highly strung young man, full of guilt at the consequences of behavior contrary to his familial and religious code and to the pious commandments of his less troubled friends. It is even probable that it was written under the influence of opium, since drug-taking was prevalent then. Anton von Doblhoff wrote to Schober in the spring of 1823 remembering a time when he had been with "dear Bertl" (another nickname for Schubert) in a café, where they had had a coffee and "a long Turkish pipe," which could have been a hashish pipe, the hookah. It may be that Schumann's comment about the story (in 1839) was one of the wiser ones: "The 'Dream' does allow a deep interpretation; let it be the concern of those involved."[89]

THE POEMS OF WILHELM MÜLLER

In 1823 Schubert came upon the poems of Wilhelm Müller. Many non-German speakers have used his setting of these poems to prove, as they would put it, that Schubert had little literary taste. They cite from translations such as this early one of "Ungeduld" (Impatience). "I'd carve it on the bark of every tree / On ev'ry stone it should engraven be / I fain would sow it in each garden green / In early cress it should be quickly seen." It may make one smile, but it rhymed. Germans have been re-assessing Müller as a poet, and one great singer wrote: "His poems have form, imagination, and, above all, they are singable."[90]

Schubert was now and then in the hospital in 1823, when he began what he told Schober were "a few songs on poems by Wilhelm Müller" that would appear in four small volumes (later they became five) with vignettes by Moritz von Schwind. They actually appeared between February and August 1824, dedicated to the tenor-baritone Baron Karl von Schönstein.[91] Liszt was moved to tears by Schönstein's singing of parts of the cycle *Die schöne Müllerin* in 1838, while Julius Stockhausen was the first to sing the full cycle in Vienna in 1857. Wilhelm Müller's cycle was published in his *Seventy-seven Poems from the Posthumous Papers of a Traveling Horn-player* (1820), and is ironically subtitled "To be read in Winter." He is thought to have taken the basic idea from Goethe's poem *The Young Apprentice and the Miller-Girl* of 1797. Müller supplied an ironical prologue and epilogue to his twenty poems that tell the sad story of the miller's boy who sets off on his travels accompanied by his beloved brook. He finds a girl in her father's mill, falls in love, but loses her to a hunter dressed in green, and finds solace in the watery arms of the brook. Müller's cycle, spoken originally as an ironic, Heine-esque parody of lost love, was set as a serious, sad, almost tragic story, reflecting Schubert's mood at the time. He omitted Müller's prologue and epilogue, but it is difficult to believe that he did not appreciate their irony. He must have felt that they would detract from the effect of his mood, as indeed they would have. Moved by the deeper interpretation of the poems, Schubert wrote music that has served generations as the epitome of Romantic music, a combination of "What if?" and "If only." When sung, as it is nowadays, without sentimental portamentos or final rallentandos, this cycle can move any listener prepared to listen to the music and the German words together; words alone, music alone, do not communicate the composer's message.

Thus, once again: What if . . . ? Wilhelm Müller visited Goethe on 20 September 1827? If it is true (and we doubt it) that Goethe only liked strophic songs, what would have happened had Müller shown him Schubert's settings of his poems? Of the twenty poems, no fewer than sixteen are strophic or modified strophic. Alas, Müller never knew of Schubert's settings, and he too died young in late 1827. On 8 October 1815 Müller wrote in his diary: "I can neither play nor sing, and yet, when I write poetry, I both play and sing. If I could find my own melodies, then my poems would be more popular than they are now. But, courage, one day a like-minded soul might come along who will hear the melodies in the words and give them back to me." How right he was.[92]

THE FINAL YEARS

As the brook closed over Schubert's wandering lad, Schubert's final struggle against illness, neglect, and frustration began. Just as the previous years of disappointment had brought forth music of the highest order, so would the few years left to him. Behind him, in 1824, lay something like seven symphonies, nine masses, fourteen string quartets, seventeen stage-works, and more than 450 of the final total of some 630 Lieder, for solo or mixed voices. In front of him lay what would be a lifetime of work for any other composer, until, at his death, the catalog of his works produced originally by Deutsch, and brought up to date by Aderhold, Dürr, and Feil, would number 998 (with queries about many other works outstanding).

As was the case with syphilitic sufferers in those times, Schubert went through several stages of the illness—now seemingly healthy and cheerful, now sick and depressed. (McKay quoted the name cyclothymia ("swings of mood") for the condition.)[93] On 14 August 1823, Schubert wrote to Schober from Steyr. "I'm quite well. But I doubt whether I shall ever be completely well again." On 9 November, Schwind wrote to Schober that Schubert is ill in bed again, but, on 18 November, Johanna Lutz, the fiancée of their friend Leopold Kupelwieser, wrote to him in Italy: "Schubert is well and healthy again." Being forced to wear a wig after his disease had removed his hair did not improve the little composer's self-confidence and fortunes. He could not dispose of the wig until January 1824.[94]

The publication of his song cycle Die schöne Müllerin (D. 795) in 1824 seemed to have intensified Schubert's depressive condition. His friend Bauernfeld printed in his memoirs deeply disturbing entries which, he said, Schubert had made in a notebook at the time (now lost), although one has to question the reliability of such claims made many years later. What was reliable was the letter Schubert wrote to Leopold Kupelwieser on 31 March 1824, in which we read:[95]

In a word, I feel myself to be the unhappiest, most miserable person in the world. Just imagine a person whose health will never improve, and who, out of sheer despair, always makes matters worse rather than better, just imagine a person, I say, whose most dazzling hopes have come to nought, for whom the happiness of love and friendship can offer nothing but pain at the most, for whom enthusiasm for all that is beautiful (at least, what moves one to it), threatens to disappear, and ask yourself, if this is not an unhappy, miserable man.

Then he turns to his Goethe and writes: "My peace is gone, my heart is heavy, I'll never find it again, never" (quoting from *Gretchen am Spinnrade*). One critic remarked that the letter was not all pessimistic, that it does not indicate "unalleviated misery."[96] It seems to mirror Schubert's miserable condition.[97]

Schubert turned to Goethe again in a letter to Schober from Zseliz on 21 September 1824 and quoted the line from Goethe's sad little poem *Erster Verlust* (First Loss): "Who can bring back just an hour of that divine time?—the time when all friends were together" (and perhaps, too, the time with Therese). Now he has no one with whom he can exchange "one sensible word," and he enclosed one of his poems titled *Klage an das Volk* (Complaint to the People). It is a heart-rending plea from a man who feels that he has been neglected by his nation. Writing to Schober, who wrote the poem *An die Musik* (To Music) with its devoted thanks to the "divine art," Schubert ends by claiming that only "holy art can lessen the pain which never reconciles it with fate."[98]

The picture seems to be one of sadness, frustration, and neglect. Yet, when one turns to the various books that document Schubert's life, one finds that, far from being neglected at this time, more reviews of and comments on his work were appearing than ever before, although, of course, very few of his major instrumental works had been published, and the Singspiele that he had hoped would make his name had not met with much commercial success. Indeed, by the end of 1823, he seems to have lost any hope of ever becoming an established composer of stage-works.

The second visit to the Esterházys in Zseliz in May 1824 had given him a modicum of solace. Schubert was now, seemingly, restored to health. Countess Caroline was eighteen, and it is fairly certain that Schubert became very fond of her. Whether those feelings remained platonic is not really known. He left no written comment behind; his friend Bauernfeld wrote in his diary later, in February 1828: "Schubert seems to be really in love with the Countess E. I like that about him. He is giving her lessons."[99] Schönstein wrote, however, that Caroline did not reciprocate Schubert's love and mentioned Schubert's one declaration of his feelings. When she once asked the composer why he had not dedicated a composition to her, he replied: "What's the point? Everything is dedicated to you anyway."[100] One critic claimed that Schubert's Fantasie in F Minor (D. 940, 1828), which was eventually dedicated to her, "composed for four hands," contains the "suffering, pain, hopelessness, and indecision" that characterizes both the work and Schubert's feelings for Caroline.[101] Once again, the truth is hard to come by, and the affair is one that has become linked to the discussion of Schubert's sexuality.

Some critics see the Caroline episode as proof of Schubert's heterosexual proclivities.[102]

The earlier favorable reviews of his songs led Schubert to believe that the cycle of twenty songs that made up *Die schöne Müllerin* would also meet with approbation, but, alas, no. The accompaniments to some songs may have been too difficult for the average pianist. The critic G. W. Fink certainly wrote about the unnecessarily violent desire to "modulate, and again to modulate, again and again, without rest or pause." He thought that this "modulation mania" had become a "real illness of the age."[103] On the other hand, the local *Wiener Allgemeine Zeitung* of 17 February 1824, praising the cycle, wrote of "the novelty of his melodies united with that ease of comprehension," which was attractive both to the expert and the "educated music-lover." Schubert wanted more and, as we have seen, he complained bitterly about the decline in the public's taste, but he was not the first or the last composer to do so. Beethoven, cruelly fate-struck, had a right to complain. Schubert had always believed himself to be in Beethoven's shadow and he had worshipped him from his earliest days. Indeed, Deutsch smiled to himself when he calculated that the very first music that Schubert must have heard, at seventy-six days old, was the band's rendition of Beethoven's *Battle Song of the Austrians* outside his house, on 4 April 1797.[104] Schubert often wondered whether there was any point in going on at all as a composer after Beethoven.[105] He studied Beethoven's Lieder avidly and may have gleaned some hints for his settings of Goethe poems from the older composer's works.

Schubert's elder brother Ferdinand stated categorically, "He often met Beethoven," and added that Beethoven "often praised his Lieder."[106] Anton Schindler wrote in 1857 that four months before Beethoven died in 1827, he (Schindler) took him (Beethoven) sixty of Schubert's Lieder. After looking through them, Beethoven is reported to have said, "Truly, there is a divine spark in Schubert!"[107] Whether the two composers knew each other personally is still uncertain. What is certain is that Schubert was invited to be one of the torchbearers at Beethoven's grand public funeral on 29 March 1827, some sign, surely, that there was some connection there. Furthermore, Beethoven had been rejected by Goethe, too, as Schubert was, when, in 1825, he sent Goethe three poems asking that he might be allowed to dedicate them to him, but no answer came from the poet. The three songs *An Schwager Kronos* (D. 369), *An Mignon* (D. 161), and *Ganymed* (D. 544) carried the dedication when Diabelli published them in June 1825.

SIR WALTER SCOTT AND THE EUROPEAN
CANON OF POETS

In his letter of 14 August 1823 to Schober, Schubert mentions a name that touches on that unseen bond between Goethe and Schubert: "I am living here very simply, going on many walks, writing a good deal at my opera and reading Walter Scott."[108] Sir Walter Scott was Scotland's leading writer of ballads and novels. Like many European writers, he had been fascinated by Bishop Percy's *Reliques*, Bürger's *Lenore*, and those German plays such as Goethe's *Götz von Berlichingen* that dealt with the medieval legends of romantic chivalry. He had translated *Lenore* in 1795 and *Götz* in 1799 and then began his amazingly successful career with *The Lay of the Last Minstrel* in 1805. *The Lady of the Lake* appeared in 1810 and was followed by the long series of novels from 1814 onwards, which included *Rob Roy* (1817), *The Bride of Lammermoor* and *Ivanhoe* (1819), and *Redgauntlet* (1824). *The Life of Napoleon Bonaparte* (1827) became a particular favorite of Goethe's, who praised it ecstatically to Soret on 22 January 1830. Scott had introduced himself to Goethe in a letter of 9 July 1827, but Goethe was reading his *Kenilworth* as far back as 1821. From 1823 onwards, Schubert's interest in Scott is regularly mentioned in his, and his friends' correspondence. Scott is not an easy writer to read (even for native speakers of Scottish dialect) and the available translations obviously did not fully communicate the flavor of the original. Enough of its power and color remained to ignite the enthusiasm of both Goethe and Schubert. When the former said to Eckermann on 8 March 1831: "Walter Scott is a great talent which seeks its equal, and one cannot be surprised that he has such an extraordinary effect on the whole literary world," it was a sentiment obviously echoed in the Vienna of Schubert's day. Indeed, in that same year 1827, when Scott wrote to Goethe, a tenor named Marschall sang Schubert's 1825 setting of *Normans Gesang* (D. 846) on 8 September in Graz.[109]

By 1825 Schubert was looking for works by a poet whose poems were known beyond the Germanic countries and whose verses he might be able to underlay with a German translation, so that his Lieder might reach a wider audience. At the beginning of 1825, he had set a poem *Die junge Nonne* (The Young Nun, D. 828) by Jakob Nikolaus Craigher de Jachelutta, a Hungarian from Pest. On 23 October, Schubert and Schwind paid Craigher a visit during which he agreed to provide Schubert with "several poems from English, Spanish, French, and Italian classics with a German translation in the meter of the original," which Schubert would then set to music. Craigher had translated Colley Cibber's *The Blind Boy*, which Schubert had set that year as *Der blinde Knabe*

(D. 833). The idea came to nothing, but it displayed the direction of Schubert's thinking and that brought him to Walter Scott.[110]

Schubert found the *Lady of the Lake* poems and composed two settings, one for the English original and one for the German translation. These settings became enormously popular during the holiday visit to Upper Austria that Schubert and Vogl made in the summer and fall of 1825. The composer's parents received an enthusiastic letter dated 25 (28?) July from Steyr in which Schubert mentions the success of the Scott Lieder: "I am thinking of proceeding very differently from the usual way, which brings such little reward, with the publication of these Lieder, since they bear the celebrated name of Scott at their head and could thus arouse more curiosity and, with the addition of the English text, would make me better known in England."[111] Adam Storck's translation does not quite fit the German meter and is rarely sung in Britain. The most popular of the seven songs (D. 835–839, D. 843, and D. 846), the *Ave Maria* (Hymn to the Virgin), is usually sung in Britain to the Latin text anyway.

Although that idea came to nothing, too, we can read in a letter to his brother Ferdinand, dated 12 September 1825, how well Schubert felt he and Vogl performed together during that visit: "The way Vogl sings and I accompany is something quite new for these people." Although, from all accounts, Schubert was a notable accompanist, people would know that he was the composer, too. That the accompanist had a true role to play was yet another sign of the revolution that had taken place in the performance of Lieder.[112]

Schubert's interest in Scott seems to be a token of his wide reading and intellectual curiosity. He was obviously not just looking for poems to set to music, but was interested in the literature for its own sake. Certainly Schober may have been joking when he called him a "naive barbarian,"[113] but a memorandum from an upper-class diplomat, Anton Prokesch, granting Schubert "openness, common-sense and enthusiasm," although he was also "without education," was a similar negative assessment.[114] Anton Ottenwalt, a nearer observer who listened to Schubert's Scott settings in Linz on 27 July 1825, wrote to Josef von Spaun that Schubert sat with him and his family until almost midnight, and that they were fascinated by his conversation. He had never seen Schubert so serious and profound:[115]

> How we spoke of art, or poetry, or his youth, of friends and other meaningful people, of the relationship of ideals to life, etc. I was more and more astonished at this mind, of which people have said that its artistic achievement was so unconscious,

hardly revealed to, or understood by, itself, and so on. And yet, how simple all this was—I cannot tell you of the range and extent of his convictions—but there were signs of a view of the world that had not just been acquired, and whatever the share that his good friends might have had in it, it does not detract at all from the very special characteristics which it displays.

What a magnificent tribute from an intelligent man who went on to a high official post.

There still remained some important vocal works that demanded an understanding of new literary productions. By 1827, Schubert had set eighty Goethe texts, more than by any other poet. If one wishes to claim that Schubert was not lacking in literary taste, his early seminary education, his circle of friends, his reading, and his choice of poets all support the view that this was no ignorant rustic "fluting away" his days, setting whatever text his friends laid before him. Few composers have experienced and illustrated the power of words more than Schubert. The following remarkable list of Schubert's settings of texts by major literary figures bears witness to that:

Goethe	80	Schulze	10
Mayrhofer	47	Rellstab	10
Müller	45	A. W. Schlegel	9
Schiller	44	Stolberg	9
Matthisson	29	Scott	8
Hölty	23	Jacobi	7
Kosegarten	21	Heine	6
F. Schlegel	16	Novalis	6
Körner	14	Rückert	6
Claudius	13	Uz	5
Klopstock	13	Shakespeare	3
Metastasio	12	Herder	2
Leitner	11	Grillparzer	1
Ossian	10	Tieck	1

Schubert's eighty Goethe settings are of sixty-four separate texts, some only set as "fragments." All these poets belong to the European canon of poets. To that list must be added, moreover, those poets who are often dismissed with the derogatory sobriquet "Schubert's friends," but who, at their best, produced fine and sensitive poetry. Schubert set 140 of his friends' poems altogether.

Schubert once told his friend Bauernfeld that he would probably become like Goethe's Harper begging for bread from door to door.[116]

In 1827, he was again living with Schober who had set up a little library for the composer in which he found the fifth edition of the journal *Urania* (founded in 1823) and, in that, the first twelve poems of Wilhelm Müller's cycle *Winterreise* written in 1823. Josef von Spaun recalled (in 1858) that Schubert had become very gloomy and depressed when he met him one day in 1827. When asked what was ailing him, Schubert replied: "Come over today to Schober's. I'll sing you a cycle of frightening songs. I'm curious to see what you make of them. They've moved me more than any other songs."[117] When they heard them, his friends were moved, although Schober said he liked only *Der Lindenbaum* (The Lime Tree). (These twelve were published in January 1828.) The second twelve were composed in September 1827, and Schubert found them in *Urania* as well. Benjamin Britten rated Bach's Mass in B Minor and *Winterreise* as the greatest glories of Western music, while Richard Capell's comment has never been bettered: "A fine voice is wanted to hold the attention for so long, but the most musical tone will pall here if it is not the servant of the imagination. The singer must have sympathy with the passionate temper. For the dry of heart (the) *Winterreise* might as well not exist."[118]

As he lay on his death bed in his brother Ferdinand's damp-walled room in the Kettenbrückengasse in November 1828, Schubert corrected the proofs of the second part of *Winterreise*. He also made a strange request. He wrote to Schober on 12 November for anything by the New Jersey author James Fenimore Cooper. Schubert had read *The Last of the Mohicans* (1826), *The Spy* (1821), *The Pilot* (1827), and *The Pioneers* (1823).[119] Since Cooper's works were published in translation by C. H. Fischer in Vienna only between 1826 and 1833, Schubert must have been well versed in recent literature to have read these books.

In chapter four, we examine the various circumstances that might have brought Goethe and Schubert together, and the reasons they did not.

CHAPTER FOUR

Why Did Schubert Never Meet Goethe?

I t would be a brave or foolhardy scholar who would claim that Goethe and Schubert enjoyed a close relationship; indeed, any writer on the subject would or should begin the discussion by stating clearly and unequivocally that neither man knew the other personally. There are various reports of Schubert meeting and knowing Beethoven; there are no reports of any such bonds with Goethe. There is a faint chance that Goethe might at least have heard of Schubert; there is no doubt at all, of course, that Schubert knew a great deal about the Prince of Poets in Weimar.

Few people who know and love German Lieder would dispute the existence of that "happy bond" between the two men, of which Heinrich Panofka wrote so exultantly: "Goethe and Schubert! O happy bond, / To Germany's eternal fame!"[1] Yet this bond remained an artistic one, impersonal, unseen. What if both men had met and worked together, as Goethe did with Reichardt and Zelter, and as Schubert did with Mayrhofer and Bauernfeld? Would they not both have benefited? What musical treasures might have resulted from Goethe's close relationship with a musician of Schubert's literary sensitivity? What would Schubert have gained from working with a poet so aware of the effect of music allied to words? So, why did they never meet or correspond? We know that Schubert was not an uneducated rustic and that Goethe was not an unmusical poet-philosopher. The two men had much more in common than is generally accepted.

The critics who seek to show that Goethe was unmusical seize on those statements where the poet seemed to agree with them. In a letter to Karl Friedrich Zelter on 2 May 1820, Goethe referred to himself as "one unable to appreciate, or even, deaf to music," and to Friederike Helene Unger on 13 June 1796, he had admitted: "I cannot have an opinion on music for I lack an understanding of the technicalities which it employs to achieve its ends."[2] He could only speak of the effect

that music had on him, he added, and in that same letter to Zelter, he
wrote that he knew that he "missed a third of life" through this lack of
"understanding."

These remarks applied surely to the performance of music rather
than to the appreciation of music. In Goethe's day, most educated people were capable of performing music in an amateur fashion. We know
that Goethe even tried his hand at composing a setting of Psalm 71, but
his remarks quoted above concerned his dilettantish efforts at performance compared to the professional performances that he so regularly
witnessed. To the end of his life Goethe believed that music was an
essential element in his life and that music was essential to the full
appreciation of his poems. He would have agreed with Joachim Heinrich Campe's definition of the Lied as "a poem which is meant to be
sung or which can be sung."[3] This referred to the folk song; the art song
was first mentioned by Carl Kossmaly in 1841 in Schumann's *Neue
Zeitschrift für Musik.*[4] After Goethe had admired Zelter's settings of some
of Schiller's ballads, he wrote to the composer that "a Lied [that is, a
poem] can only be complete when set to music" (21 December 1809).

Even when critics do not completely deny Goethe's interest in music, they are quick to advance the view that he enjoyed and appreciated
only strophic settings of music. This, they then claim, was one of the
reasons why he rejected Schubert's non-strophic, through-composed
settings (if he ever saw or heard them, that is, one must add). Yet Goethe
often congratulated Reichardt and Zelter, the two professional musicians with whom he was most closely associated, on settings that are
clearly not strophic, Reichardt's tempestuous setting of *Rastlose Liebe*
(Restless Love) and Zelter's only partly strophic *Um Mitternacht* (At
Midnight), which Goethe particularly admired. Both these settings have
Schubertian non-strophic characteristics.

It is true, of course, that Goethe's original interest in musical settings went back to his early acquaintance with the mid-eighteenth-century folk song type of Lieder and its "appearance of familiarity." Yet his
love of the descriptive setting of words (as in those Mozart operas that
he admired so much) and his deep, proven and sustained regard for the
complicated musical structures of Johann Sebastian Bach belie the
description of a man who was able, or willing, to appreciate only the
simplest of musical settings. He is on record as insisting often on the
importance of the union of words and music. Contrary to some opinions, he did not expect the musician to efface himself in the presence
of the loftier poet. In the second stanza of his interesting poem of the
1790s, *An Lina* (To Lina), the poet asks the reader not "only to read (but)
always to sing": "Let the strings quickly resound / then look at the book

[the poem] / do not only read! always sing / And every page will be yours."

Goethe's pleasure in producing libretti for his many Singspiele is also evidence of the musicality of his thinking. Surely, no one who could take the trouble and who possessed the ability to write these could have done so without at least imagining in his head the music that would "support the words," as he put it. Many of his great dramatic works, *Faust, Tasso,* and *Iphigenie* among them, contain poetry that is musical in itself, but also themes that are often centered on musical images. Faust is moved, saved, by the "comforting song" of the choir of angels. Tasso's troubled soul is eased by the "joy of song" that turned "the sad feelings into harmony," and we touched, too, on the many musical images in the *Wilhelm Meister* novels. Wilhelm's remark in the *Years of Wandering* about matching the words to the rhythm of his art are relevant here.

Many poets have found their themes while out walking; Schubert found many of his in the Vienna woods round Währing and Döbling. "Das Wandern ist des Müllers Lust" (Wandering is the miller's delight), the first words of *Die schöne Müllerin,* would always remind us of Wilhelm Meister's words. As Goethe said to Eckermann on 6 April 1829: "The tempo comes unconsciously from the poetic mood." Then he added, ironically: "If one were to think about that when writing a poem, one would go mad and never write anything sensible."

That Goethe was always conscious of the possibility of having his poems set to music was shown by the comments made in that very early essay *Über den musikalischen Ausdruck* (On Musical Expression) of 1770, where he adumbrates the various aspects of the composer's task. He makes four important points. The composer must consider (1) the grammatical accentuation, the length and brevity of the syllables, to declaim correctly (that is, with the correct stress); (2) the logical divisions of the speech text to declaim intelligently; (3) the oratorical accentuation to declaim according to the intended emotion; and (4) the characteristic nature of his art to be not just a declaimer, but a musician.[5] Obviously, the musician is not thought of as a mere accompanist here, but as an independent partner in the artistic enterprise. In this context Goethe criticized the settings of his Mignon poems in *Wilhelm Meister* by Beethoven and Spohr: "I cannot understand the poem when they throughcomposed it; the differentiating marks which occur in each stanza in the same place should (I thought) have been sufficient for the composer to show him that I just expect a Lied [the normal 'strophic' Lied] from him."[6] For Goethe such a through-composed setting disturbed the harmony of the "whole" by emphasizing the "parts," and thus destroyed the general lyrical character of the poem.

The accompaniments that Zumsteeg, Reichardt, and Zelter wrote to Goethe's Lieder are clear indications that they were fully aware that Goethe would welcome any accompaniment written by a composer who produced "a radical (that is, faithful) reproduction of the poetic intentions" (as he put it to A. W. Schlegel on 18 June 1798), and who, in so doing, remained faithful to his professional creed as a musician. The musicologists of the day went a step further and would have added that the composer must not only reproduce these "poetic intentions," but, in so doing, "he will become a poet himself," as E. T. A. Hoffmann wrote in a review of Lieder by the composer Riehm.[7]

By this time, it was becoming generally recognized that the composer (as accompanist) had gained an entirely new and improved status. This was, above all, the importance of Schubert's setting of Goethe's *Gretchen am Spinnrade* (D. 118) on 19 October 1814. For many, the seventeen-year-old Schubert's setting had "reproduced the poetic intentions" of Goethe's ballad, while providing an amazingly advanced type of accompaniment. It had, of course, little resonance for the world of music at the time (it was only published as Op. 1 in 1821), but his professional musician friends recognized its importance. Its effect was pioneering, as we can now appreciate, paving the way for the great Lieder of Schumann and Wolf—and Brahms—although the latter always declared the strophic Lied to be the "highest form of art." Brahms, too, declared (with reference to Schubert's settings) that no composer could really add anything to Goethe's poems: "They are all so finished, there is nothing one can do to them with music," he is reported to have said to the singer, Georg Henschel.[8] We know that, because of his proven love of the German folk song, Brahms often condemned through-composed Lieder and accused Hugo Wolf of "formlessness." The interesting point here is that such comments were made by a composer generally held to be "un-literary" or less literary than his immediate predecessor, Robert Schumann (and, we would add, than Franz Schubert). Brahms certainly chose to set poems by poets who could only be called "minor" figures, but his remark to Henschel suggests that he would have shared the views of some that a great poem cannot be improved upon.

For this reason it is quite incorrect to think of Schubert as an uneducated rustic. He was a man who, through his association with poets and thinkers of status in Vienna, his considerable reading, and his attendance at operas and concerts, was indeed what Franz Liszt called him, "the most poetical musician ever."[9]

From Schubert's reading of *Faust I* in the autumn of 1814 and a study of Goethe's poems in volume seven of the 1810 edition of the *Collected Works* published in Vienna, Schubert's poetic tastes were largely formed by the Weimar master. We have stressed that *Gretchen* did not arise out of the blue; Schubert would have paid homage to the earlier Lieder of composers such as Zumsteeg, and the two who were close friends of Goethe, Reichardt and Zelter, but the development of his art over the next fourteen years showed an ever-increasing sensitivity to poetic values. (In the final chapter we shall be mentioning those "faults" in his settings that critics such as Lief Ludwig Albertson have been keen to point out, namely, Schubert's *mis*reading of some of the poems, the omission or addition of words to suit the settings, his alterations of certain key words in Goethe's texts, and so on. Albertson is kind enough to add that this is "the price that one pays for immortality!")[10]

Throughout his life and career, Schubert was to return regularly to Goethe's poems. There was a period, around 1818, when the literary men with whom he was associating began to display some signs of irreverence towards the great man. In fact, there are no Goethe settings in 1818, but Schubert's bond with Goethe always remained strong.

It is perhaps the setting of Goethe's *Erlkönig* (D. 328), probably composed in October 1815, which provides the nearest, albeit faint promise of an even closer bond. Spaun's breathless description of Schubert's setting of the ballad has become famous: "We found Schubert all aglow reading *Erlkönig* aloud from a book. He walked back and forwards several times with the book in his hand; suddenly he sat down and *in no time at all* (italics added) the wonderful ballad was on paper."[11] There have been many arguments over whether Schubert could possibly have composed the song so quickly. Maurice Brown thought it highly unlikely and believed that even copying out the song "would surely take three hours or so"; Fischer-Dieskau was not so sure, since Schubert "did not usually write out all the repeats in the accompaniment," and it is known that he composed at great speed.[12]

Goethe heard Schubert's setting of *Erlkönig,* sung by Wilhelmine Schröder-Devrient on 24 April 1830. The poet recalled having heard it before and not being much impressed, but "performed like that, the whole thing becomes a visible image," he said.[13] This was a simple remark in itself, but one that led to the generalization that Goethe disliked non-strophic Lieder. According to a record of a conversation with Johann Gottlieb von Quandt in Spring 1826, Quandt wrote:[14]

Inter alia, Goethe mentioned: Your Madame (Devrient) was here a little time ago and sang me a *Romanze* [*Erlkönig*]—one has to say that the composer has expressed the horse's gallop excellently. One cannot deny, that in very many admired compositions, fearfulness is exaggerated into ugliness, especially when the female singer intends to let herself be heard.

This took place when *Erlkönig* fever was still at its height. Much nearer the poem's publication date in 1821, twenty-three-year-old Max Löwenthal, a Viennese contemporary and friend of Goethe, visited Weimar on 20 October 1822 and had a short conversation with the poet. Goethe admitted that he was now unwilling to take up new relationships because of his advanced age (he was then seventy-three) and the increased pressure of his administrative duties. We know that he had an ambiguous attitude towards Austria, although he often said that he regretted not having visited Vienna especially, since "there must be an enormous mass of music in Vienna, and the fine instruments which are made there tempt one" to visit the city. This comment came, wrote the diarist, after "my mention of the Schubert compositions of his poems which he didn't know." Only a "few words" were exchanged on the subject.[15]

Thus, Goethe had certainly at least heard of Schubert in 1822, but had he heard of him before then, and, more importantly, had he heard any of his songs?

Some critics, mainly instrumental musicians, with no great knowledge of Goethe and, it seems at times, not much more of Schubert's Lieder, can write sentences such as "we have first-hand evidence that Goethe strongly disliked some of the greatest settings of Schubert and Beethoven."[16] The British biographer McKay wrote of Schubert's 1825 letter to Goethe (which will be discussed shortly) that "as Goethe could see at a glance that Schubert's settings did not conform to his *preferred strophic settings* (italics added) of the poetry, favored also by his composer friends, Zelter and Reichardt, the songs warranted no reply from him. He returned them without comment."[17]

THE 1816 LETTER TO GOETHE

The Deutsch catalog lists eighty separate numbers of Goethe settings, although many poems were set more than once and some settings remained fragments. For example, "Nur wer die Sehnsucht kennt" (Only those who know what yearning is) from *Wilhelm Meister* was set six times for various voices. Few of these settings and fewer of the fragments are ever performed.[18] Schubert immersed himself in Goethe's poetry in the years 1814–1816, during which he wrote some forty or so settings of Goethe texts, of which, it must be said, few are as innovative as either *Gretchen am Spinnrade* or *Erlkönig*. Many were quite straightforward strophic songs of two or more stanzas, which makes what took place in 1816 all the more surprising.

Contrary to some opinions, Goethe's taste in Lieder was not restricted to strophic songs. As long as a setting was faithful to the poet's original intention(s) in writing the poem, he would accept it. The notion that Goethe was a staid, humorless, dinosaur-like conservative is very wide of the mark, as a detailed study of his correspondence would show. His printed works were certainly something different; these were written in the style expected of a leading European man of letters, and this was reflected too in the reverential reports of Johann Peter Eckermann's conversations with Goethe, which were published in Leipzig in 1836 (volumes one and two), and in Magdeburg (volume three) in 1848 (supplemented by additional material from Frédéric Soret). This was the image of Goethe projected on the mid-nineteenth-century world. In his unbended correspondence, however, and particularly that with his musician friend Zelter (whom he called "du," a rare tribute from Goethe), the humor and sheer down-to-earthness of both men are very evident. Clearly Schubert saw and appreciated this side of his "master," too.

To the outside world, however, it was undoubtedly the persona of the sage of Weimar that became widely known, and, on the whole, this was the persona that Schubert and his friends in Vienna expected and accepted when Goethe's poetry was being read and discussed, and then set to music by Schubert. Josef von Spaun had watched Schubert's development with pride and felt certain that a man so sensitive to poetic values as Goethe would be sure to appreciate the acuteness of these settings of his poems. The other friends, Albert Stadler and Anton Holzapfel, shared his admiration, and often called at the Schubert house in the Säulengasse to listen to and sing some of the compositions.

Such meetings led Spaun to consider approaching Goethe. Were the great man to listen to, and perhaps even publicly praise these Lieder, then Schubert's at that time very modest existence might be transformed. The composer's love affair with Therese Grob was at its height in 1816; any improvement in his prospects, both as regarded status *and* finances, might enable them to marry. Accordingly, Spaun encouraged Schubert to prepare copies of his Lieder, arranged according to the poets represented. The composer planned eight volumes, and Spaun decided to send the first two to Goethe with an explanatory letter. The Lieder sent were *An Schwager Kronos* (D. 369), *Jägers Abendlied*

(D. 368), *Der König in Thule* (D. 367), *Meeres Stille* (D. 216), *Schäfers Klage-lied* (D. 121), *Die Spinnerin* (D. 247), *Heidenröslein* (D. 257), *Wonne der Wehmut* (D. 260), *Wandrers Nachtlied* ("Der du von dem Himmel bist") (You who are from Heaven, D. 224), *Erster Verlust* (D. 226), *Der Fischer* (D. 225), *An Mignon* (D. 161), *Geistes-Gruss* (D. 142), *Nähe des Geliebten* (D. 162), *Gretchen am Spinnrade* (D. 118), *Rastlose Liebe* (D. 138), and *Erl-könig* (D. 328). It is remarkable that, with the possible exception of *Die Spinnerin* and *An Mignon,* all these Lieder are still regarded as among Schubert's finest and feature regularly in Schubert Lieder recitals all over the world.

Spaun's accompanying letter is often regarded by non-German speakers as "somewhat stilted" (perhaps because of Eric Blom's awk-ward English translation of 1946), but the German of the letter would be fairly normal for an ordinary Viennese of 1816 to write to an "Excel-lency." The Viennese have always had (and, indeed, still have) an exag-gerated respect for titles; some of their famous citizens have not been above adding a "von" (that is "of") to their names from time to time. Spaun's letter dated 17 April 1816 read:[19]

Your Excellency,
    The undersigned dares to rob Your Excellency of a few moments of Your so valuable time with these present lines, and only the hope that the enclosed collection of Lieder might be a perhaps not unpleasant gift for Your Excellency can excuse him for this enormous liberty.
    The compositions included in the present volumes are by a nineteen-year-old composer named Franz Schubert, whom nature has endowed from his most tender childhood with the most remarkable gift for composition, which Salieri, the Nestor of composers, with his exceedingly unselfish love of the art, brought to its wonderful maturity. The general praise which the young artist has received for the present Lieder as for his other, already numerous compositions, came from the most critical experts of the art, as well as from amateurs, from men as well as from women, and the general wishes of his friends moved the modest lad finally to commence his musical career by publish-ing some of his compositions, with which he will without doubt raise himself in a short space of time to that position among Ger-man composers which his great talents assign him.
    A choice collection of German Lieder is the beginning, to be followed by larger instrumental compositions. It will contain eight volumes. The first two (of which the first is enclosed as an

example), contain poems of Your Excellency, the third will contain poems by Schiller, the fourth and fifth by Klopstock, the sixth by Matthisson, Hölty, Salis etc., etc., and the seventh and eighth will contain the odes of Ossian, these last excelling all the others.

The composer now wishes to dedicate this collection most humbly to Your Excellency to whose so magnificent works he not only owes the creation of a great part of it, but also, in essence, his development as a "German song" composer. Yet as he himself is too modest to consider his works to be worthy of the so great honor of bearing such a name, celebrated wherever the German tongue is spoken, he has not the courage to beg this favor himself of Your Excellency, and I, one of his friends, permeated by his melodies, dare to beg this of Your Excellency in his name: an edition worthy of such a favor will thus be assured. I refrain from any further recommendation of these Lieder, they must speak for themselves; I would only say that the volumes to follow are in no wise inferior to the present one as far as melody is concerned, but may even be superior to it, and that the pianist who will play them to Your Excellency must not lack agility and expressiveness.

Should the young composer be so fortunate as to receive the praise of him whose praise would honor him more than that of any other person in the whole wide world, so I may dare to request to let me have the wished-for permission in two words.

I remain, with unbounded admiration,
    Your obedient servant,
        Josef Edler [nobleman] von Spaun

That letter, and its consequences, have remained one of the unsolved mysteries of Schubertian scholarship. Most writers on Schubert pass it off with a remark such as "Goethe did not even acknowledge the letter, only returned the volume of Lieder,"[20] or "The songbook was sent back without acknowledgement,"[21] or "The packet was returned without being granted an answer from Goethe,"[22] and most writers then go on to criticize Goethe's conservative musical taste (or lack of any) in the manner already referred to.

But is there more to Goethe's lack of response than that? It is true that there is no mention of the songs, either in his diary for April 1816 or in his otherwise fully informative correspondence on musical matters with Zelter.[23] Yet there were many other more important matters weighing on Goethe in those days; it is doubtful whether he ever got over the death of his friend Schiller in 1805, when he had declared that he was now standing "on the edge of existence." Certainly, his diaries, which he began to keep with meticulous regularity from that time forward, contain details of one illness after another, which led to unusually critical and acerbic remarks. For example, when his *Theory of Colors* was reviewed in the *Quarterly Review* by Thomas Young (1773–1829), the British physicist who revived the wave theory of light, Goethe wrote on 21 January 1816: "It [the review] is written by a man who is just not up to it." On 26 January, he is inveighing against the Jena professors who had "sinned" in his eyes. On 18 February, there was a violent disagreement with his Weimar theater orchestra, after which Goethe forbade any performance of his Singspiele. Then we read on 25 March of his need to gain the emperor's permission for the publication of the Viennese edition of his works, which need displeased him greatly, and that was quickly followed on 27 March by yet another dispute in the theater, when an actor "dared" to address the public without Goethe's permission. This led in the next year, 1817, to Goethe's resignation from the directorship after thirty years' service.

On 2 April, Goethe took to his bed with "a strange, not dangerous, but severe rheumatic illness," and remained there till 5 April. On top of all this, along with a debilitating disorder in his left eye, he had to stand by Karl August's throne at the opening of the Weimar Congress on 7 April 1816, the type of duty that was becoming ever more distasteful to him. Most works on Goethe concentrate, of course, on his burgeoning love affair with Marianne von Willemer up to 1815; they tend to overlook the steadily deteriorating state of health of his wife, Christiane. Certainly, not much is to be read about her in the diaries; now and then, we read the entry: "Midday for us," which indicates a measure of domestic contentment.

It is not known when the packet of Lieder arrived in Weimar. No record exists, either in Weimar of their arrival or in Vienna of their return. Our investigations in both cities revealed that the incident has become just one of those stock citations for every biography, particularly, of course, of Schubert.

It would be false, and, we think, unfair to use the incident to calumniate Goethe. If Spaun sent the packet off around 17 April, we might assume that it arrived towards the end of the month. We have indicated a few of the concerns that Goethe had on his mind at the time, but a further major concern occurred on 26–27 April, when the house of his friend in Berka, the baths inspector Johann Heinrich Schütz, caught fire. Goethe had visited the inspector to listen to his beloved Bach as recently as on the 17th. He hurried over by coach to Berka on hearing the news to find that Schütz's treasured scores of Bach and Handel had been destroyed; fortunately, the beautiful Streicher piano was saved, but both men were obviously distraught.

In the back of Goethe's mind also was the continually growing tension caused by his wife's illness. Their life together had been, to say the least (and for those days), peculiar. Only one of their five children, August, had survived childhood, and he brought his father little joy, while his death in Rome, reported on 26 October 1830, led to a hemorrhage that undoubtedly hastened Goethe's death in 1832. Goethe clearly loved his wife; his letters prove this, and one feels that she meant more to him than what his mother called her, his "bed-darling."

Then came the news of the death of his friend Zelter's youngest son, Adolf, from an infectious disease contracted during the Napoleonic Wars that had just ended. To no one did Goethe write with such honest, caring familiarity as he did in his answer to Zelter's news on 26 March, seen again in that frightening letter that he wrote to Zelter after Christiane's death on 6 June. Christiane had suffered grievously for five days before she died on 6 June, "on her birthday in the hour of her birth," as her brother wrote to a friend on 11 June. "We are all weeping and her husband cannot be comforted," he added.[24]

We repeat that comment in Goethe's diary on 6 June that gives some idea of what he had gone through in the earlier months of his wife's illness: "Approaching end for my wife. Last terrible struggle of her nature. She passed away about midday. Emptiness and the silence of death in and around me." When later that summer, the axle of his coach broke on a journey to southern Germany, Goethe took it as yet another "hint of fate," and decided against any further long journeys. Goethe was sixty-six, Christiane fifty-one at the time of her death.

When one recalls what Goethe said to Eckermann many years later about answering letters, and when one considers the above facts, it is perhaps not too surprising that Goethe did not respond to Spaun's letter. On 21 January 1827, he explained his attitude to Eckermann:

I've known great men to whom people sent many letters. They then made up certain formulae and figures of speech with which they answered everyone, and so they wrote hundreds of letters which were all the same—empty phrases. I could never do that. If I could not say something special and meaningful to the particular point at issue, I would rather not answer at all, that is why I could not answer many a good fellow to whom I would gladly have written. You can see for yourself how it is with me here, and how many letters come in every day from all ends of the earth, which would take more than a whole life-time, even if I were to answer them only superficially.

The question remains: Did Goethe ever see or hear those Schubert settings? There can be no definitive answer. One assumes that his secretary from 1812 to 1819, F. J. Kräuter, returned them to Spaun, but no documentation exists indicating when Spaun received them. The first pages of the collection have been lost, so it is not even certain, for example, that *An Schwager Kronos* was, in fact, the first song of the group. It might have been a song of similar length, to judge from the pagination. The first volume (with the sixteen songs) is in the State Library in Berlin, the second volume (May 1816) of twelve songs, including "Nur wer die Sehnsucht kennt" (Only those who know what yearning is) from *Wilhelm Meister*, and *An den Mond* (To the Moon) is, in part, in the library of the Paris Conservatory, and, in part, in the Vienna City Library. The second volume was never sent.

THE SECOND PACKET OF LIEDER

One can only guess at the disappointment felt by Schubert that Spaun's approach had met with silence. He certainly seemed to have forgiven Goethe by 14 June 1816, when he noted having taken part in a musical evening at which he had sung that *Rastlose Liebe* included in Spaun's packet, along with his setting of Schiller's *Amalia* (D. 195), but actually composed on the same day, 19 May 1815. Although *Amalia* gained the greater applause, Schubert thought that *Rastlose* Liebe was a more successful setting and attributed that to "Goethe's musical poetic genius." Another consolation came on 17 June when, as he wrote in his diary: "On this day, I composed for money for the first time"—a cantata, *Prometheus* (D. 451), for the name-day of a Professor Watteroth.[25]

Two Goethe works, one old and one new, now strengthened the unseen bond. Schubert turned in September 1816 to Goethe's *Wilhelm Meister's Years of Apprenticeship* (1783–1796) and produced his first, albeit mini-song cycle, the three Harper's songs "Wer sich der Einsamkeit ergibt" (Whoever chooses solitude), "Wer nie sein Brot mit Tränen ass" (He who never ate his bread with tears), both from chapter thirteen of Book Two, and "An die Türen will ich schleichen" (I shall steal up to the doors, D. 478, 1–3) from chapter fourteen of Book Five. Here, Schubert must have used Cotta's 1815 edition of the poems, which differed from the order in which they appear in the novel. It seems unlikely, therefore, that Schubert had read through the (very) long novel. He had set *Der Sänger* (The Bard, D. 149) from Goethe's novel, the first song of the strange old Harper, in February 1815, then two songs of Mignon's, "Nur wer die Sehnsucht kennt" (Only those who know what yearning is), from chapter eleven of Book Four, and the famous "Kennst du das Land?" (D. 321) from chapter one of Book Three, in October 1815. He kept returning to the novel, which, as we saw, had made such an impression on all the Romantics. In April 1819, he wrote a male quintet version of "Nur wer die Sehnsucht kennt" (D. 656), in April 1821, two Mignon songs "Heiss mich nicht reden" (Don't ask me to speak, D. 726) from chapter sixteen of Book Five, and "So lasst mich scheinen, bis ich werde" (Let me look like this, until I become like this, D. 727) from chapter two of Book Eight, and finally, in January 1826, as his last Goethe settings, another cycle of poems that he had set earlier, *Sehnsucht* (D. 877a,) "Heiss mich nicht reden" (D. 877b), "So lasst mich scheinen" (D. 877c), and "Nur wer die Sehnsucht kennt" (D. 877d).

The new works were the outcome of Goethe's passionate affair with the thirty-two-year-old Marianne von Willemer (née Jung), wife of a Frankfurt banker friend of Goethe. It led to a group of love poems conceived in the then-Oriental tradition, with Goethe as the Persian poet Hafiz-Hatem and Marianne as his beloved Suleika. The poems, and those added later, made up this *West-östlicher Divan*. The Arabic lettering on the front of the book read: "The eastern divan from the western author," "divan" being an anthology of poems. The complete collection (twelve books) was published in 1819.

Goethe and Marianne's love affair reached its climax in a three-day meeting in Heidelberg in mid-September 1815. Schubert was not to know (nor, indeed, was the literary world until 1850 when Marianne herself admitted it) that two of the four poems that he set to music were not by Goethe, but by Marianne. These two were addressed to the east and the west winds and were written as Marianne made her way on the Bergstrasse eastwards to meet Goethe in Heidelberg, and then on her return westwards home to Frankfurt after the tryst. The two settings, *Suleika* I (What does this stirring mean?, D. 720) and *Suleika* II (Ah, how I envy your dampened wings, west wind, D. 717) seem to combine everything that bound Schubert to Goethe's poems—love of loving and love of nature. The two settings were (probably) written in March 1821; the autograph for D. 717 has, alas, vanished.

This is the song that, again, nearly brought about a recognition of Schubert from Goethe. On 16 April 1825, Goethe received a letter from Marianne. The memory of their meeting remained alive. She wrote: "Early this morning, I sent to a music shop for Beethoven's wonderful song *Herz, mein Herz, was soll das geben?* (Heart, my heart, what does it mean?), and they sent me a really lovely melody on the east wind, and *Geheimes* from the *West-östlicher Divan.*"[26] Alas, she did not mention the composer's name. Strangely enough, Marianne had written earlier, in June 1821, to Goethe that Beethoven should set this Suleika Lied to music: "He would understand it completely, otherwise nobody."[27] On 12 December 1824, the celebrated soprano Anna Milder-Hauptmann wrote to Schubert to tell him "how much your Lieder delight me, and with what enthusiasm they are received by the audience when I perform them." With the letter, she sent him a poem, *Der Nachtschmetterling* (The Moth), with the request that he set it to music for her. The poem held little attraction for Schubert, however, and he never took up the commission. Instead, he sent her a copy of his song *Suleika* II and the score of his opera *Alfonso und Estrella* (D. 732) to a libretto by Schober. He had finished the opera in 1822. Anna Milder-Hauptmann sang the *Suleika* with great success at her concerts in Berlin on 9 June 1825, where she had been prima donna at the Royal Opera since 1816.[28]

Goethe, who had again been taken severely ill with pleurisy ("to the point of death," wrote his son August to Zelter on 26 February 1823), took to Marienbad for the waters in July. In mid-August, Anna Milder sang "four little Lieder" to Goethe, which "she managed to make so great that the memory of them still brings tears to my eyes," he wrote to Zelter on 24 August. Then Goethe added: "The most marvelous thing! The enormous power of music on me at this time." Goethe regularly wrote how envious he was of Zelter's regular attendance at operas and concerts in Berlin. The musician had reported to him on 22 May 1815 of Anna Milder's arrival from Vienna: "I am looking forward to the wonderful golden voice," and Goethe answered, on 16 June, "I envy you on account of Milder. When one grows older, one should live in a big town, and with you." Much later, on 17 July 1827, he is still calling himself "a far-distant hermit."

This correspondence that regularly touched on topical musical matters makes it seem unlikely that, as has been suggested, Goethe looked at Spaun's packet and then sent them to Zelter for his opinion and advice. (Zelter is usually blamed for leading Goethe to ignore Schubert's songs.) Zelter, the outspoken musician, would surely have given his views in writing, or Goethe would have reported these in his meticulously kept diary.

Schubert's eight Goethe settings of 1817 were followed by another nineteen between 1819 and 1822, proof that his interest in Goethe never really waned. No matter how many other settings (and there were many), or other instrumental works intervened, no matter his state of health (and we are now in the first period of his syphilitic infection in 1822–1823),

Schubert continued to return to what might well be called his true love. On 30 April 1821, Cappi and Diabelli published *Gretchen am Spinnrade,* to be quickly followed by four more Goethe Lieder on 22 May, and another five on 9 July. (Of course, *Erlkönig* had been published, on commission, as Op. 1, on 2 April 1821.) But, although the unseen bond was bringing its rewards, Schubert still sought Goethe's recognition. Having been elected a "performing member" of Vienna's prestigious Society of the Friends of Music in March 1821, having seen many of his Lieder published, and perhaps also having gained in intellectual confidence from the reading-circle sessions held thrice weekly at Schober's house, Schubert's world was about to collapse with the onset of the dread illness.

Despite the publication of his song cycle *Die schöne Müllerin* (D. 795) in 1824, that terrible letter to Leopold Kupelwieser in Rome on 31 March 1824 about his miserable state betrayed his state of mind. Significantly, it was to Goethe that he turned to describe it: his peace was gone forever, too, and he was now "the unhappiest, the most miserable person in the world." One biographer suggests that the letter does not indicate unalleviated misery in the writer, because of Schubert's reasonably optimistic plans for the future contained in the later lines, but, even granting that, the letter sounds very desperate.[29]

By 1825 Schubert seemed to have recovered, albeit only temporarily, his usual good spirits, and it was then that he decided to approach Goethe, this time personally, to seek recognition. He was due to go on holiday to Upper Austria with his mentor Vogl at the end of May 1825. Before he left, he prepared for Goethe two beautifully printed copies— on satinated paper with gold borders—of three of his settings: *An Schwager Kronos* (D. 369), which some believe was never sent with the 1816 packet, *An Mignon* (D. 161), and *Ganymed* (D. 544). They were left for dispatch with his publisher, Anton Diabelli, with the following letter:

> Beginning of June 1825
> Your Excellency,
>   If I should succeed in showing my unbounded respect for Your Excellency through the dedication of these compositions of Your poems, and perhaps gain some recognition for my unworthy person, then I should count the favorable outcome of this wish as the happiest event of my life.
>   With deepest respect
>   Your obedient servant
>   Franz Schubert

Schubert then left for Upper Austria.[30]
The packet arrived in Weimar on 16 June 1825 and (presumably)

Goethe's secretary at the time, C. F. John, entered in the diary: "Packet from Felix from Berlin, quartets. Packet from Schubart [sic] from Vienna: Compositions of my Lieder" [poems].[31] This is the only mention of Schubert in Goethe's works, and even this entry betrays a mistake. C. F. D. Schubart (1739–1791) had been a well-known composer of the folk song type of Lieder in the 1770s, and thus a familiar name to Goethe, which is perhaps why the diary entry was so spelled (or dictated). On 18 June, a long letter of thanks went from Goethe to sixteen-year-old Felix Mendelssohn-Bartholdy, who had incidentally just played part of his Piano Quartet in B Minor, Op. 3, for Goethe on 20 May. Not a word was sent to Schubert.

Did Goethe see, hear, or play these settings? We know that, when Spaun's packet arrived in 1816, Goethe had no piano in the house on the Frauenplan. In 1825, however, a fine Viennese Streicher piano, bought in 1821, had become a central feature of the Juno Room, his music room; the piano stands there to this day. Goethe was now seventy-five, and, although we know from Eckermann's report that he kept busy writing and receiving his many visitors, he was naturally no longer so receptive to requests and suggestions. Furthermore, in that year 1825, his peace was disturbed when his beloved theater was burned down, in the night of 21–22 March. He confided to Eckermann: "The scene of my almost thirty years of labor left in ashes and ruins."[32] Shortly after that, he had to take to his bed again.

A gap in the record of Goethe's conversations with Johann Peter Eckermann (and Frédéric Soret) exists between 11 June and 15 October 1825, when their friendship was temporarily disturbed. This means, therefore, that there is no record for the time that Schubert's songs arrived. Stranger still, the three Schubert Lieder had been published (as Op. 19 on 6 June 1825) and dedicated to Goethe. Since Schubert knew that he would be away from Vienna until the October of 1825, it seems he did not expect an answer from Weimar. Before and during that holiday, Schubert had discovered a new poetic inspiration, Walter Scott, and had set poems from his The Lady of the Lake (D. 837–839) between April and July 1825.

Strangely enough, Goethe, too, was taking an interest in the Scottish writer just at this time. On 3 December 1824, he asked Eckermann: "Where will you find in Germany three literary heroes who can be placed on a level with Lord Byron, Moore, and Walter Scott?" It was about the other Scottish writer, Robert Burns, that Goethe made the remark most relevant to our theme, when, on 3 May 1827, he spoke of how Burns' poems and songs still lived on "in the mouths of his people." Then he added: "Of my own Lieder [poems], how many will live on? One or the other will be sung by a pretty girl at the piano, but among our own people, all is quiet." How wrong he was to be.

WHAT IF THE TWO ARTISTS HAD MET?

IF ONLY . . . ? WHAT IF . . . ? These words might stand as a summary of our study of the relationship between Goethe and Schubert. We have documented the many occasions on which the two artists might have been brought together. What benefits would such a meeting have brought to the two men?

The recognition of Schubert by Goethe in 1816 might have set the young composer on a happier life path; he might have been able to marry Therese Grob and thus avoid the dark pit into which Franz von Schober drew him in the 1820s. Recognition by Goethe would almost certainly have awakened both the public's and publishers' interest and given intimation that the music world had a new and worthy successor to its great sons. Schubert's desire to make a name for himself in the musical theater might have come to fruition had he been allowed to set some of Goethe's Singspiel libretti; that would have opened many doors to him.

And Goethe? He might have found the composer who was in harmony with these libretti and who had the genius to marry the texts to great music. This would have given Goethe recognition in one of the few worlds that he failed to conquer: the world of musical theater. Then again, Schubert might have managed to emulate Goethe's life-time hero, Wolfgang Amadeus Mozart, and put Goethe's planned continuation to *The Magic Flute* to music. It would not have been difficult for Goethe to have emulated the libretto of Emanuel Schikaneder to Mozart's opera.

Goethe might not have gained so much from a collaboration with Schubert in his life time, but who could deny that Schubert's settings of Goethe's poems have kept the name of the poet in front of a non-German public who will never have read a word of his other works? How many people have been moved to learn German just to appreciate Schubert's Lieder?

The "happy bond" that was to remain unseen was to ensure that many of Goethe's finest poems would be known and loved throughout the world. Let us look finally at the result of this bond: the Goethe Lieder of Franz Schubert.

PART TWO

CHAPTER FIVE

The Goethe Lieder of Franz Schubert

$\mathbf{S}$chubert set eighty Goethe texts to music (see list below). When he decided in March 1821 (and again in 1824) to set two poems from Goethe's recently published *West-östlicher Divan*, consisting of twelve volumes and a supplement, Schubert (and the rest of the literary world) was not aware that they had, in fact, been written by Goethe's paramour, Marianne von Willemer, personified in the collection as Suleika, the beloved of the poet Hafiz-Hatem. Thus, although we know that Nos. 79 and 80 are not two "Goethe Lieder of Franz Schubert," Schubert did not. We therefore append them as "intended" Goethe Lieder.

Song no.	Title	Deutsch number	Date composed
1.	*Gretchen am Spinnrade*	D. 118	19 October 1814
2.	*Nachtgesang*	D. 119	30 November 1814
3.	*Trost in Tränen*	D. 120	30 November 1814
4.	*Schäfers Klagelied* (a/b)	D. 121	30 November 1814
5.	*Sehnsucht* "Was zieht mir das Herz so?"	D. 123	3 December 1814
6.	*Szene aus Faust* (a/b)	D. 126	a: December 1814 b: 12 December 1814
7.	*Rastlose Liebe (a/b)*	D. 138	19 May 1815
8.	*Geistes-Gruss* (a–f)	D. 142	(?)1815; March 1816(?)
9.	*Der Sänger* (a/b)	D. 149	February 1815

Song no.	Title	Deutsch number	Date composed
10.	*Am Flusse* I	D. 160	27 February 1815
11.	*An Mignon* (a/b)	D. 161	27 February 1815
12.	*Nähe des Geliebten* (a/b)	D. 162	27 February 1815
13.	*Die Liebe*	D. 210	3 June 1815
14.	*Jägers Abendlied* I	D. 215	20 June 1815
15.	*Meeres Stille* I	D. 215a	20 June 1815
16.	*Meeres Stille* II	D. 216	21 June 1815
17.	*Wandrers Nachtlied* I	D. 224	5 July 1815
18.	*Der Fischer* (a/b)	D. 225	5 July 1815
19.	*Erster Verlust*	D. 226	5 July 1815
20.	*Tischlied*	D. 234	15 July 1815
21.	*Claudine von Villa Bella* a) "Hin und wieder fliegen die Pfeile" b) "Liebe schwärmt auf allen Wegen"	D. 239a D. 239b	Begun on 26 July 1815 July/August 1815
22.	*Die Spinnerin*	D. 247	August 1815
23.	*Der Gott und die Bajadere*	D. 254	18 August 1815
24.	*Der Rattenfänger*	D. 255	19 August 1815
25.	*Der Schatzgräber*	D. 256	19 August 1815
26.	*Heidenröslein*	D. 257	19 August 1815
27.	*Bundeslied*	D. 258	(?4)/19 August 1815
28.	*An den Mond* I	D. 259	19 August 1815
29.	*Wonne der Wehmut*	D. 260	20 August 1815
30.	*Wer kauft Liebesgötter?*	D. 261	21 August 1815
31.	*Hoffnung* I	D. 295	1815/1816(?); (?15–16 October 1819)
32.	*An den Mond* II	D. 296	ca. October 1819(?)

Song no.	Title	Deutsch number	Date composed
33.	*Sehnsucht* I "Nur wer die Sehnsucht kennt" (1) (a/b)	D. 310	18 October 1815
34.	*Mignon* "Kennst du das Land?"	D. 321	23 October 1815
35.	*Harfenspieler* I "Wer sich der Einsamkeit ergibt" (1)	D. 325	13 November 1815
36.	*Erlkönig* (a–d)	D. 328	October 1815(?)
37.	*Sehnsucht* II "Nur wer die Sehnsucht kennt" (2)	D. 359	1816
38.	*Der König in Thule*	D. 367	Early 1816
39.	*Jägers Abendlied* II	D. 368	Early 1816(?)
40.	*An Schwager Kronos*	D. 369	(?)1816
41.	*Chor der Engel*	D. 440	June 1816
42.	*Mignon* "So lasst mich scheinen, bis ich werde" (1, 2)	D. 469	September 1816
43.	*Gesänge des Harfners* I "Wer sich der Einsamkeit ergibt" (2)	D. 478, No. 1	September 1816
44.	*Gesänge des Harfners* III "An die Türen will ich schleichen"	D. 479 (D. 478, No. 3)	September 1816
45.	*Gesänge des Harfners* II "Wer nie sein Brot mit Tränen ass" (1–3)	D. 480 (D. 478, No. 2)	September 1816; Fall 1822
46.	*Sehnsucht* III "Nur wer die Sehnsucht kennt" (3)	D. 481	September 1816

Song no.	Title	Deutsch number	Date composed
47.	*Gesang der Geister über den Wassern* I	D. 484	September 1816
48.	*Gesang der Geister über den Wassern* II	D. 538	March 1817
49.	*Auf dem See* (a/b)	D. 543	(?)March 1817
50.	*Ganymed*	D. 544	March 1817
51.	*Mahomets Gesang* I	D. 549	March 1817
52.	*Liebhaber in allen Gestalten*	D. 558	May 1817
53.	*Schweizerlied*	D. 559	May 1817
54.	*Der Goldschmiedsgesell*	D. 560	May 1817
55.	*Gretchen im Zwinger*	D. 564	May 1817
56.	*Sehnsucht* IV "Nur wer die Sehnsucht kennt" (4)	D. 656	April 1819
57.	*Die Liebende schreibt*	D. 673	October 1819
58.	*Prometheus*	D. 674	October 1819
59.	*Gesang der Geister über den Wassern* III	D. 704	December 1820
60.	*Gesang der Geister über den Wassern* IV	D. 705	December 1820
61.	*Im Gegenwärtigen Vergangenes*	D. 710	March 1821(?)
62.	*Gesang der Geister über den Wassern* V, VI	D. 714	V: December 1820; VI: February 1821
63.	*Versunken*	D. 715	February 1821
64.	*Grenzen der Menschheit*	D. 716	March 1821
65.	*Geheimes*	D. 719	March 1821
66.	*Mahomets Gesang* II	D. 721	March 1821

Song no.	Title	Deutsch number	Date composed
67.	*Mignon* I "Heiss mich nicht reden" (1)	D. 726	April 1821
68.	*Mignon* II "So lasst mich scheinen, bis ich werde" (3)	D. 727	April 1821
69.	*Johanna Sebus*	D. 728	April 1821
70.	*Der Musensohn* (a/b)	D. 764	December 1822
71.	*An die Entfernte*	D. 765	December 1822
72.	*Am Flusse* II	D. 766	December 1822
73.	*Willkommen und Abschied* (a/b)	D. 767	December 1822
74.	*Wandrers Nachtlied* II (Ein Gleiches. Auf dem Gickelhahn)	D. 768	(?)December 1822; before 25 May 1824
75.	*Gesänge aus Wilhelm Meister Sehnsucht* V "Nur wer die Sehnsucht kennt" (5)	D. 877, No. 1	(?)January 1826
76.	*Lied der Mignon* II "Heiss mich nicht reden" (2)	D. 877, No. 2	(?)January 1826
77.	*Lied der Mignon* III "So lasst mich scheinen, bis ich werde" (4)	D. 877, No. 3	(?)January 1826
78.	*Lied der Mignon* IV "Nur wer die Sehnsucht kennt" (6)	D. 877, No. 4	(?)January 1826
79.	*Suleika* I (a/b)	D. 720	March 1821
80.	*Suleika* II	D. 717	(?)December 1824; March(?) 1821

1. *Gretchen am Spinnrade* (D. 118)
(Gretchen at the Spinning Wheel)
19 October 1814
D minor
120 measures
ca. 3.30 minutes

Text

The first fragments of Goethe's long poem *Faust I* were probably written between 1769 and 1775 at the height of the Storm and Stress movement. The text was completed in 1806 after which the poet destroyed all his earlier manuscripts, forgetting that he had loaned a draft to Luise von Göchhausen, a lady at the Weimar court. Her copy, discovered in 1887 by Erich Schmidt and published in the same year, is known as the *Urfaust* (*Ur* means original, or first) and contains the "Gretchen tragedy."[1] Goethe had just left the young Friederike Brion in Strasbourg in 1771 and was suffering pangs of guilt. It is clear now that he did not leave her pregnant, but the public execution of a young woman, Susanna Margaretha Brandt, in Frankfurt in 1772 for the murder of her illegitimate child, no doubt became linked in his mind with his abandonment of Friederike. In *Faust I*, Goethe describes how the aging professor Faust makes both a pact and a wager with the Evil Spirit, the sardonic Mephistopheles, who will grant him years of rejuvenated life, on condition that, when Faust declares himself "satisfied with life," Mephisto may claim his soul. Dressed as a French cavalier, Faust meets Gretchen (or Margarete as she is named at first), an innocent, small-town girl, seduces her, making her pregnant, and finally abandons her to her death for having drowned their illegitimate child. It has been suggested that Gretchen could not have been so innocent, since she gave her mother a sleeping potion to enable her to "sleep with" Faust and, of course, in the *Urfaust* it is her "loins" which "yearn for him," not her "bosom" (cf. stanza no. 8 of the translation). Certainly, there is no doubt that this monologue (spoken, not sung, in the work), is, indeed, a "frank and physical declaration of passion."[2]

Music

Almost certainly, Schubert found the text in the edition of *Faust* published by Anton Strauss as volume one of Goethe's *Collected Works* in Vienna in 1810. He was infatuated at the time with Therese Grob, who had sung in his Mass in F Major (D. 105) in the autumn of 1814, and he must have written the song shortly after that performance. The original is now lost. He made a copy for Goethe in 1816, and the first sixteen measures of that are now in the State Library in Berlin. This had formed

Gretchen am Spinnrade.

Edition Peters

Gretchen am Spinnrade (D. 118), 19 October 1814.

Edition Peters.

Gretchen am Spinnrade (D. 118), 19 October 1814. Note the phrase "und ach, sein Kuss!" when Gretchen stops spinning to think of Faust's kiss.

the basis for the version published in Vienna by Cappi and Diabelli as Op. 2 in 1821.

Setting

Schubert had read the monologue that autumn and had obviously been excited by the relevance and the musicality of the text. Here, truly, for the first time in the history of the German Lied, text and music share the honors; the music does not just illustrate the poem, it is indeed self-contained and "reproduces the poetic intentions," as Goethe had demanded of a setting. Thus, it forms an art song, which is a higher synthesis of the two art forms.[3] In ten stanzas in the simple folk song meter of the day, Goethe allows Gretchen to pour out her feelings after meeting Faust. She speaks as she spins. The spinning wheel is personified by the monotonous allegro non troppo whirring of the sixteenth-notes' accompaniment, in 6/8 time, which only ceases at the most miraculous moment in song literature—when Gretchen thinks of Faust's kiss. She cries ecstatically: "und ach, sein Kuss!" (And, oh, his kiss!). The dramatic pause, which comes after the high G, is followed by the resumption of the spinning wheel motif in the accompaniment, until Gretchen sinks back exhausted, and Schubert (not Goethe) makes her repeat, "my peace is gone, my heart is heavy," as the very last words. Because of these sections in the higher register, the song has tended to become the preserve of dramatic sopranos, and it might be felt that what often sounds like an operatic aria is inappropriate for the love song of a simple working girl—but it rarely fails to move a concert-hall audience.

Translation

1. My peace is gone, my heart is heavy, I'll never find it again, never.
2. Where I'm not with him is the grave for me, the whole world has turned to gall.
3. My poor head is in a whirl, my poor wits are all to pieces.
4. (Goethe repeats stanza one).
5. Only for him do I look out of the window, only for him do I leave the house.
6. His lordly gait, his noble figure, the smile on his lips, and the power of his eyes.
7. And the magic flow of his words, the squeeze of his hands, and, oh, his kiss!
8. My bosom yearns for him. Oh, if I could only clutch and hold him,
9. And kiss him, just as I wanted to, and die under his kisses.
10. (Schubert repeats stanza one).

2. *Nachtgesang* (D. 119)
(Night Song)
30 November 1814
A-flat major
14 measures
ca. 3.30 minutes

Text

This beautiful poem seems to encapsulate all Goethe's poetic and musical gifts at their height in March or May 1802, yet it is not entirely his own. It was adapted from Reichardt's setting of an Italian folk song *Tu sei quel dolce fuoco,* with its refrain "Dormi, che vuoi di più?" (Sleep, what more do you desire?). It was published in Schiller's *Musenalmanach* of 1804. The poet sings to his beloved accompanied by his zither, but softly so as not to wake her. The poem takes on the form of a cradle song.

Music

Schubert found the poem (and five of his next six settings) in volume seven of Goethe's *Collected Works* in Vienna in 1810. To make it a better commercial proposition, Diabelli transposed the first published edition in volume forty-seven of the 1850 *Nachlass* to G major, with his trivial prelude and postlude. The manuscript contains D. 120, D. 123, and D. 124 as well. The song was in the second volume prepared by Josef von Spaun for Goethe in 1816 but never sent to him.

Setting

The poem had five stanzas, which Schubert set as a strophic Lied, keeping the same questioning refrain, "Sleep, what more do you desire?" Diabelli's version had only three stanzas. It can be seen from the structure of the poem, where the third line of each stanza becomes the first of the next, that the singer must really sing all five stanzas to "reproduce the poetic intentions." The fourteen measures of the melody, in 2/4 time, should also be varied in tonal intensity to match the varying sentiments. The final line, sung *pianissimo,* should have an incantatory effect.

Translation

1. As you lie dreaming on your soft pillow, lend but half an ear to the melody of my zither. Sleep! What more do you desire?
2. To the melody of my zither, the starry host blesses our eternal emotions. Sleep! What more do you desire?
3. Our eternal emotions raise me high and sublime above the world's turmoil. Sleep! What more do you desire?
4. From the world's turmoil, you banish me only too well to this cool air. Sleep! What more do you desire?

5. You banish me to this cool air and listen to me only in your dreams. Oh, sleep on, on your soft pillow, Sleep! What more do you desire?

3. *Trost in Tränen* (D. 120)
(Consolation in Tears)
30 November 1814
F major
23 measures
ca. 3.40 minutes

Text
Again, as with song no. 2, this poem was taken from a folk song set to a new melody by Reichardt in 1777, which then reappeared in 1800, set to a popular Swiss song melody. Goethe's parody version of March 1803 was published in the *Taschenbuch auf das Jahr 1804* (Pocketbook for the Year 1804), edited by Goethe and Wieland. It is in the form of a conversation, alternately between the poet and his friends, the one mourning an undefined loss, the others consoling him.

Music
The music is very much in the former simple folk song style, and a reminder that Schubert was still a child of his age and not always so innovative as in *Gretchen am Spinnrade*. As with D. 119, a copy for Goethe was made in 1816 for the second volume of songs, which was not sent to the poet. One does wonder how Goethe would have greeted this almost perfect example of what he was accustomed to from the eighteenth century. Schubert took this poem, the second song written on this day, from volume seven of the 1810 *Collected Works* of Goethe.

Setting
The eight stanzas are divided equally between poet and companions. The 6/8 rhythm and the simple melody can become soporific, particularly in translation, although Goethe's musical poetry lightens the melancholic sentiments in the German.

Translation
1. Why are you are so sad when all around are happy? We can see in your eyes, you've been crying?
2. "And if I have been crying, then my pain is my own, and the tears which flow so sweetly, lighten my heart."
3. Your merry friends invite you to come and join us. Whatever it is you've lost, tell us about it.
4. "You're a noisy, drunken lot and cannot guess what troubles my poor soul. Oh no, I've not lost anything, however much I miss it!"

5. Come on then, pull yourself together, you're still a young lad. People of your age have the strength and the courage to go on and achieve things.
6. "Oh no, I can't go on—all that is beyond me. It's all up there, shining so bright, like that star above."
7. But people don't ask for stars, they just enjoy their beauty and love to look up at them in the comforting nights.
8. "And I like to look up there too, during the many lovely days; but let me weep the nights away as long as I can weep."

4. *Schäfers Klagelied* (D. 121) (a/b)
   (Shepherd's Lament)
   30 November 1814; Spring 1818(?)
   a: C minor; b: E minor
   a: 61 measures; b: 65 measures
   ca. 3.00 minutes

Text

This poem also is based on a well-known folk song, *Dort droben auf jenem Berge* (Up there on that mountain), that Goethe heard at a party. His version was written in Jena on 17 (or 19) February 1802 to fit the old melody. It is possibly one of the Lieder mentioned in his letter to Schiller on the 19th: "I have once again written a few Lieder [poems] to well-known melodies."[4] It was published in the *Taschenbuch auf das Jahr 1804*. The poem certainly reminds one of the beautiful hilly landscape round Weimar and Jena in Thuringia.

Music

There are two versions, written on the same day; the first in C minor, the second in E minor. The first has no introduction and was included in Spaun's 1816 packet to Goethe. On 28 February 1819, a Schubert song was to be performed for the first time in public by the twenty-three-year-old tenor, Franz Jäger. For the event, Schubert transposed this song into the higher key of E minor and added the four-measure introduction. The C minor version was published by Cappi and Diabelli as Op. 3, No. 1, in 1821, but both versions are in the Old and New Complete Editions. The *Berliner Gesellschafter* for 22 March 1819 wrote: "*Schäfers Klage*, composed by the young Schubert and sung by our fine young tenor Jäger, afforded most pleasure"—and Schubert was named as "the hopeful composer."[5] So, foreign newspapers were now becoming aware of Schubert, and Zelter, Goethe's friend, planned to visit Vienna in July of that year.

Setting

Schubert's modified strophic setting preserves the folk song identity of the poem. Its six stanzas are grouped in three sets of two and move gently in his favorite 6/8 time, painting a beautiful rural, yet also melancholic picture. Such a song would be very familiar to native German speakers of the period—but the passion of the storm in the fourth, the genuine anguish in the last stanza, and the wonderful modulations throughout mark it out as something different—a true Schubertian Lied. In this setting as in others, Schubert altered many of Goethe's lines, which has led to some criticism from lovers of German poetry.

Translation

1. I stand a thousand times up there on that mountain, leaning on my crook and looking down into the valley.
2. Then I follow my grazing flock, watched over by my little dog. I've come down into the valley—but I don't know how I did so.
3. The whole meadow is full of lovely flowers. I've picked them, but don't know to whom I should give them.
4. And rain storms, thunder, and lightning shower down, while I shelter under this tree—but that door over there stays closed; for, alas, all is but a dream.
5. A rainbow stands above that house, but she has gone away, away to a far-distant land.
6. Away to a distant land—and, perhaps even further, over the sea. Pass by, oh, pass by, my flock, your shepherd's heart is heavy. (Repeat the last lines.)

5. *Sehnsucht* (D. 123)

(Yearning)
"Was zieht mir das Herz so?"
(What is tugging at my heartstrings so?)
3 December 1814
G major
69 measures
ca. 3.00 minutes

Text

In 1798, Goethe had purchased an estate in Oberrossla, not far from Weimar: "At the end of March," he wrote in his diary in 1801, "a stay in the country was very refreshing."[6] He sold the estate in 1803, feeling that one must be "born to the earth" to enjoy country life completely. The five stanzas suggest a Goethean love affair, but his roving eye had simply been gladdened by the sight of a "sweet child," Silvie von Ziegesar, the sixteen-year-old daughter of an aristocratic friend. (See also song no. 57.)

Music
The original manuscript is in G major and was divided in the 1880s. A copy was made for Goethe in 1816, but was never sent. The song was published in volume thirty-seven of Diabelli's *Nachlass*, in June 1842, in F major (and in the Peters edition, too). It was restored to G major in 1887.

Setting
Schubert was again attracted by a poem about a pretty girl and a possible happy outcome to a love affair. Beethoven had written a very successful setting in 1810 (Op. 83, No. 2), and perhaps Schubert should have left the poem alone. The many (twelve) changes of key, rhythm, and style detract from Goethe's pastoral, light-hearted stanzas. One has the feeling that Schubert was trying too hard here. This setting is one of his few failures.

Translation
1. What is tugging at my heart strings so? What is pulling me out of doors, and is wrenching and wresting me from my room and my house? Look how the clouds are floating away from the rocks! I'd love to go over there, oh yes, over there!
2. Now the ravens are flitting by, all happy together; I'll mingle with them and follow their flight. We'll wing over the walls and the hills; she is waiting down there, I'll look out for her.
3. Here she comes, walking along; I'll hurry along right away, a singing bird in the bushy wood. She waits there, listens and smiles to herself: "He is singing so beautifully, and he's singing for me."
4. The sinking sun gilds the mountain tops, the beautiful girl, deep in thought, lets it go. She wanders by the brook, over the meadow; the path twists and turns, and grows ever darker;
5. Suddenly, I appear—a shining star. "What is that shining up there, so near, and yet so far?" And when you have watched the gleam in astonishment, then I'll lie at your feet, and I'll be happy!

6. *Szene aus Faust* (D. 126) (a/b)
    (*Scene from Faust*)
    a: December 1814; b: 12 December 1814
    C major
    b: 100 measures
    ca. 8.30 minutes

Text

"Mozart should have composed Faust," Goethe said to Eckermann on 12 February 1829, and when one listens to the most popular opera on the theme, Gounod's (1859), one grants that he was probably correct. In the *Urfaust* (before 1775), this Requiem Mass in the cathedral was being sung for Gretchen's mother, which heightens the tension and the awareness of Gretchen's guilt. Is the Evil Spirit just Gretchen's "troubled conscience," as Mason suggested,[7] or some Christian condemnation? It is certainly a powerful picture of a woman seized by an inner terror, a type of religious panic for which Goethe had little time in real life. Its major significance for us is the proof of Goethe's awareness of operatic conventional treatment, which then inspired Schumann, Spohr, Gounod, Berlioz, Liszt, Wagner, Mahler, Pousseur, and Busoni to write works on the *Faust* theme.

Music

The music is likewise proof that Schubert was thinking here of a full operatic treatment of the theme. His first draft for soprano and alto has the instructions "chorus," "organ," and "trombones" marked for the obvious places, although the piece was published without these, as a solo song, in December 1832, in volume 20 of Diabelli's *Nachlass*. Graham Johnson's version introduces the Evil Spirit (sung by Thomas Hampson) and a chorus, thus making the "scene" into a true "scena."[8]

Setting

Although rarely performed, the music is extraordinarily effective, especially when the Evil Spirit is sung by a man. One is forced again to wonder why Schubert had no real success as a composer of operas—and returns to the reason already advanced: he never found a good enough librettist. And why did Goethe never have any real success as a Singspiel librettist? He never found a good enough composer. Goethe said once, on 9 October 1828, to Eckermann: "I cannot enjoy an opera unless the story is as perfect as the music, so that the two can go together."

Translation

The work is headed "Cathedral. Mass. Organ and choir singing. Gretchen in the crowd. Evil Spirit behind Gretchen."

   Evil Spirit: How different you were, Gretchen, when, full of innocence, you came up to the altar, and lisped your prayers from that old Bible, your heart half-filled with childlike ideas, half with God. Gretchen! What are you thinking now? What sin is in your heart? Are you praying for your mother's soul who fell asleep into a long night of pain because of you? Whose blood lies at your door? And is something not stirring already under your heart, frightening you and itself with the presentiment of the present?

Gretchen: Oh, woe, woe is me! If I could only be rid of these thoughts that plague me through and through!

Choir: Dies irae, dies illa / Solvet saeclum in favilla. (Day of wrath and terror looming / Heaven and earth to ash consuming).[9]

(Organ sounds.)

Evil Spirit: Anguish seizes you! The trombone sounds! The graves quiver! And your heart, fanned from the dead ashes in the flames of torment, trembles too!

Gretchen: Oh, were I no longer here! I feel as if the organ is stealing my breath away and the singing loosening my heart strings in its depths.

Choir: Judex ergo cum sedebit / Quidquid latet adparebit / Nil inultum remanebit. (Then the judge will sit, revealing / Every hidden thought and feeling / Unto each requital dealing.

Gretchen: I cannot breathe! The cathedral pillars are stifling me! The ceiling is crushing me! Air! Light! Woe unto you!

Choir: Quid sum miser tunc dicturus? / Quem patronum rogaturus? Cum vix justus sit securus. (What shall wretched I be crying / To what friend for succor flying / When the just in fear are sighing?)

Evil Spirit: Those who are blessed turn their faces away from you. The pure in spirit fear to reach out their hands to you! Oh, woe unto you!

Choir: Quid sum miser tunc dicturus? (What shall wretched I be crying?)

(At the end of Goethe's scene, Gretchen, after asking: "Neighbor! Your flask!" falls in a faint. Schubert omitted this conclusion.)

7. *Rastlose Liebe* (D. 138) (a/b)
(Restless Love)
19 May 1815
a: E major; b: D major
a/b: 93
ca. 1.20 minutes

Text
Ilmenau is a charming little village set at the foot of the Thuringian forest, some twenty-five miles (forty kilometers) southwest of Weimar. It became a favorite retreat of Goethe from the burdens of his administrative work at the court. This poem was written just a few months after his arrival in Weimar in November 1775. He had met Charlotte von Stein,

then thirty-three and the mother of seven children (although only three had survived). Goethe, twenty-six, fell deeply in love with her and believed at one point that they had been man and wife in another life. "I have no names for us," he wrote to C. M. Wieland in 1776, "the past—the future—the All."[10] This tempestuous love poem, written in Ilmenau on 6 May 1776 in an unseasonal snowstorm, mirrors the impression that Goethe gave to the staid Weimar court—an impetuous youth, still flaunting his reputation as the author of the sensational novel *Die Leiden des jungen Werther* (1774). The poem appeared in his *Collected Works* in 1789; a copy by Herder showed some variations.

Music

Eduard von Bauernfeld wrote in 1829 of the effect that reading this poem had on Schubert. Goethe's poem "fell like sparks of fire," but met in Schubert's soul "something that caught fire."[11] The music was on paper in no time at all, and a performance lasts just over a minute. The original was included, in revised and simplified form, in Spaun's packet for Goethe in 1816. When Baron von Schönstein agreed to sing it in May 1821, Schubert transposed the song to D major, but the original key was restored for the publication as Op. 5, No. 1, by Cappi and Diabelli in July 1821. The song was dedicated to Schubert's old teacher, Antonio Salieri, then seventy-one. One wonders what the dignified old "Nestor of composers," as Spaun had called him in that letter to Goethe, would have made of the pounding sixteenth notes and the on-rushing tempo. Would Goethe have made no comment to Zelter had he seen the song?

Setting

The song was heard for the first time when Schubert sang it on 13 June 1816 at a gathering of musical friends. His diary entry for 14 June said: "I played some Beethoven variations, sang Goethe's *Rastlose Liebe* and Schiller's *Amalia*. Unanimous applause for the latter, less for the former. Although I regard my *Rastlose Liebe* as more successful than *Amalia*, one cannot deny that Goethe's musical poetic genius contributed much to the applause."[12] This fragment was later found to have been written on the original manuscript of the song. Herder's copy mentioned above has "Wie? Soll ich fliehen?" (*What?* Am I to flee?). If no pause is made when singing, then the meaning must surely be "*How* am I to flee?" which (*pace* Albertson) seems wrong.[13] That is only one of the many problems of interpretation and performance here. Fischer-Dieskau wrote that it needed a singer "with a trained voice and interpretative skills,"[14] a slight understatement. Schubert possessed neither, which might have accounted for the song's immediate lack of success. Even today, it is not a number one choice among singers. The accompanist's problems are manifold, particularly in the second stanza where the poem moves from impetuosity to reflection, the music modulates to G major, is marked *piano,* and changes to triplets. This text is one of the Goethe poems set as through-composed by both Reichardt (in 1794) and Zelter (in 1812).

Translation

1. Against the snow, against the rain, against the wind, through the steaming, misty gorges, ever onwards! Ever onwards! No rest, no peace!
2. I would rather fight with suffering than bear so much of the joys of living. All this love from one heart to another, oh, how much pain it causes!
3. What—am I to flee? Rush off into the forest? All, all in vain! Crown of my life, happiness without peace, love, that is you! (The last words are repeated three times before the short stormy postlude).

8. *Geistes-Gruss* (D. 142) (a–f)
   (Ghostly Greeting)
   (?)1815; March 1816(?)
   E major
   25–33 measures
   ca. 2.00 minutes

Text
The poem was written during a journey (starting from Ems on the Lahn) down the river Rhine, which Goethe made with a dozen friends, chief among them the influential Swiss clergyman J. K. Lavater, on 18 July 1774. Goethe "improvised rhymes as they went,"[15] and as they passed the ruins of the castle of Lahneck, he dictated this ballad. It appeared in his *Collected Works* in 1789, under the one-word title *Geistesgruss.*

Music
There are six versions in all, but it is usually sung in E major. It was sent to Goethe in 1816, but only published in 1828 as Op. 87 (later Op. 92), No. 3, by Leidesdorf, at a time when many of Schubert's works, including the first twelve songs of *Winterreise,* Op. 89 (D. 911), were being published. The longer versions have extended introductions.

Setting
Goethe might just have been pleased with Schubert's pseudo-medieval setting. It is very simple, stately, and singable, but probably too simple for recital purposes. Schubert's six versions seem to indicate the prob-

lems of finding a satisfactory setting. Most listeners would probably prefer Heine's poetic descriptions of the river Rhine—in Schumann's settings of his *Dichterliebe* (Poet's Love), Op. 48, for example.

Translation

1. The noble spirit of the hero stands high up on the old tower, and, as he watches the ship sail by, bids it a fond farewell:
2. "Look, this sinew was so strong, this heart so firm and wild, these bones so full of knightly vigor, this beaker full of wine.
3. I fought my battles for half of my life, spent the last half in peace, so you, ship of mankind, sail on, ever onwards!"

9. *Der Sänger* (D. 149) (a/b)
(The Bard)
February 1815
D major
a: 129 measures; b: 151 measures
ca. 7.00 minutes

Text
Chapter three dealt in detail with Goethe's novel *Wilhelm Meister's Years of Apprenticeship* (1795–1796), which grew out of his earlier attempt *Wilhelm Meister's Theatrical Mission*. In chapter twelve of Book Four in the earlier work (and chapter eleven in Book Two of the later), Wilhelm and his friends are drinking in an inn when an "old, balding man" with "large blue eyes, peering gently from under white eyebrows" and with a "long white beard, which fell from under a finely shaped nose" is admitted. He is dressed ("like a Papist or a Jew," some think) "in a long dark brown cloak that covers his slim body from head to foot." The company is jovial, and the old man entertains the drinkers with this medieval ballad, accompanied on his harp. The ballad praises the innocence of poetry. The Harper and Mignon are, wrote Nicholas Boyle, "the image of a power of heartfelt poetry, that may yet draw meaning and magic out of a desperately prosaic existence."[16] As we learn, tragedy grows out of seeming happiness and joviality, which makes this first song of the Harper all the more poignant.

Music
Chapter three points out how much the *Wilhelm Meister* scenarios illustrate and underline Goethe's musicality. Schubert, like most of that generation of the early 1800s, thought highly of *Wilhelm Meister*, and he set several of the songs. There are two versions of *Der Sänger*, one made for Spaun's (second) 1816 packet for Goethe, and another revised for the

publication by Josef Czerny in June 1829, as Op. 117. It is twenty-two measures longer than the 1815 version, but in the same 4/4 time. Since Schubert was a member of the reading circle during those years, it is likely that that experience, along with his knowledge of Reichardt's and Zumsteeg's ballads, influenced his choice of texts with medieval themes. In January 1816 (possibly), he composed *Bardengesang* (The Bard's Song, D. 147) from Ossian's *Comola* as a terzet, and on the 17th of the same month, *Lodas Gespenst* (Loda's Ghost, D. 150), a solo song, from Ossian's *Carric-Thura*.

Setting

Both settings ask for a tempo of "cheerfulness." The prelude imitates the harp before the recitative begins. When the bard starts up his song, in the third stanza, we only read of its effect on the knights and their ladies—we never know what he actually sang. As one critic put it, "everyone feels cheated!" We only know that the bard "sings like the bird sings" and his only reward will be a glass of wine, which he quaffs with obvious enjoyment. The song proceeds as a mixture of recitative and aria, full of medieval courtly grace and charm. The didactic message, that song can soothe the savage breast, is never very far away.

Translation

1. "What do I hear outside the gate, what is that commotion on the bridge? Let that song be heard before us in the hall!" The king spoke, the page ran to do his bidding; the boy came in, the king cried: "Let the old man come in to me!"

2. "Greetings, my noble lords! Greetings, fair ladies! What a wonderful heaven! full of stars! Who knows their names? Eyes, close yourselves, in this hall full of grandeur and magnificence; this is not the time to look around in joy and amazement."

3. The bard closed his eyes and sang out in full voice; the knights watched him gallantly, while the ladies lowered their eyes. The king, delighted with the song, had a golden chain brought, to thank the old man for his performance.

4. "Do not give me the golden chain; give it to the knights before whose brave countenances the enemy lances are shattered; give it to your chancellor to add this golden burden to the others."

5. "I sing as the bird sings which lives in the branches; my song, which flows from my throat, is my rich reward. Yet, if I may beg one favor: give me your best wine in a goblet of pure gold."

6. He took it up and drained it empty: "Oh, a drink of sweet comfort! Oh, blessings on such a happy house where this is but a little gift!

Keep well, and think of me, and thank God as warmly as I thank you for this drink."

10. *Am Flusse* I (D. 160)
(By the River)
27 February 1815
D minor
30 measures
ca. 1.15 minutes

Text
This tiny poem recalls Goethe's love affair with Käthchen Schönkopf during his student years, 1765–1768, in Leipzig. On his birthday, 28 August 1768, the poet returned home to Frankfurt, broken in health after a hemorrhage, and saddened by the loss of Käthchen. This poem was intended to be the epilogue to the poems he wrote for her. It appeared in Schiller's *Musenalmanach* of 1799.

Music
Schubert wrote two settings of this text; the other is song no. 72 (D. 766). This setting is one of the first to mirror Schubert's lifelong love affair with water, brooks, and rivers. The second version shows how the affair had deepened in seven years. The miniature concentrates on what we held to be one of his major themes: lost love. Goethe suffered this too, only, his lifestyle offered him consolations denied to Schubert. The song was published in the *Complete Edition* in 1894.

Setting
Goethe's verses are a perfect example of his "musical poetic genius," to quote Schubert. The theme is "song," the rhythm and the rhyming are musical; Schubert's through-composed setting in 3/8 time, marked "wehmütig" (sadly), matches the charm of the poem.

Translation
1.   Flow on, my beloved songs, towards the sea of oblivion! No happy boy will sing to you again, nor any girl in the springtime of her youth.
2.   You sang only of my beloved; now, she mocks my faithfulness. You were written into the water; go, flow away with it!

11. *An Mignon* (D. 161) (a/b)
(To Mignon)
27 February 1815
a: G-sharp minor; b: G minor

19 measures (5 stanzas)
ca. 3.15 minutes

Text

The poem was written in 1796 at the time of the publication of *Wilhelm Meister's Years of Apprenticeship*, which features the little Italian waif Mignon. This raises the immediate question: To whom is this poem addressed? And by whom? Graham Johnson, following von der Hellen's 1902 thesis, believes that Goethe was thinking back to his "beautiful Milanese," Maddalena Riggi, whom he met and was attracted to in October 1787 in Rome.[17] Hearing that she was engaged, Goethe decided to avoid a repetition of the Werther story and left her alone. Later, he had a serious erotic affair with Faustina Antonini, a twenty-four-year-old mother of a three-year-old child who was immortalized, particularly, in the fifth of his *Roman Elegies*, whose original title was, significantly, *Erotica Romana*. Maddalena told Goethe how she used to "watch the ships coming and going in the Ripetta," Rome's old harbor (cf. the third stanza). The poem was sent to Schiller on 28 March 1797 and was published (along with Zelter's setting) in the *Musenalmanach* of 1797. The Goethe-Zelter correspondence began in 1799.

Music

All the above would not, of course, have been known to Schubert, who found the poem with most of his early Goethe choices near one another in the Goethe 1810 edition, where they appear under the title "Lieder." The beginning of the melody is immediately recognizable to Schubertians as a variant of the beginning of song no. 5 of *Die schöne Müllerin,* "Am Feierabend" (After Work): "Hätt' ich tausend Arme zu rühren" (If I had a thousand arms to use). That song is marked "ziemlich geschwind" (pretty fast), and this one "etwas geschwind" (quite fast). Both are in 6/8 time. There are two versions, the first in G-sharp minor, but the song was published in G minor, as Op. 19, No. 2, by Diabelli, in 1825. It was sent to Goethe in 1816, and again in 1825, with Schubert's letter, requesting permission to dedicate it and two other songs to the poet.

Setting

Schubert set the poem as a strophic Lied; the five stanzas respond to this treatment, since they are all on the same theme: the sorrow of separation. It may be that too bright an attack by the singer would convey too much optimism, hence the composer's instruction, not "ziemlich" but "etwas geschwind."

An Mignon.

An Mignon (D. 161), 27 February 1815.

Translation
1. Borne across vale and stream, the sun's carriage moves serenely on. Oh, in its course, it stirs up both my and your sorrows, deep in our hearts, every morning anew.
2. Nor is night of any help to me, for my dreams themselves arrive so sadly clad; and I feel the secretly waxing power of those pains in the stillness of my heart.
3. For many a year now, I've watched the ships sail past below, each one arriving at its port; but, oh, these pains fixed in my heart never swim away in the river.
4. I must come in fine clothes taken from the wardrobe, because today is a holiday; no one suspects that, in my heart of hearts, I am racked by terrible pain.
5. So, I must always weep alone, yet I can seem to appear quite happy, ever healthy and rosy faced; but if these pains had been fatal to my heart, I should have long since died.

12. *Nähe des Geliebten* (D. 162) (a/b)
(Nearness of the Beloved)
27 February 1815
G-flat major
a: 19 measures; b: 10 measures
ca. 3.15 minutes (4 stanzas); ca. 2.15 (2 stanzas)

Text
Goethe heard a setting of a poem by Karl Friedrich Zelter in 1796. The original poem by Friederike Brun was not to his taste, although Zelter's melody was. Goethe therefore wrote a more suitable poem for Schiller's *Musenalmanach* of 1796.

Music
As happened more than once in Schubert's way of working, a group of Lieder was composed on the same day and often contained one jewel among more mundane products. In this case, the composer produced two versions of this song—the first in 6/8 time, the second in 12/8—along with *Am Flusse, An Mignon* and a setting of Körner's *Sängers Morgenlied* (Singer's Morning Song, D. 163). He eventually chose the second version for publication by Cappi and Diabelli in July 1821 as Op. 5, No. 2 (with *Rastlose Liebe*). Both pieces were dedicated to his old teacher, Antonio Salieri, and included in Spaun's 1816 packet to Goethe.

Setting
This strophic song has the truly limpid simplicity of the great Schubert

Lieder. Here, too, is that perfect balance between voice and accompaniment that makes a Schubert song inimitable. One waits breathlessly for the entry of the voice after the long introduction: a passionate declaration of devotion, "I think of you." As we know, there was a large number of women in Goethe's life to whom these words of love might have been addressed; in Schubert's strophic setting, they somehow sound more genuine, more personal. The wonderful descent from D flat to G flat on the "da" (here) of "O wärst du da" (Oh, if only you were with me here) in the last line, conveys so magically the impression of loving longing. From time to time, Schubert, like many setters of poems, is accused of altering his poet's texts to suit his music. Here, he adds but one word in the third stanza; Goethe's text—"Im stillen Haine geh' ich" (I often walk in the quiet grove)—does not quite fit the melodic structure, so Schubert adds "*da* geh' ich," but this does not alter the meaning.

Translation
1. I think of you, when the sun shimmers on the sea; I think of you, when the moon is reflected in the brook.
2. I see you, when the dust is raised on the distant roads; in the depths of the night, when the wanderer stands trembling on the narrow bridge.
3. I hear you, when the waves break over there with a dull roar; I often walk in the quiet grove to listen, when all is still.
4. I am with you; however far away you are, you are near me! The sun sinks, soon the stars will shine on me. Oh, if only you were with me here!

13. *Die Liebe* (D. 210)
(Love)
3 June 1815
B-flat major
21 measures
ca. 1.25 minutes

Text
Goethe's comment to Charlotte von Stein in 1782 graphically describes the seven years' struggle he had with his play *Egmont* (finally published in 1787): "It is a strange play. If I had to write it again, I would write it differently—and perhaps not at all."[18] It is a war story set in the Low Countries in 1566–1568. Count Egmont, famed for his victories against the French, is charged by the court with high living and irresponsibility. The Spanish Duke of Alba marches on the Low Countries, captures Eg-

mont, and sentences him to death. Asleep before his execution, Egmont has a vision of "freedom," which bears the features of his beloved, Klärchen, and he goes to his death, certain that right will triumph in the end. Outside German-speaking countries, the play is perhaps known only because of Beethoven's dramatic settings (Op. 84) of 1810–1811, particularly of the overture, and the end of act 5, the "Victory" Symphony. Klärchen is a symbol of female devotion in eighteenth-century Germany, a woman who stands by her man. In act 3, scene 2, she is reminded by her mother of her promise to marry the less flamboyant Brackenburg, but, like Gretchen by Faust, she too is blinded by her love for the aristocratic Egmont and would like to follow him into battle. The song has no title in the play, but it is known as *Klärchen's Lied* (Clara's Song).

Music
Reichardt set the words as *Die Liebe* in 1804, and Schubert probably knew this. Beethoven's music was played for the first time in Weimar in 1814, but there is no record of Schubert having seen the play in Vienna, although a letter of 1823 suggests that he knew the overture by then. He certainly heard it a few times after that. The song was published in volume thirty of Diabelli's *Nachlass* in 1838.

Setting
Beethoven's dramatic settings were obviously intended for the stage; Schubert's setting here is lyrical, a love song that mirrors the key words "himmelhoch jauchzend, zum Tode betrübt" (rejoicing to heaven, sorrowful unto death), although there is a dramatic ascent to a B-flat on "glücklich" (happy) to underline Schubert's title.

Translation
Full of joy and pain and deep thoughts; longing and languishing, always in agony; rejoicing to heaven, sorrowful unto death; happy alone is she who is in love.

14. *Jägers Abendlied* I (D. 215)
   (Hunter's Song at Evening)
   20 June 1815
   F major
   17 measures
   ca. 1.30 minutes

Text
The original title of the poem was *Jägers Nachtlied* (Hunter's Song at

Night). Written in 1775–1776, a second version was printed for Goethe's *Collected Works* in 1789. Two women stand behind this poem: Lili Schönemann, Goethe's fiancée in Frankfurt till the September of 1775, and his love-to-be, Charlotte von Stein, in his new surroundings in Weimar, from November 1775. In 1815, Goethe told the singer Eduard Genast how this poem (in Reichardt's setting) should be sung: "The first and third stanzas must be accented with a sort of wildness, the second and fourth stanzas softer, for a different emotion comes in here."[19] Goethe proved there that he realized that strophic songs had to be sung with an understanding of the text. Schubert chose a different path. He knew nothing, of course, of Goethe's dictum, which was not, in fact, unreasonable, when all four stanzas are set.

Music
The autograph is lost. The copy in Berlin, made in 1906, is dated 20 June 1815. The song was published by the Schubert scholar Eusebius Mandyczewski in *Die Musik,* Volume VI/7, in 1906 and 1907.

Setting
There is a second version (D. 368, song no. 39), which, like this one, omits the third verse. Schubert keeps here to a modified strophic lyricism, in 4/4 time, which (we feel certain) Goethe would have felt did not distinguish between the hunter's (or the grieving lover's) two moods. Schubert was wise to make a second version.

Translation
1. I steal around the field, quiet and fierce, my rifle at the ready. And then your loving image, your sweet image, floats before me.
2. You wander now, quiet and peaceful, through the fields and the lovely valley, and, oh, does my fast-fading image never appear before you?
3. (Omitted by Schubert) That image, of a man who, full of anger and frustration, wanders through the world from east to west, because he has to leave you.
4. I seem to be looking at the moon, whenever I think of you; a gentle peace descends on me, and I don't know what has happened to me.

15. *Meeres Stille* I (D. 215a)
(Calm Sea)
20 June 1815
C major
35 measures
ca. 3.00 minutes

Text

The poem was written (in 1795?) as the memory of a treacherous sea journey from Messina to Naples made during Goethe's Italian journey. He and his friend, the artist C. H. Kniep, undertook the voyage on 14 May 1787 at the end of their stay in Sicily. Having passed Vesuvius, and after a spell of unpleasant seasickness, they were coming in sight of a "dark" Capri, when, caught by the currents, the ship was becalmed and seemed to be drifting towards the rocks. After much shouting (and praying), the "gentlest puff of wind" guided the ship safely into Naples. The poem, with its companion *Glückliche Fahrt* (Prosperous Voyage), was probably written in 1795 and appeared as an epigram in Schiller's *Musenalmanach* of 1796, and then in the *New Poems* of 1800.

Music

Beethoven's contemporaneous setting for four voices and orchestra of the two poems (Op. 112 of 1814–1815) was performed in Vienna on 25 December 1815. It and Mendelssohn's Op. 27 setting of 1828 have made the poem(s) famous. Schubert's setting was found on the reverse of *Jägers Abendlied* (D. 215), composed on the same day, 20 June 1815. Otto Erich Deutsch published it as late as 1952 in the *Schweizerische Musikzeitung*.

Setting

The poem was described by R. M. Meyer as a "masterpiece of tone painting,"[20] and Fischer-Dieskau wrote that the score of the second version looked like a drawing that illustrated the air of "fearful deathly silence."[21] The composer made two settings on successive days (D. 216)—and one must wonder why, since this first one is quite magical. Like the second version, this first one is marked "fearfully," in ¢ time, conveying the poet's terror, but, at the same time, his wonder at the natural phenomena. Goethe, and Schubert too, for that matter, were strangers to the sea, of course.

Translation

Profound silence reigns over all the water, the sea lies motionless, and the anxious boatman looks out over the smooth surface. No wind from any direction! A deathly frightening calm! In the whole vast expanse not a wave stirs.

16. *Meeres Stille* II (D. 216)
(Calm Sea)
21 June 1815
C major

32 measures
ca. 3.15 minutes

Text and Translation
As for song no. 15.

Music
This second version by Schubert was sent to Goethe in 1816. The marking is as for the first one (song no. 15), "Sehr langsam, ängstlich" (very slow, fearfully), but the first version has "leise" (quietly) added. Both versions are in ¢ time. The second version was published in May 1821 by Diabelli as Op. 3, No. 2.

Setting
This version is really a quite separate song. The broken chords of the accompaniment and the fearful harmonies of "in der ungeheuren Weite" (in the whole vast expanse) make this an almost perfect example of the word-painting that Goethe told Zelter on 2 May 1830 he so admired: "to put the listener in the mood suggested by the poem."

17. *Wandrers Nachtlied* I (D. 224)
(Night Song of a Wanderer)
5 July 1815
G-flat major
11 measures
ca. 1.45 minutes

Text
The poem was written in February 1776 as an expression of Goethe's early love for Charlotte von Stein and sent to her in a letter on 14 April 1776 when the poet was beginning to realize that this woman was no fly-by-night, but a serious-minded person who demanded respect. He, in turn, was "tired of all this struggling" and was seeking peace and happiness. It was published in the *Christliche Magazin* in 1780.

Music
Schubert wrote the song on the same day as *Der Fischer* (The Fisherman, D. 225) and *Erster Verlust* (First Loss, D. 226). It was sent to Goethe with the Spaun packet in 1816 and eventually published by Cappi and Diabelli in May 1821 as Op. 4, No. 3.

Setting
With his now usual sensitivity to words, Schubert saw intuitively what lay behind the words on the page and set them as a through-composed

Wandrers Nachtlied.

Edition Peters.

Wandrers Nachtlied I (D. 224), 5 July 1815.

prayer that subtly mirrored the poet's changing sentiments. Whether Goethe would have approved the repetition of the last two lines is doubtful; it does seem to detract unnecessarily from the prayerlike atmosphere. Schubert also altered Goethe's "Erquickung" (comfort) to "Entzückung" (rapture) in the fourth line. Leif Albertson and most Germanists take great exception to this *lèse-majesté*. Albertson even suggested that this change proved that Schubert had no literary feelings, but only used Goethe for prestige reasons.[22]

Translation
You who are from heaven, who soften all grief and suffering, you fill him who is doubly miserable, doubly with rapture. Oh, I am tired of all this struggling! What use is all this pain and joy? Sweet peace, come, oh, come into my heart. (bis)

18. *Der Fischer* (D. 225) (a/b)
(The Fisherman)
5 July 1815
B-flat major
a/b: 18 measures
ca. 2.30 minutes

Text
Cornelia, Goethe's beloved sister, died on 8 June 1777, aged only twenty-six. "Dark, lacerated day," the poet wrote in his diary.[23] There followed a period of wild debauchery, but also of intense mental activity that produced many important works, including this poem, written in January 1778. Shortly before this, another young woman, Christel von Lassberg, had been found drowned in the river Ilm in Weimar. A copy of Goethe's 1774 novel *Die Leiden des jungen Werther* was found in her pocket, and her death was thought to have been a sad case of unrequited love. Goethe, always sensitive to the charge of immorality often brought against *Die Leiden des jungen Werther*, was very distressed by the suicide. This poem and its companion, *An den Mond* (To the Moon), employ the image of the river as a portent of death, exercising a magic spell over human beings. Goethe's friend Herder published the poem in his *Stimmen der Völker* in 1779 as a model folk song.

Music
This was one of three songs written on 5 July 1815 and sent to Goethe in 1816. The composer must have felt certain that the poet would believe that the music "reproduced the poetic intentions," matching the quality of the ballad. It was published, with four other Lieder, by Cappi and

Diabelli as Op. 5, No. 3, in July 1821, a year of great publishing successes for Schubert, and was dedicated to his old teacher, Antonio Salieri.

Setting

Schubert managed to produce an archetypal folk song, which, at the same time, fulfills all the prerequisites of the art song. The four stanzas are set to what appears to be a cheerful melody in 2/4 time, but the singer must try to convey also the dread of the water in the third and fourth stanzas, by acting out the blandishments of the mermaid. Water was to become one of Schubert's favorite themes; Ilija Dürhammer listed forty-six Lieder on "water" themes.[24]

Translation

1. The water roared, the water swelled, a fisherman sat there looking at his line and feeling cold. As he was sitting and watching, suddenly the waters part and a wet mermaid rises out of the rushing waters.
2. She sang to him, she spoke to him: "Why are you tempting my family to their deaths with your human guile and human treachery? Oh, if you but knew how happy the fish are down here, you would come right down as you are, and you would be really happy, too."
3. "Don't our darling sun and moon bathe themselves in the sea? And don't their faces look twice as lovely when they come back up again after breathing in the waves? Does not this heavenly deep, this watery, transfigured blue color, tempt you? Are you not tempted to bathe your own face in the eternal dews?"
4. The water roared, the water swelled and wet his naked feet; his heart grew so full of longing, as if a beloved were calling him. She spoke to him, she sang to him; and that was his end: she half dragged him, he half sank, and was seen no more.

19. *Erster Verlust* (D. 226)

(First Loss)
5 July 1815
F minor
22 measures
ca. 1.45 minutes

Text

Fired by the performances of Mozart's *Die Entführung aus dem Serail* (*Il Seraglio*, 1782), which reached Weimar in 1785, Goethe began work on his second Singspiel libretto: *Die ungleichen Hausgenossen* (The Mismatched Lodgers). This little jewel is an aria from yet another unsuccessful libretto. The poem was published in 1789 in Goethe's *Collected Works.*

Music
Schubert would accept the poem as poem and would be unaware of its provenance. It was printed under the heading "Lieder" in his edition of Goethe's poems with the vast majority of these early settings. The manuscript is lost, but the copy made for Goethe in 1816 is extant in Berlin.

Setting
Schubert's musical evocations of longing for a love lost came, of course, from a full heart in July 1815. Possibilities of ever marrying Therese Grob were fast fading and, although artistically it was a most productive year with nearly 150 Lieder, three symphonies, and versions of four Singspiele to its credit, he was earning nothing, and the art did little to compensate for the heartbreak. The song was published eventually as Op. 5, No. 4, by Cappi and Diabelli in July 1821 and dedicated to his old teacher, Antonio Salieri. It is a simple but evocative setting, one long sigh, one could say, with precious little hope behind it—even although the vocal part ends on a (hopeful) major chord. Schubert added the word *wer* (who) to the last line to suit his melody; it does not make much sense there.

Translation
1. Ah, who can bring back the lovely days, those days of first love; ah, who can bring back one hour of that divine time!
2. Alone, I feed my wound, and, complaining ever anew, I mourn my lost happiness.
3. Ah, who can bring back the lovely days [who], that divine time back again?

20. *Tischlied* (D. 234)
(Drinking Song)
15 July 1815
C major
19 measures per stanza
ca. 0.30 minutes per stanza

Text
If there is one feature of life in Germany that would say "German" to foreign observers, it would be the communal drinking sessions with much hilarity and banging of beer mugs on the long tables. Goethe was certainly no stranger to conviviality; his diaries and conversations

abound with references to good food and drink. He intended this 1802 poem to be a parody of the medieval song "Mihi est propositum in taberna mori" (I intend to die in the inn), which had been included in J. A. P. Schulz's 1782 collection *Lieder im Volkston*. There are at least twelve other settings of this popular historical text, which is included in Goethe's (long) list of Songs of Companionship in his *Collected Works*.

Music

Schubert, too, was (or became) a regular visitor to Vienna's inns; contemporary reports of his over-indulging do not seem to be exaggerated, and, indeed, they contributed without doubt (with his pipe smoking) to what McKay called his "self-neglect," partly the cause of his early death.[25] They did not lead to his being called *Schwammerl* ("Tubby"); that was simply a genetic matter. The song was sent to Goethe in 1816, obviously as a solo for a lead singer to accompany the table-thumping at the end of each stanza.

Setting

The setting was published by Josef Czerny in June 1829 as Op. 118, No. 3. The relish of Schubert's beery melody, in ¢ time, might serve to remind some people of Schubert's very down-to-earthness. There were eight stanzas in the original poem; anyone wishing to perform the song in public today should limit the "agony" to three or four perhaps. Schubert did not stipulate a number.

Translation

1. I don't know how, I'm heavenly happy, Am I going to be carried up to the stars? Yet, I'd rather stay here—honestly—and thump the table while we're singing and drinking our wine.
2. Dear friends, don't be surprised by my behavior; it's really fine down here on our dear earth. So I'll swear solemnly without any reservations, that I won't steal away like a criminal.
5. How I'll greet her, the one and only, and each of you can think in knightly fashion of your girl. See how lovely she is, mine I mean, so let her nod to me: long live my man!
8. Since we are all gathered together now, let others do as well as we do, in their fun and games! Many a mill will grind from the source to the sea—and it's the weal of the whole world that I bear in mind!

21. *CLAUDINE VON VILLA BELLA* (D. 239a/b)

a: "Hin und wieder fliegen die Pfeile"
   (The arrows fly to and fro)

Begun on 26 July 1815
F major
35 measures
ca. 1.10 minutes

Text

Goethe wrote *Claudine von Villa Bella,* the most charming of his Singspiel libretti, in 1774–1775, just before leaving for Weimar and after breaking off his engagement to Lili Schönemann in Frankfurt, in September 1775. With reminiscences of Mozartian operatic intrigues, aided by the Spanish ambience, it gives some idea (again) of what a great composer could have achieved with a Goethe libretto. The work had three acts: Goethe asked Philipp Kayser to make it into a full Italianate opera in Rome in 1787, then Reichardt took a hand in 1789, but neither managed to make a theatrical success out of it.

Music

Schubert worked on the libretto in 1815 and had it completed by the first week of August; sadly and, for our major theme, tragically, the music for acts 2 and 3 was stupidly burned (as fuel) by servants of his friend Josef Hüttenbrenner, in his absence during the 1848 revolution. It is possible the work received an amateur performance shortly after it was composed. The song "Hin und wieder fliegen die Pfeile" is an arietta sung by the character Lucinde, Claudine's cousin, and is number three in the score.

Setting

The two stanzas fly past like the arrows they describe; the strophic setting suits the light-hearted text. Schubert committed one of his sins here by the addition of "die" (the) to Goethe's title "Hin und wieder fliegen Pfeile" (The arrows fly to and fro).

Translation

1. (The) arrows fly to and fro. Cupid's light arrows fly from the slender, golden bow! Maiden, are you not hit by them? It is chance! Nothing but chance!
2. Why does the arrow fly so fast? Cupid wants to conquer her over there. He has flown by already. Her bosom remains unscathed and carefree—but, look out! He'll be back.

b: "Liebe schwärmt auf allen Wegen"
     (Love goes roving on every highway)
     July/August 1815
     D major

43 measures
ca. 1.10 minutes

Text
This poem is the sixth number in act 1 of Goethe's libretto *Claudine von Villa Bella* and is sung by the main character, Claudine, daughter of Alonzo, the lord of Villa Bella. She is a girl with a roving eye, who falls in love with a Sicilian bandit while engaged to another man—a familiar situation to Goethe. The text might even be construed as a minor expression of guilt about Lili Schönemann.

Music
The song is in C major in the Peters edition. It is called "Ariette" in the score of the Singspiel.

Setting
Although not technically a Goethe Lied, this charming song, thrown off by a good soprano voice, would grace any recital. With its oboe and bassoon accompaniment in the opera score, it would make an even greater hit.

Translation
Love goes roving on every highway. Constancy dwells alone. Love comes quickly towards you. Constancy has to be sought out.

22. *Die Spinnerin* (D. 247)
   (The Spinning Woman)
   August 1815
   B minor
   11 measures
   ca. 2.45 minutes

Text
After returning from his Italian journey of 1786–1788, Goethe composed several poems that could rightly be termed "erotic." It seemed that his sexual experience(s) in Italy had turned his mind in that direction. This led probably to his starting a liaison with the twenty-three-year-old Christiane Vulpius (1765–1816), who fashioned artificial flowers—very different from Goethe's usual circle of acquaintances. This was much to the consternation of his friend, Charlotte von Stein, and the Weimar court in general. The poems of the period, in particular, *Der Besuch* (The Visit) and *Morgenklagen* (Morning Complaint), describe the early erotic stages of the affair. One critic found this poem "at once, playful and serious," but did not seem to wish to probe further.[26] *Die Spinnerin* (1793)

was published in 1800. The sexual implications are certainly concealed, but the fifth stanza surely makes the basic connotation plain.

Music
It would be difficult to believe that Schubert failed to notice these implications in his state of mind in August 1815. His settings in that month almost all concern that aspect of love and loving. The song was published in June 1829 by Josef Czerny as Op. 118, No. 6. A copy was made for Goethe in 1816.

Setting
The seven stanzas to the same melody in 2/4 time make the perfect balladlike Lied, with a folk song feel. The charming melody has a Gretchen-like spinning-wheel accompaniment, which mirrors the earlier tale of working-class drudgery, seduction, and guilt. Only a top coloratura soprano could manage the original key. That, and perhaps the feeling that Goethe's "Ionic" reputation might suffer (because of stanza five?), seems to have prevented many performances.

Translation
1. As I sat still, quietly spinning away without ceasing, a handsome young man came up to my spinning wheel.
2. He praised what there was to praise—was there any harm in that?—my flaxen-like hair and thread.
3. He wasn't happy with just that and wouldn't leave it there—and the thread which I had kept for so long, snapped in two.
4. And the heavy weight of the distaff went on working for a time—but oh, I could no longer boast about the results.
5. When I took them to the weaver, I felt something stir within me, and my poor heart beat ever faster.
6. Now, in the heat of the sun, I bring my work back to be bleached, and I bend down with difficulty to the nearest pool.
7. What I span so fine and quietly in my little room, will come—how can it not?—into the light of day at last.

23. *Der Gott und die Bajadere* (D. 254)
(The God and the Prostitute)
18 August 1815
E-flat major
26 measures
ca. 4.00 minutes

Text

Goethe's interest in Oriental literature, manifested most strikingly in his collection of poems, *West-östlicher Divan*, published in 1819, goes further back in his career as a poet. He translated Voltaire's *Mahomet* and, on 8 June 1797, in the so-called Year of Ballads, he wrote this remarkable poem. Once again, as in *Die Spinnerin*, the theme is an erotic one, in this case, the fate of what is, in effect, a Hindu prostitute. Many writers prefer to view the poem as an expression of Goethe's universal humanity, which encompassed an interest in other lands and religions. It was published in Schiller's *Musenalmanach* of 1798, with Zelter's setting at the back of the book.

Music

Schubert's three Goethe Lieder (D. 254–D. 256) of 1797 are all of ballads, a song form well known to the young composer from his study of Zumsteeg's and Reichardt's compositions. This music is mantralike and requires much patience from the listener, since there is precious little variation from beginning to end. Here, indeed, there is more "length" than "heavenliness," to paraphrase Robert Schumann's adulatory remark about Schubert's music. The song, in ¢ time, was published in 1887 by Weinberger and Hofbauer in Vienna. A copy was sent to Goethe in 1816.

Setting

The nine lengthy stanzas are summarized below. They are set in strophic form with little light or shade suggested. Schubert himself wrote on the manuscript: "In these verses as in the others, the content must determine the *piano* and *forte*."[27] In Graham Johnson's recording for Hyperion, a female voice sings the Bajadere, a male singer the god Mahadöh, and two male singers the temple priests, thus creating the light and shade that we felt were missing.[28]

Synopsis

The ballad tells of the incarnation of the Hindu god Mahadöh (Siva) as a human being, his befriending of a temple dancer, their night of love, followed by his death in their bed, her grief, and her attempt to commit suttee on his funeral pyre. The god then miraculously returns to life and bears the girl aloft, a symbol of redemption through love. Mahadöh means "the great god."

24. *Der Rattenfänger* (D. 255)
(The Rat-Catcher)
19 August 1815

G major
21 measures
ca. 2.00 minutes

Text

This ballad is dated 1804 and bears an obvious relationship to *The Pied Piper of Hamelin*, best known to Anglo-Saxon readers from Robert Browning's poem, published in his *Dramatic Lyrics* of 1842, itself based on the folk song *Der Rattenfänger von Hameln*, Goethe's source. Goethe's version varies in several ways. First, the rat-catcher is a singer, well known to all and sundry. Second, although he is a "child-catcher," he uses a lute, not a pipe. Third (and this makes the ballad Goethe-esqe), he is also a "woman-catcher" who can capture unmarried and married women alike. The ballad was published in the *Taschenbuch auf das Jahr 1804*.

Music

Schubert wrote a strophic setting of three stanzas. It is a jaunty tune with just a sufficient amount of dissonance in the accompaniment to remove it from folk song to art song status. Indeed, it has more of the Singspiel manner. The song was published in volume forty-seven of Diabelli's *Nachlass* in 1850 (in F major) and included in Spaun's packet for Goethe in 1816.

Setting

A good interpreter will underline the differing tones of the rat-catcher in the first stanza, the child-catcher in the second, and the woman-catcher in the third, but will at the same time strive to avoid the coyness that creeps into so many interpretations.

Translation

1. I am the well-known singer, the much-traveled rat-catcher, whom this famous old town certainly needs. And even if there were lots of rats, and even weasels too, I'd clean the town of them all.
2. But the good-tempered singer is also, now and then, a child-catcher, who can tame the wildest children by singing them his golden fairy tales. And even if the boys are cheeky, and the girls suspicious, they'll follow me when I pluck my strings.
3. Then the versatile singer is also, now and then, a woman-catcher; he never comes into a town without attracting a few. And even if the girls are stupid and the wives prudish, they'll all become lovesick when they hear his magic strings and songs.

25. *Der Schatzgräber* (D. 256)
(The Treasure-Hunter)
19 August 1815
D minor
46 measures
ca. 3.45 minutes

Text
One of the Goethe ballads from 1797, the Year of Ballads, this poem also was published in Schiller's *Musenalmanach* of 1798. Goethe sent the ballad to Schiller on 23 May 1797. In his answer on the same day, Schiller called the poem "absolutely beautiful and round and perfect."[29] A very Germanic Protestant work ethic is present here; it extols the virtue of hard toil over the chance of quick riches. Unemployed young Germans of the twentieth century might smile ironically at this advice from a wealthy, middle-class, eighteenth-century poet!

Music
The second of the Goethe ballads set to music on 19 August 1815 was published in the Peters edition in 1887.

Setting
Schubert tried to devise a modified strophic ¢ setting which, alas, barely rises above the sobriquet "interesting." It was one of the few 1815 Lieder not sent to Goethe; Schubert was perhaps equally unfavorably impressed by the results of his work. Ballads obviously attracted him, and this one has that touch of medieval mystery—caves and midnight magic—that appealed to the young Romantics, too.

Synopsis
Five stanzas relate the story of a poor young man who has decided to dig for treasure; preparing a spell of herbs and bones, he begins to dig on a wild and stormy night. At twelve o'clock, a beautiful boy enters the cave, carrying a light and a cup. As he drinks from it, the poor lad is sure that the beautiful boy cannot be the Evil One. He is told to drink the cup dry for "a life of purity." "Do not stay here," he is told, "but, work hard during the day and enjoy good company in the evening. Hard work, happy holidays"—that is the magic formula. A perfect piece of advice from employer to employee.

26. *Heidenröslein* (D. 257)
(Wild Rose)
19 August 1815

G major
16 measures
ca. 1.45 minutes

Text

No one accurate version of this most famous of Goethe's poems survives. The poet's first version of the old folk song certainly goes back before 1771; it was printed by Herder in 1773, but only from memory, since Herder had never seen it written down. This was part of the excitement of those heady days of 1771 in Strasbourg, when he and Goethe were busily discovering the old songs of Alsace. Goethe, however, saw more in the poem than Herder; as he wrote in Book Ten of *Poetry and Truth*, this began a trend "to turn everything that pleased or tormented me into a poem." The first version had the boy pick the little rose, the rose defends itself and pricks him, but the boy forgets that "beim Genuss," in his enjoyment of his action. Goethe's final version, of 1788–1789, makes it quite clear that, although the boy is pricked by the rose, the rose is "deflowered" and the boy feels no pain at all. Goethe remembers, with some feelings of guilt, his abandonment of Friederike Brion in Sesenheim in 1771.

Music

It is not known in what order Schubert wrote the five songs on 19 August; it seems unbelievable that this jewel could have been created among the other dross. It is by far the best song in the 1816 volume sent to Goethe, which makes us believe that Goethe could never have seen the collection. How could a man with Goethe's sensitivity to music and to words fail to have recognized this perfect evocation of what he had been looking for in the 1770s—the folk song? Cappi and Diabelli published the song as Op. 3, No. 3, in May 1821, along with three other Goethe settings: *Schäfers Klagelied, Jägers Abendlied,* and *Meeres Stille.*

Setting

Schubert achieved here the artless simplicity of the true folk song, although it is naive to believe that in his state of mind in August 1815 he was unaware of the sexual undertones. The simple 2/4 strophic setting of the three stanzas with that irresistible refrain has charmed generations of music-lovers, although today not all these music-lovers are aware that the 6/8 version they usually sing is the imitative version published in 1827 by Heinrich Werner. Moser listed more than 150 settings of the poem.[30]

Translation

1. A boy noticed a little wild (briar) rose growing on the heath

Heidenröslein.

Edition Peters

Heidenröslein (D. 257), 19 August 1815.

(meadow), a rose on the heath. It looked so fresh and beautiful in the morning that he ran up to look at it more closely. *Refrain:* (Little) rose, rose, rose, so red, rose on the heath.

2. The boy said: "I'll break you, little briar rose!" The rose said: "I'll prick you, so that you will always think of me, and I shan't have to suffer." *Refrain.*

3. And the naughty boy broke off the little rose on the heath. The rose defended itself and pricked him—but no moaning or groaning helped it—it just had to suffer. *Refrain.*

27. *Bundeslied* (D. 258)
(Song of Good Cheer)
(?4)/19 August 1815
B-flat major
20 measures
ca. 2.00 minutes (solo)

Text
Goethe returned to Frankfurt from his short visit to Switzerland on 22 July 1775, well aware that his engagement to Lili Schönemann was on its last legs. He wrote this ironic song of good cheer for the wedding of a mutual clergyman friend, J. E. Offenbach, only too well aware that he would not be celebrating one himself, even although Lili and he sang the song after the ceremony.

Music
Schubert dated the manuscript 19 August 1815. It was one of the Lieder sent to Goethe in 1816 and was eventually published by Weinberger and Hofbauer in 1887.

Setting
Schubert accepted the poem as a straightforward Song of Companionship (in Goethe's *Collected Works*), for convivial entertainment in the Viennese inn. His jovial ¢ setting of the five stanzas has all the features of a typical German get-together, something that we know Schubert was much to enjoy, particularly from 1819 onwards, and something that Goethe enjoyed also. Is it not part of the unseen bond that both men belie their handed-down image: Goethe, the stiff, staid, conservative German, and Schubert, the shy, retiring, rustic Viennese? Perhaps they would have enjoyed each other's company.

Synopsis
The original subtitle of the poem was: "A song sung to a young couple

by four friends." The singers, inspired by love and wine, ask that the good Lord keep them all together. They clink glasses in the happy hour and renew old friendships. Who cannot be happy in such company, in friendship never disturbed by trivialities? God has blessed them with their independent minds—they are never distracted by fine things. So, they must never be bothered by small mishaps and must remain good companions.

28. *An den Mond* I (D. 259)
(To the Moon)
19 August 1815
E-flat major
20 measures
ca. 3.15 minutes

Text
One of the greatest Goethe poems, this was written between 1776 and 1778 and was found in an undated letter to Charlotte von Stein. With it was a strophic Lied setting by Philipp Kayser, made for a poem by Heinrich Wagner (1747–1779) known in literary circles for one play *Die Kindermörderin* (The Child Killer, 1776). Goethe usually had a melody in his head for the poem he was writing. There are two versions of the poem: this one, the second version, was published in 1789 and is much more peaceful, looking back on vanished happiness and incorporating lines from Charlotte's version, which was found in her papers after the breakup of her close friendship with Goethe in 1788. Those who have visited Weimar will recall the evocative image conjured up by the river Ilm in the park outside Goethe's little garden house.

Music
This was one of five songs written on 19 August. *Bundeslied* (D. 258) was on the other side of this manuscript. A copy went to Goethe with the 1816 packet, and the song was published in volume forty-seven of Diabelli's *Nachlass* in 1850.

Setting
This, Schubert's first version, is a surprisingly unreflective response to what is obviously a fine poem. Indeed, one would think that this is a prime case for the argument that he set texts without much forethought. The melody is undistinguished, and Schubert's method of setting every two of the nine stanzas together means that he had to omit a stanza, number five in this case—another example of *lèse-majesté* for his critics.[31] All in all, it is an uninteresting piece of work which has, with jus-

tice, been grouped with three of the settings of this day as "copy exercises"; the fifth song, the splendid exception, was *Heidenröslein*.[32]

Translation
1. Once again, you quietly fill the bushes and the valley with your misty gleam, and at last my soul, too, is set quite free.
2. You cast your healing glance over the fields, just as a friend's gentle gaze observes my passing life.
3. My heart feels the echo of every sad and happy time, I hover in my loneliness 'twixt joy and pain.
4. Flow on, flow on, dear river! I shall never be happy; that was how our laughter, kissing—and our faithfulness—flowed away, too.
5. I possessed once something so precious! Something that one, alas, never forgets.
6. Flow on, river, through the valley—without pause or rest, flow on and whisper a melody to my poem
7. When in the wintry night, you angrily flood the fields, or when you pour over the young buds in their springtime glory.
8. He is blessed who hides himself away from the world without hate, or who clasps a friend to his bosom and, with him, enjoys
9. What men do not know nor have ever envisaged, and which wanders by night through the labyrinth of the heart.

29. *Wonne der Wehmut* (D. 260)
(Joy of Sadness)
20 August 1815
C minor
20 measures
ca. 1.00 minute

Text
Written in 1775 and published in his *Collected Works* in 1789, the poem embraces the theme that engrossed Goethe in his post–Lili Schönemann period. The tears have, however, a "crocodile"-like effect on knowledgeable readers. The 1789 version is much altered from the more genuine 1775 original.

Music
Schubert set this poem on the day after that exhausting 19 August when he composed five Goethe Lieder. It is possible that the words meant something more to him than they did to Goethe, who quite easily found a replacement for Lili—Schubert found none for Therese. A copy was sent to Goethe in 1816, and the song was published by Leidesdorf only

in 1829, after Schubert's death. It appeared as Op. 115, No. 2. Schubert used the song as an aria [No. 13] in his opera *Der Graf von Gleichen* (D. 918) of 1827. It had a libretto by one of his more intellectual colleagues, Eduard von Bauernfeld, but, because of Schubert's deteriorating health, the opera was neither completed nor performed.

Setting
Most commentators find Schubert's 2/4 setting insipid beside Beethoven's very fine version (Op. 83, No. 1), of 1811. Certainly the poem cried out for a through-composed treatment; Schubert's strophic setting turns the poem into a trite folk song.

Translation
Do not dry, do not dry, tears of eternal love! Oh, how empty, how dead the world appears when one eye is half-dried. Do not dry, do not dry, tears of unrequited love! (bis)

30. *Wer kauft Liebesgötter?* (D. 261)
(Who Will Buy My Gods of Love?)
21 August 1815
C major
24 measures
ca. 2.30 minutes

Text
This poem is one of the direct proofs of Goethe's interest in and concern for music. In chapter two, we referred to his devotion to Mozart; this little aria was intended for his planned continuation of *The Magic Flute* in 1796. The aria was to be an erotic duet for Papageno and Papagena with all the quick-fire wit and repartee of a Mozart. Goethe wrote eight scenes for his Part II—but never found the composer he was looking for. Was Schubert his man here?

Music
Schubert knew nothing of what lay behind the poem. His first attempt, in the impossibly high key of C major, was made for Goethe in 1816 but was never sent. It has been suggested that it was written with Therese Grob in mind (who could reach a D in alt), and there is, of course, no indication that it was ever meant as a duet. The song was published, in A major, in volume forty-seven of Diabelli's *Nachlass* in 1850.

Setting
Here, too, there are sexual overtones and undertones in Goethe's poem and in Schubert's setting. Earlier critics like Capell write, with delicate,

well-bred English reserve, how successful the song might have been if it "had not been an anecdote inadmissible in the nineteenth-century drawing-room";[33] "saucy" is another term regularly used and the tune itself has been called "pert."[34] The five stanzas should certainly be sung at break-neck speed—with consequent problems of articulation for singers with less than adequate German.

Translation

1. Of all the beautiful wares that are brought to market, none will please you more than these brought from far-off lands. Oh, hear what we are singing and look at the lovely birds! They are all for sale.
2. First, look at the big one, that merry, cheeky fellow! He is hopping about, light and happy, from tree to bush; now he's back up there again—but we won't praise him. Oh, do look at this happy bird! He's for sale.
3. Now look at the little one; he is pretending to be shy, but he's as good as the big one. He shows up best when all are quiet. And this clever little bird is for sale.
4. Oh, look at the little dove, the lovely little turtle-dove! The females are so dainty, so intelligent and well-mannered; they love to spruce themselves and to return your love. The delicate little bird is on sale here.
5. We don't want to praise them all, they are all here for inspection. They love new things; yet they don't need letters or seals to prove that they are genuine; they all have wings. How well behaved the birds are, how attractive to buy!

31. *Hoffnung* I (D. 295)
(Hope)
Usually 1815/1816(?), but more likely 15–16 October 1819
F major / E major
a/b: 34 measures
ca. 1.30 minutes

Text
A strange poem written in 1776, shortly after Goethe's arrival in Weimar. The 1789 version in the *Collected Works* differs from that original, which was more concerned with the actual hard work in his new English garden by the river Ilm than the difficult administrative work—and hard work generally—to which the later version refers, albeit metaphorically.

Music

For the poem, Schubert found an almost religious, four-square, chorale melody that has a more German than Austrian ring to it. If it was composed in the autumn of 1819, its air of responsible earnestness would marry with the sentiments expressed in Antonio Salieri's letter of recommendation of 21 September 1819, in which he wrote of Schubert's "morally good character."[35] Alas, that was soon to change. The song was published in 1872 by J. P. Gotthard as No. 14 of his *Forty Songs*. The second version is in E major.

Setting

The onward-striding bass creates the choralelike atmosphere, while the (preferably bass or baritone) voice evokes the Protestant work ethic.

Translation

I do my daily work with my hands, oh, good fortune, may I complete it! Oh, do not, do not let me grow lazy! (bis). No, these are not idle dreams: the trees which are now only saplings will one day give fruit and shade. (bis)

32. *An den Mond* II (D. 296)
(To the Moon)
ca. October 1819(?)
A-flat major
60 measures
ca. 4.30 minutes

Text and Translation
As for song no. 28.

Music

The rather carefree first setting has been replaced by one of Schubert's finest, most moving melodies. One must believe that he had now sat down for some time with the poem and realized its superior quality. Here we sense the true marriage of minds as we listen to the magical development of the setting. The poet's heartfelt prayer to the moon as it sails over that beautiful park and river in Weimar, mirroring his longing for what was, but can never be again, is literally reflected in the composer's music. If one commentator was once so carried away that he confused Charlotte von Stein with Gertrude (von) Stein, who could blame him? The date of Schubert's setting is uncertain. Paper examination now suggests ca. October 1819.

Setting
Schubert again combines two stanzas into one in this 3/4 modified strophic setting, but much more rationally than in his first setting. Marked "langsam" (slowly), stanzas one to five are in the marked key, stanzas six and seven modulate to G flat and C flat, until stanzas eight and nine return to the original key. The haunting beauty of this setting, the literal illumination of the magical verses, make this a perfect example of the often-reviled word-painting.

33. *Sehnsucht* I (D. 310) (a/b)
    (Yearning)
    "Nur wer die Sehnsucht kennt" (1)
    (Only those who know what yearning is)
    18 October 1815
    A-flat major
    a: 35 measures; b: 39 measures
    a: ca. 2.15 minutes; b: ca. 2.25 minutes

Text
The song is sung by Mignon and the mysterious Harper in chapter eleven of Book Four of *Wilhelm Meister's Years of Apprenticeship* as an "irregular duet with the most intense expression." Wilhelm was recovering from a mugging by bandits. Goethe's first version of 1785 (in *Wilhelm Meister's Theatrical Mission*) was a solo song, interpreted by one of Goethe's biographers as a "half-strangled cry," put into Mignon's mouth, but which Goethe told Charlotte von Stein "is now mine, too."[36]

Music
Goethe placed the three Harper songs with the title *Harfenspieler, drei* under the general title of "From *Wilhelm Meister*" in his *Collected Poems* of 1815, where Schubert found them. It is unlikely, therefore, that Schubert had read the whole novel at this stage; he was simply setting the poems as he found them in this collection. The three Mignon songs are here in the order in which they appear in the novel. Schubert took Mignon more as an archetypal Romantic figure of mysterious provenance than the tragic character of Goethe's popular and widely read novel. Arch-Romantic Friedrich Schlegel in his *On Goethe's Wilhelm Meister* (1789) called Mignon "a divinely light point" in the work, one of those beings "who give to the whole (novel) magic and music, and who go to their deaths in the excesses of the glowing fire of their souls."[37] There are two versions of this setting—both written on the same day, and both published in the *Complete Edition* of 1895.

Setting

Of the many settings of these words, perhaps Tchaikovsky's "None but the lonely heart," Op. 6, No. 6, is the best known to Anglo-Saxon music lovers. These two versions of this first setting, although worthy efforts, lack the emotional depth of Schubert's later settings, and, in particular, of D. 877, No. 1 (song no. 75), where he solved the major problem—how to balance the pathos of the major part of the poem with the emotional outburst on "Es schwindelt mir, es brennt mein Eingeweide" (I feel dizzy, my entrails are burning), a curious passage for the foreign listener. In the first version, this becomes a mere addendum; the stormy chords of the second introduce it more effectively. Since these settings are usually sung and recorded by the great international sopranos, it means that few recreate the simplicity of Goethe's poor little Mignon—who is twelve or thirteen. As Goethe said to the composer Wenzel Tomaschek, on 6 August 1822: "Mignon's character can allow her to sing a Lied, but not an aria."[38]

Translation

Only those who know what yearning is, know what I am suffering! Alone, and robbed of all happiness, I look around the world. Oh! He who loves and knows me is far away. I feel dizzy, my entrails are burning. (bis) Only those who know what yearning is, know what I am suffering! (bis)

34. *Mignon* (D. 321)
 (Mignon)
 "Kennst du das Land, wo die Zitronen blühen?"
 (Do you know the land where the lemon trees bloom?)
 23 October 1815
 A major
 81 measures
 ca. 3.30 minutes

Text

Goethe's father had done the grand tour of Italy as a young man and filled his son in the early years with thoughts of doing it himself one day. In those boring years around 1782–1783, Goethe's thoughts often turned to escaping from his administrative drudgery in Weimar. He wrote this poem in 1782 or 1783 for Book Four of the early version of *Wilhelm Meister's Theatrical Mission*. It then appeared at the very beginning of Book Three of the later *Wilhelm Meister's Years of Apprenticeship* (1795–1796). The child Mignon enters Wilhelm's bedroom and sings this

Mignons Gesang.

Edition Peters.

Mignon's song, "Kennst du das Land, wo die Zitronen blühen?" (D. 321), 23 October 1815.

song to her zither accompaniment. In the novel, Goethe gave precise indications how she sang the song: "Do you know the land?" was "mysterious and thoughtful"; in "There! There," was an irresistible longing, and "Let us go" was modified each time, now "longing and urgent," now "persuading and hopeful."

Music

Schubert found the poem, not with the other *Wilhelm Meister* poems under the heading "Mignon, drei," but separately as the first of the "Ballads" section. Spaun sent a copy to Goethe in 1816; it was finally published in volume twenty of Diabelli's *Nachlass* in December 1832, where it was transposed to F major.

Setting

After Wilhelm had heard Mignon sing, he thought that "the charm of the melody was beyond compare." Schubert probably did not know that when he composed the song; there is certainly a charm to his melody, a wistfulness in the opening measures of each of the first two stanzas, while the music describing the dragon's caves is suitably chilling. What ruins the setting (for us) is the out-of-character rushing triplets for the "dahin, dahin" lines. Schubert adopts here a Beethovenian characteristic, seen at its most extreme perhaps in the German's setting of C. F. Weisse's *Der Kuss* (The Kiss), where the final phrase "doch lange hinterher" (but only much later), is repeated ad nauseam. Schubert is only a little less enthusiastic. Nevertheless, his version remains popular with audiences, if a little less so than Hugo Wolf's magisterial version of 17 December 1888, published in 1899.

Translation

1. Do you know the land where the lemon trees bloom, where golden oranges glow amidst the dark foliage, where a gentle breeze drifts out of the blue sky, and the myrtle stands quiet and the laurel high? Do you know it all? It's there! There, that I long to go with you, my love!

2. Do you know the house? Its roof rests on pillars, the hall gleams, the room shimmers, and marble statues stand there, looking at me; What have they done to you, my poor child? Do you know it all? Oh, it's there! There, that I want to go, my protector!

3. Do you know the mountain and its cloud-shrouded path? The mule seeks its way in the mist; in the caves lives the ancient breed of dragons; the cliff plunges downward, and the water pours over it. Do you know it all? It's there! There, that our path leads! Oh father, let us go!

35. *Harfenspieler* I (D. 325)
(Harper's Songs)
"Wer sich der Einsamkeit ergibt" (1)
(Whoever chooses solitude)
13 November 1815
A minor
40 measures
ca. 3.00 minutes

Text
Goethe wrote this poem for his earlier novel *Wilhelm Meister's Theatrical Mission* in 1783. It appeared in the later novel, *Wilhelm Meister's Years of Apprenticeship*, as the second Harper's song in chapter thirteen of Book Two, when Wilhelm finds the strange old man sitting alone on a straw bed in a shabby inn. He asks him not to stop weeping, but to sing whatever he feels suits him. Wilhelm admires his courage in accepting his art as a consolation for his loneliness and exclusion from society. Then, "the old man looked at his strings, and, after he had gently played a prelude, he tuned his harp and sang."

Music
Schubert had two attempts at the poem on 13 November before the final one (D. 478, song no. 43 below) in September 1816. This song was published in the *Old Complete Edition* in 1895.

Setting
The poem is printed in four stanzas of four lines each in the novel, and in the *Collected Poems* as two stanzas of eight lines each. The 6/8 through-composed setting has a certain mournful simplicity about it. In fact, it is marked "klagend" (mournfully), and one cannot deny that it has the characteristics of the situation described in the novel. The harp is also represented in the chords of the accompaniment. Generally, however, it cannot match the later versions.

Translation
1. Whoever chooses solitude, alas, he is soon alone. Each man lives, each man loves, and leaves this one to his agony. / Yes! Leave me to my agony! And if I can be just once in solitude, then I shall not be entirely alone.
2. A lover steals quietly around, listening: Is his beloved alone? So, by day and by night, my pain creeps up on me, the lonely one / my torment on me, the lonely one. Oh, when I am once in the grave, then it will leave me alone!

36. *Erlkönig* (D. 328) (a–d)
(Erl-King) (King of the Alders)
October 1815(?)
G minor
a–c: 145 measures; d: 148 measures
ca. 4.15 minutes

Text

In April 1779 Goethe made a terrifying night ride on horseback from Weimar to Tiefurt with the seven-year-old Fritz von Stein in the saddle before him. The son of Goethe's close friend, Charlotte von Stein, Fritz was educated by Goethe for three years, from 1783 to 1786, and in Goethe's house, which led to many prurient rumors in Weimar. The frightening memory of that ride, along with the mis-translation by his friend Herder of a Danish folktale *Ellerkonge* (King of the Elves) as *Erlkönig* (King of the Alders), contributed to this poem written before August 1781 and published in 1782. It has been called "the most terrifyingly erotic poem" of Goethe's life, since he was in the midst of a quarrel with Charlotte, which was exacerbated by the attentions that he had paid to a very attractive visitor to Weimar, the Marchioness Branconi.[39] It seemed a strange choice to insert in one of Goethe's contributions to the cultural evenings of Grand Duchess Anna Amalia in her new summer seat at Tiefurt, a short distance from Weimar. There, in the summer of 1782, Goethe produced his little Singspiel *Die Fischerin* about a fisherwoman, Dortchen, who hides herself so that her father and her lover will think that she has drowned. This would shock them and repay them both for having stayed out too late. The Singspiel was held in a grotto in a bend on the river Ilm—a beautiful, tree-lined spot—and the ballad was sung by Corona Schröter, the soprano, to her simple eight-measure melody, which fitted Goethe's requirements: one that "the singer knows by heart" and which everyone can easily remember.

Music

We have discussed, in chapter three, Spaun's celebrated description of the writing of the song and how authorities differ in their views of it. John Reed, for example, believed that it was written in Anton Stadler's parents' house in late autumn 1815,[40] and there are other conjectures. When Schubert decided to send a copy to Goethe in April 1816, he and Spaun obviously assumed that only the very best of pianists would be able to play the difficult accompaniment in triplets. Even Schubert found the accompaniment difficult and played the right hand in eighths, the version they sent to Goethe. Spaun's letter had mentioned that the pianist "must not lack agility and expressiveness." The song exists in

Erlkönig.

Edition Peters

Erlkönig (D. 328), October 1815.(?)

four versions: the first is a copy made by Stadler, the second is the version for Goethe, the third is a copy for Breitkopf and Härtel, and the fourth was published by Cappi and Diabelli in March 1821, as Op. 1. Three hundred or so of the six hundred copies offered for sale were sold by October 1822.

Setting

Lovers of German poetry make less of the ballad than do musicians, for obvious reasons perhaps. For some literary critics, the form is fairly commonplace as was the theme, while the treatment is felt to be exaggerated.[41] Others naturally disagree. There must be few musicians who do not marvel at Schubert's ingenuity. He followed his masters Zumsteeg, Zelter, Reichardt, and even Salieri, but emulated them in his daring. The poem's built-in dramatic qualities—the terror of the child, the calming voice of the father, the three inveiglements of the Erl-King, and the factual tones of the narrator—were all combined in an onrushing 4/4 rondo form to make a music masterpiece. The sensuous, erotic elements, in both ballad and setting, have been more stressed recently, some critics considering the poem's treatment to have been almost pedophilic—"Ich liebe dich, mich reizt deine schöne Gestalt" (I love you, your lovely body tempts me), whispers the Erl-King to the little boy.[42] What is indisputable and of importance for our major theme is that the publication of this result of the bond between Goethe and Schubert gave the composer the first taste of true fame and ensured that the name Goethe would be known to future generations who had never read a word of his literary works.

Translation

1. Who is riding so late through night and wind? It is a father with his child; he has the child safe in his arms, he holds him sure and keeps him warm.

2. "My son, why are you hiding your face?" "Father, don't you see the Erl-King? The Erl-King with his crown and his tail?" "My son, it's only a wisp of mist."

3. "You, dear child, come, go with me! I'll play really lovely games with you; there are lots of brightly colored flowers on the banks. My mother has lots of golden clothes."

4. "My father, my father, don't you hear what the Erl-King is promising me so quietly?" "Be calm, stay calm, my child; it is the wind rustling in the bare branches."

5. "My fine, little lad, will you come with me? My daughters will wait on you, my daughters will dance at night, and cradle and dance and sing you to sleep."

6. "My father, my father, don't you see over there—Erl-King's daughters in that dark place?" "My son, my son, of course I see it; it's the old willow trees gleaming gray."
7. "I love you, your lovely body tempts me; and, if you're not willing, then I'll use force." "My father, my father, now he's got hold of me! Erl-King has hurt me!"
8. The father is terrified, he rides on quickly. He holds the moaning child in his arms. Reaches the farm in great distress; in his arms the child was dead.

37. *Sehnsucht* II (D. 359)
(Yearning)
"Nur wer die Sehnsucht kennt" (2)
(Only those who know what yearning is)
1816
D minor
45 measures
ca. 2.15 minutes

Text and Translation
As for song no. 33.

Music and Setting
We do not have the autograph of this second setting of the duet between Mignon and the Harper from *Wilhelm Meister*, but there is a copy in the catalog of the Society of Friends of Music in Vienna, dated 1816. It was published in J. P. Gotthard's *Forty Songs* as No. 13, in 1872. It is in 6/8 time and marked "mässig" (moderato). It is not a complete failure, but clearly just another attempt, again to be discarded.

38. *Der König in Thule* (D. 367)
(The King in/of Thule)
Early 1816
D minor
34 measures
ca. 3.00 minutes

Text
During Goethe's journey down the Rhine in July 1775 with his Swiss friend Johann Lavater and others, a stop was made in Cologne on 24 July. The group repaired to the Holy Ghost inn, where, in the growing dusk, Goethe squatted on a table and recited Scottish ballads in transla-

tion, at that time all the literary rage. He included his ballad, *Der König in Thule*, written between 1771 and 1774 when he was suffering from feelings of guilt over abandoning Friederike Brion in Sesenheim. "This poem," he wrote in *Poetry and Truth* (Book Fourteen), "lay deep in my heart" and "could only rarely be recited." For this reason, it easily found its way into the *Urfaust* and then, as scene 8 of Part I, where the simple girl Gretchen, having just met the "impertinent" Faust, sings it while musing beside her lamp, and wishing that her mother would come home. But she also scolds herself for being so "stupidly fearful." Thule, the ancient Norse kingdom, represented, both for Gretchen and Goethe, a place of true and constant love—Gretchen's hope and Goethe's sorrow.

Music

The Spaun volume that included this song was sent to Goethe on 17 April 1816, so the song must have been written before that date, probably in February or March. It was published with four other Goethe settings by Cappi and Diabelli as Op. 5, No. 5, in July 1821, when so many of the Goethe settings appeared.

Setting

A review of March 1822 described the song—accurately, we believe—as "naively sad."[43] Schubert was obviously trying to emulate Zelter's well-known setting of 1812. The simple strophic ballad form in 2/4 time was achieved by amalgamating the six stanzas into three groups of two. It can be made wonderfully evocative by a sympathetic, non-operatic soprano voice.

Translation

1. There was once a king of Thule who was faithful even unto the grave. When his beloved was dying, she gave him a golden goblet.
2. It became his favorite goblet, and he emptied it at every meal; he wept openly whenever he drank out of it.
3. And when he came to die, he counted up the cities in his realm, and gave everything—except the goblet—to his heirs.
4. He sat there at the royal table, surrounded by his knights in the huge hall of his fathers in the castle by the sea.
5. The old tippler stood up and drank his last life's glow, and threw the sacred goblet down into the waves.
6. He saw it fall, fill up, and sink deep into the sea. His eyes glazed over, and he drank not one drop more.

39. *Jägers Abendlied* II (D. 368)
(Hunter's Song at Evening)
Early 1816(?)
D-flat major
13 measures
ca. 2.30 minutes

Text and Translation
As for song no. 14.

Music
This setting, the one usually performed, was written a year after the first version, and published by Cappi and Diabelli as Op. 3, No. 4, in May 1821.

Setting
This strophic love song, in 2/4 time, is one of pensive stillness. By omitting Goethe's third stanza, Schubert misses the real point of the poem: the poet is, in fact, *un*happy, for he knows that he has lost his loved one. Schubert's very beautiful setting reflects only very beautiful thoughts. There is an earlier version where all four stanzas were set.

40. *An Schwager Kronos* (D. 369)
(For Coachman Chronos)
1816(?)
D minor
140 measures
ca. 2.45 minutes

Text
Goethe's *Die Leiden des jungen Werther* had been published in 1774 and had established the poet's fame in Germany as a fiery, innovative writer. He had visited the celebrated poet Klopstock in Frankfurt, accompanied him to Darmstadt, and, in the postchaise on 10 October, on his return visit, wrote this poem. *Schwager* is a pun: it means both "brother-in-law" and "coachman," and Goethe intended the poem to indicate that he would "rather go to hell quickly while young and drunk, than become a gray beard in a slow trot."[44] ("Spuden/Sputen" is a Frankish dialect word, meaning "to drive a coach.") The original German has always caused problems of interpretation, although clearly the poem is directed to Goethe's times, "die Zeit," personified as "the coachman Time" (Chronos).

Music

The original music is lost, and there are no contemporary copies; an extant copy in Vienna asserts the date as the "beginning of 1816," possibly because it was assumed that it had been sent to Goethe in April 1816, but doubts have been expressed. The first pages of Spaun's 1816 collection have vanished, alas, and one can therefore only surmise. We know that Schubert included the song (with *An Mignon* and *Ganymed*) with his letter to Goethe in June 1825. It was finally published by Diabelli in the summer of 1825 as Op. 19, No. 1.

Setting

Hugh Macdonald has described what he called examples of Schubert's "volcanic temper,"[45] and one can certainly think of many such intrusions in his works—in the otherwise idyllic Adagio of the String Quintet in C (D. 956), for example—or was it Schubert's attempt to emulate his rival Rossini's outbursts? Here too, we have unusually violent music from the normally placid composer, who, like the young Goethe—who was twenty-five in 1774—was trying out his strength as his command of his medium developed. The marking is "nicht zu schnell" (not too quickly), which not all singers, alas, observe as they are carried along on the 6/8 driving eighths of the setting. It is certainly not the most popular Schubert Lied, particularly when bellowed out by insensitive baritones, but the setting does convey the excitement and the sheer animal vitality of the Storm and Stress writers of the 1770s. Again, the key is D minor, the key of so many of Schubert's "powerful dramatic masterpieces."[46]

Translation

1. Drive on, Chronos! Onwards at a rattling trot! The way leads downhill; your slow speed makes me sick and dizzy—so, ever onwards, we're stumbling over sticks and stones, right into life!
2. Now, once again, that exhausting tiring climb uphill, so up, ever upwards, don't be lazy, go on striving and hoping!
3. Far, high, magnificent, is the view into life; from mountain top to mountain top, the eternal spirit hovers over us, intimating eternal life.
4. At the side, the shadow of a rest house pulls you towards it, and you espy a glance offering refreshment at the girl's threshold. Enjoy it!—give me a drink too, my lass, this foaming drink, this refreshing, healthy glance!
5. Away now, ever faster downhill! See, the sun is sinking! Before it does, before the mist of the moors seizes me, graybeard, with my toothless, gnashing jaws and tottering legs;

6. Drunk by the last rays, let me be snatched through the darkened doors of hell, a boiling sea over my watery eyes, me, blinded and staggering.
7. Sound your horn, brother postilion, clatter on your noisy way, so that Orcus can hear us coming, so that my host can welcome us at the door.

41. *Chor der Engel* (D. 440)
(Choir of Angels) (Christ is Risen)
June 1816
C minor
59 measures

Text
This poem is the Easter scene from *Faust* Part I, when Faust is about to drink the poisoned chalice (phial). He hears the choir of angels and, laying down the chalice, proclaims: "My tears flow, the earth has won me back!"

Music and Setting
Although the setting is, technically, not a Lied, we include it for sake of completeness. It was set as a four-part choral item and published in 1839 in the *Neue Zeitschrift für Musik*, 10. It is rarely performed.

Translation
Christ is risen! Joy to the mortal man whom the wasting, creeping, inherited needs encircled.

42. *Mignon* (D. 469) (a/b)
(Mignon)
"So lasst mich scheinen, bis ich werde" (1, 2)
(Let me look like this, until I become like this)
September 1816
A-flat major
a: 7 measures; b: 11 measures
a: 20 seconds; b: 40 seconds

Text
The song occurs in chapter two of Book Eight of *Wilhelm Meister's Years of Apprenticeship*. For a twins' birthday party, Nathalie, Wilhelm's lady friend, had dressed Mignon as an angel in a long white robe with a golden girdle, and a golden diadem in her hair. She was to bring gifts to the two children. They looked at her in amazement. We realize that

Mignon's life is nearing its end when she takes up her zither and sings the song with unbelievable grace.

Music

Two of Schubert's four attempts to set this elusive text are found in D. 469 (a/b). Both remained fragments; there are only seven measures, in A flat, of the first, and eleven of the second, in G, which stops at the "Ich" (I) of "I shall leave this pure raiment." Both are in the revised section of the *Complete Edition* and have been completed by Pater Reinhard van Hoorickx. (See D. 877, No. 3, song no. 77.)

Setting

The text is difficult enough for experienced literary experts, let alone for a twenty-five-year-old Austrian—even if he had read the entire, very long novel. It is not certain whether Schubert did or not, although his treatment of some of the other *Wilhelm Meister* poems suggests that he did (cf. song nos. 43–45). Schubert's setting has "dark" house for Goethe's "secure" or "safe" house.

Translation

1. Let me look like this, until I become like this; don't take off my white dress! I shall hurry from the beautiful earth down to that dark house.
2. There I shall rest a little while, then a fresh view will open up and I shall leave this pure raiment, the girdle and the diadem.
3. And those heavenly figures will not ask whether I am a man or a woman, and no clothes, no folds will encircle my transfigured body.
4. True, I lived indeed without a care, yet I felt enough of the deep pain; I aged too early from my worries; make me eternally young again!

43. *Gesänge des Harfners* I (D. 478, No. 1)

(Harper's Songs)
"Wer sich der Einsamkeit ergibt" (2)
(Whoever chooses solitude)
September 1816
A minor
52 measures
ca. 4.30 minutes

Text and Translation

As for song no. 35.

Music

The first version was marked "langsam" (slow). The second version, published by Cappi and Diabelli as Op. 12, No. 1, in December 1822, is marked "sehr langsam mit der Verschiebung" (very slow, with soft [*una corda*] pedal).

Setting
Schubert was now moved to write what Alfred Einstein called his "first great song cycle."[47] Beethoven's song cycle *An die ferne Geliebte* (To the Distant Beloved), Op. 98, to poems by Aloys Jeitteles, had been published in early 1816. The prelude to Schubert's second setting of the poem corresponds to the description given in the novel, which suggests that Schubert must have read the whole novel, since the prelude does not appear with the poem in the collected edition of Goethe's poems. The pianist strikes up chords that sound like the tuning chords of a harp, before the wonderful song begins, in A minor, Schubert's key of desperation or death. The Harper's tormented mind is set on the grave, his punishment for his sins on earth. We discover later that his sin was to commit incest with his sister, Mignon's mother. He is found later lying in his blood with his throat cut. Although he recovers then, he is discovered dead shortly afterwards (chapter ten of Book Eight). The sinister bass line seems to guide the passage to his end; and if, as so often with Schubert, the repetition of the last four lines seems to be unnecessary, one could argue that they, with the now dominant piano, will signify the final closing of the door: "Then they will leave me alone."

44. *Gesänge des Harfners* III (D. 479; D. 478, No. 3)
(Harper's Songs)
"An die Türen will ich schleichen"
(I shall steal up to the doors)
September 1816
A minor
50 measures
ca. 2.00 minutes

Text
We find this song in chapter fourteen of Book Five of *Wilhelm Meister's Years of Apprenticeship*. Wilhelm had feared that the crazed Harper had been lost in the raging fire, which Wilhelm suspected him of having started. Wilhelm hears someone crying in a nearby alley: "the consolation of an unhappy man who feels himself very near to madness." He hears only the last stanza of the song. The song was printed as the second of the Harper's songs in Goethe's *Collected Poems* and is dated 1795, but it is the third of the three songs in the novel. Schubert set it as the sec-

ond, which makes one wonder whether he took the text from the novel or from the *Poems*. More than likely he used the 1815 edition of the *Poems*, in which the three Harper's songs follow Mignon's trio, but the evidence is inconclusive.

Music

Schubert's copy of this song, which had been sent to the printer, is missing. He then revised the song for publication by Cappi and Diabelli in December 1822 as Op. 12, No. 3, changing the tempo marking only from "mässig" (moderate) to "mässig, in gehender Bewegung" (moderate, in walking tempo).

Setting

Although a song of madness, D. 479 has a peculiarly soothing quality. One has the impression of total inevitability, as with so much of Bach's music. In this case the inevitability is that the wanderer's fate is sealed and that the rest of the world will leave him to his fate, but will wipe away a tear. At the same time, the walking rhythm, produced by symmetrical quarter notes in the bass, conjures up a very Schubertian image of the wanderer now a beggar, alienated and isolated. Schubert reproduced this image in *Gute Nacht* (Good Night), the first song of his *Winterreise* (D. 911) of 1827–1828. The music to the second stanza supports the poet's description of the people who see, not a beggar, but one who, but for the grace of God, might be themselves. Here again we are reminded of *Winterreise*, this time, of the last song *Der Leiermann* (The Hurdy-Gurdy Man), which is also in that key of A minor, the key of alienation and madness. Goethe would surely have approved of the use of the minor for this tragic episode.

45. *Gesänge des Harfners* II (D. 480; D. 478, No. 2)

(Harper's Songs)
"Wer nie sein Brot mit Tränen ass" (1–3)
(He who never ate his bread with tears)
September 1816; Fall 1822
A minor
66 measures
ca. 5.00 minutes

Text

This poem is the Harper's second song in *Wilhelm Meister*, after *The Bard*, and comes from chapter thirteen of Book Two. Wilhelm, upset and disgruntled, was looking for the Harper to put him in better spirits. He was told that he would find him (as he did) in a disreputable inn on the out-

Gesänge des Harfners.

Gesänge des Harfners ("An die Türen will ich schleichen," D. 479; D. 478, No. 3), September 1816.

Edition Peters.

skirts of the town. There, he heard heart-rending, mournful sounds, accompanied by a sad, worried song. The old man, often choked with tears, then half-sang, half-recited a sort of fantasy, which he repeated continually. Goethe wrote the poem for the earlier novel, *Wilhelm Meister's Theatrical Mission*, in November 1783, when he was still struggling with guilt feelings at the life he had led and the women whom he had loved and left: Friederike Brion in Alsace, Lotte Buff in Wetzlar, and Lili Schönemann in Frankfurt. There were also the repercussions of his immoral novel, *Die Leiden des jungen Werther*, of 1774. "Am I then in the world only to writhe in never-ending innocent guilt?" he wrote in his diary after leaving Frankfurt in 1775 for Weimar.[48] "For all guilt is avenged on earth," was always his firm belief and was what his friend Wieland called his "gnawing worm within."

Music

As previously mentioned, Schubert first set this poem as the third song in his little song cycle, but later placed it second. He wrote three versions in all, two in September 1816. The last and final version, written in the fall of 1822 (D. 480, No. 3), was published in December 1822 as Op. 12. This was a new version.

Setting

Schubert's two 1816 versions move from the first, a fairly simple balladlike setting (in many ways, a more accurate representation of the circumstances of Goethe's song in the novel), to the second setting, which is more detailed and more expressive, indeed, perhaps too much so. Then came the wonderfully moving third (1822) version, known to all lovers of Schubert. Again, the piano chords bring us the old man's harp prelude. The first stanza sounds almost like a Lied in itself until the "Ihr führt ins Leben uns hinein" (You lead us into life), of the second stanza takes the poor man away again from the world and plunges him into his solitude, where he utters the great, heart-piercing cry of guilt, "denn alle Schuld rächt sich auf Erden" (for all guilt is avenged on earth). There are few more poignant songs in Lieder literature, and fewer still which so perfectly reproduce the poetic intentions. Here, if anywhere, Schubert became the poet that Bauernfeld had seen in him.[49]

Translation

1. He who never ate his bread with tears, he who never sat weeping on his bed through these anguish-filled nights, he will never know you, you heavenly powers.
2. You lead us into life, you let the poor man become guilty, then you leave him to his agony. For all guilt is avenged on earth.

46. *Sehnsucht* III (D. 481)
(Yearning)
"Nur wer die Sehnsucht kennt" (3)
(Only those who know what yearning is)
September 1816
A minor
45 measures
ca. 2.00 minutes

Text and Translation
As for song no. 33.

Music
Schubert did not set this third version very successfully either. The set-ting is headed "Sehnsucht. Mignon" and is marked "slow," in 2/4 time. It is in the *Complete Edition* (1895) in 2/4 time.

Setting
Again, there is the agitation at "Es schwindelt mir" (I feel dizzy), but, as a whole, one misses the true Schubertian lilt to the melody and the com-poser's usually sensitive reaction to the words. The few recordings take the song quite briskly.

47. *Gesang der Geister über den Wassern* I (D. 484)
(Song of the Spirits over the Waters) (Fragment)
September 1816
A minor
64 measures
ca. 4.45 minutes

Text
In 1779, Goethe embarked on a journey with his duke, Karl August, first intending to visit Düsseldorf, but changing plans and heading for Swit-zerland, where they visited the now celebrated tourist traps: Lauter-brunnen, the Jungfrau, and Grindelwald. When they returned to Thun on 14 October, Goethe sent this poem to Charlotte von Stein, reflecting his emotions after viewing the Staubbach and Reichenbach waterfalls. The poem, written on 9 October, is a meditation on man's soul, which is pictured as a rush of water tumbling between heaven and earth.

Music
Once again, a Goethe poem struck a resonance in Schubert's soul. He never had a very deep faith—his settings of Catholic Masses always omitted that cardinal Roman Catholic line: "Et unam sanctam catholi-

cam et apostolicam Ecclesiam" (And [I believe in] one holy Catholic and apostolic church), and it seems that the Goethean pantheistic attitude appealed more to him.

Setting

This setting was for solo voice and is the first of four. The manuscript is not complete. We only have sixty-four measures of the original, from the end of the second stanza to the beginning of the sixth (and last) stanza. It even includes other 1816 Lieder, while the music, with its two-and-a-quarter-octaves' range in 4/4 time, is too ambitious for the solo bass voice. Only the middle section marked "geschwind" (fast) has a true Schubertian vivacity and charm—but the torso suggests "that a really great song lies here unwritten."[50] It is one of a few Lieder completed (not to everyone's satisfaction, it must be said), by Pater Reinhard van Hoorickx. It appeared in the 1895 *Complete Edition*.[51]

Translation

1. The soul of man is like the water; it comes down from heaven, and then rises to heaven, and back again to earth it must go, eternally changing.
2. When the pure stream pours down from the high, steep, cliff face, it breaks up into cloudy spray like a gentle veil against the smooth rock, and, as it is gently embraced, it rushes down in a veil of spray to the depths below.
3. The cliffs loom up against its fall, but the water foams in rage as it descends in steps to the abyss.
4. On its level bed, the stream glides along the meadowed vale, and all the stars mirror their images in the smooth lake.
5. The wind is the wave's darling lover; the wind loves to mingle with the foaming waves!
6. Soul of man, how like you are to the water! Fate of man, how like you are to the wind!

48. *Gesang der Geister über den Wassern* II (D. 538)

(Song of the Spirits over the Waters) (Fragment)
March 1817
A major
129 measures

Text and Translation

As for song no. 47.

Music and Setting
We include this second setting for the sake of completeness, as a Schubert setting of a Goethe text. It was set for two tenors and two basses unaccompanied, and marked "sehr langsam" (very slow). It was published in the *Complete Edition* in 1891.

49. *Auf dem See* (D. 543) (a/b)
(On the Lake)
(?)March 1817
a: E major; b: E-flat
a: 80 measures; b: 91 measures
b: ca. 3.00 minutes

Text
Christian and Friedrich Stolberg arrived in Frankfurt on 8 May 1775 and quickly persuaded Goethe to accompany them on a tour of Switzerland. Goethe was torn at the time between his love for Lili Schönemann, the moralistic sixteen year old, and his more ordinary sexual instincts—so he joined the group without a word to Lili.[52] His friend Lavater and others joined them in Zurich on 15 June, where they started their tour in a boat on the lake. Goethe kept a notebook and, on the boat, and after a walk on the banks, drafted the poem, now regarded as one of his finest. The title of Herder's copy is "In the Boat on Lake Zurich." Each of the wonderful modulations corresponds to the poet's amazing chameleon-like ability to register changes of moods—iambics move to trochaics, the ecstatic joy of life in nature to somber contemplation of the worries of living life on earth. When, at the height of the tour, Goethe caught a distant view of Italy, from the St. Gotthard Pass, it was as if his destiny lay before him—and that was to be his Italian journey of 1786–1788.

Music
The original manuscript is lost. Schubert, however, made a copy for Josef Hüttenbrenner in March 1817, when he was setting other Goethe poems, and this probably justifies the dating above. There are two versions. The first, in E major, is marked "mässig, ruhig" (moderate, peaceful). The second, published with *Der Musensohn* (D. 764) and *Geistes-Gruss* (D. 142) as Op. 92, No. 2, by Leidesdorf in July 1828, is in E-flat and marked "mässig" (moderate) only.

Setting
The 6/8 tempo of the second quatrain gives us the rocking motion of the boat, while the sixteenth notes of the accompaniment represent the

Auf dem See.

Auf dem See (D. 543), (?)March 1817.

Edition Peters.

gentle lapping of the waves against the boat before it enters rougher waters at "the wave cradles our boat." The change into the minor at "Eye, dear eye, why are you so cast down?" as the poet contemplates his far-off fiancée Lili, marks the memory of happy, but also painful, times—until another change of mood welcomes the morning breeze in the ripening fruit by the side of the lake. Schubert's repetition of the third stanza means that the two parts of the composition are of equal length. It is a setting that shows the composer in perfect harmony with the poet's mind—an unseen bond indeed.

Translation
1. And I take in fresh victuals, new blood from this new, wide world; how divine and good Nature is, holding me to her bosom! The wave cradles our boat as we row up the lake, and the mountains, cloud-capped, meet us as we go. Eye, dear eye, why are you so cast down? Golden dreams, will you ever return? Begone, you dream, however golden you are; love and life are here, too.
2. A thousand twinkling stars are mirrored in the waves; faint mists drink in the distant mountains; the morning breeze wings o'er the shady bay, and the ripening fruits are mirrored in the lake.

50. *Ganymed* (D. 544)
(Ganymede)
March 1817
A-flat major
121 measures
ca. 4.00 minutes

Text
The poem, "a meditative incantation,"[53] is based on the Greek legend of Ganymede, the most handsome of men, who was spied asleep on Mount Ida by Zeus. The god sent a cloud down to earth, wrapped the sleeper up in it, and bore him up to the heavens to become cupbearer to the gods on Mount Olympus. In astrology, Ganymede is Aquarius. Thus, he is a symbol of man reaching up to the higher powers, who, in turn, reach down to receive him, in a reciprocal gesture of love, it seems. This poem is Goethe's 1774 statement of his pantheism in a more strident and independent declaration than in the Greek legend. Man's defiance of the gods was later to be even more forcibly declared in a companion poem to *Ganymed* titled *Prometheus* (D. 674).

Music
Schubert was busy in 1817 setting the poems of his friend Johann Mayr-

hofer on classical themes, so Goethe's *Ganymed* fitted into this work scheme. Again, the original of the song is missing—one of the great problems for those who had wanted to support Schubert in the nineteenth century—but there are two copies, dated March 1817. It was published by Diabelli in that fateful year 1825, as Op. 19, No. 3—in June indeed, the very month that Schubert sent the song to Goethe. This setting made the great baritone Johann Michael Vogl take notice of the insignificant little composer.

Setting
Starting off at a walking pace, in 4/4 tempo and in A-flat major, the song, marked "etwas langsam" (somewhat slowly), becomes ever more passionate as the composer follows the cupbearer up into the heights. The triplets of the breeze then challenge the seductive song of the nightingale; the composer follows each flashing turn of the poet's thought, culminating in the rapturous apotheosis of "I'm coming, I'm coming." Schubert's 1817 settings display his intense involvement with great literature and his uncanny sensitivity, not only to words, but to the deepest philosophical, albeit non-Christian, thinking.

Translation
1. You glow all around me like the rosy dawn, Spring, my beloved! The holy intimation of your eternal warmth, its unending beauty, steals into my heart with its myriad delights of love!
2. Oh, that I might hold you in these arms!
3. Ah, I lie, languishing, at your breast, and your flowers, your grass, pierce my heart. You cool the burning thirst of my bosom, darling breeze of the morning, while the nightingale calls lovingly to me from out the misty valley. I'm coming, I'm coming! Where to? Oh, where to?
4. Upwards! ever upwards, I strive. The clouds drift down, they bend down to my yearning love. To me! To me! Upwards into your lap! Embracing and embraced! Upwards into your bosom, all-loving father!

51. *Mahomets Gesang* I (D. 549)
(Mohammed's Song) (Fragment)
March 1817
E major
114 measures
ca. 4.00 minutes

Text
Goethe's mind was in a whirl in the years 1771–1774. Christian theology, the Koran, pantheism, and, of course, the affairs of the heart, vied for his attention. He considered writing a drama with Mohammed as the main character, but it remained a fragment. His poem, really a song *for* Mohammed, paints a wonderful picture of the prophet's life, like a river from its source to its arrival at the great ocean. It is yet another glorification of the individual, the genius; indeed, this period in German culture is termed the Age of Genius(es).

Music
This version, like Schubert's second (D. 721, song no. 66) was never completed. This first fragment has 114 measures in 2/4 time and was published in the *Complete Edition* in 1895.

Setting
One thinks at once of the setting that Schubert was certainly working on at the same time: *Song of the Spirits over the Waters* (D. 538). It is very likely that Schubert found this poem too abstract and complicated for his taste. Nevertheless, this first (considerable) fragment is a noble effort with a dazzling and very difficult accompaniment. The whole fragment is as long as *Erlkönig*. Schubert set the first thirty-five lines only.

Translation
1. Look at the spring, up in the cliffs, joyful and bright as the twinkling of a star! Way above the clouds, the good spirits nourished its youth in the bushes between the cliffs.
2. Youthfully fresh, it dances out of the cloud down to the marble rocks, and, exulting, back again to heaven.
3. It chases brightly colored pebbles through the gaps in the mountain peaks, and, like a leader, makes its brothers follow.
4. Flowers blossom in its path down in the valleys, and the meadow comes alive from its breath. Yet no shaded valley can detain it, no flowers wind round its knees, flattering it with love's glances, its course brings it snakewise to the plains.
5. Brooks cuddle up to it. Now, it enters the plain, silver-bright, and the plain is just as bright, and the rivers from the plains, and the streams from the mountains, exult with it, and cry: Brother! Brother, take your brothers with you . . .

52. *Liebhaber in allen Gestalten* (D. 558)
(Lover in All Shapes and Sizes)
May 1817

A major
20 measures
ca. 2.00 minutes

Text

The more earnest students of Goethe tend to look down on his comic verses, just as the older ones used to try to ignore his erotic poems. Schubert obviously enjoyed both sides of his art. Goethe knew the classical theme of metamorphosis very well indeed and used it in his philosophical *Metamorphosis of Plants* (1798). This little poem, written in 1810, and found under "Lieder" in his works, has nine stanzas, each describing a different guise of the lover, and is very Goethean.

Music

Schubert set the first three stanzas, then the final one, in strophic form. It has thus become the province of soubrette-like sopranos, particularly as an encore. Some make it just too coy. It was published in volume seven of the Peters edition in 1887.

Setting

The strophic setting, with its bouncy 2/4 tempo, matches the almost childlike bonhomie of the text. For those who still believe that either poet or composer or both were over-serious artists, this work should make them think anew. The final measures of the accompaniment always raise the spirits—and the roof of the concert hall.

Translation

1. I wish I were a fish, so nimble and so fresh; and when you came to fish, I should be there. I wish I were a fish, nimble and fresh.
2. I wish I were a horse, then you'd value me. Oh, were I a coach, I could carry you comfortably. I wish I were a horse, then you'd value me.
3. I wish I were gold, always in your account. And when you wanted to buy something, I should be available. I wish I were gold, always in your account.
9. Yet I am just how I am, so take me as I am. If you want a better, then have yourself one made to measure. I am just how I am, so take me as I am.

53. *Schweizerlied* (D. 559)
(Swiss Song)
May 1817
F major

12 measures
ca. 1.15 minutes

Text

Goethe found the first stanza of a little Swiss poem in the Brentano-Arnim collection *Des Knaben Wunderhorn*, which he reviewed enthusiastically in 1806 in his *Writings on Literature*, and from which many nineteenth-century composers, such as Gustav Mahler, took their Lieder texts. Goethe sent it to Zelter in 1811 to set to music; he hoped that the poems printed in the collection might lead to a revival of interest in the German folk song. Goethe knew little of the Swiss German language (*Schwyzerdütsch*), but he did for this poem what he did for those folk poems gathered in 1771 in Alsatian dialect: "Good, said I," (he said), "even if I could not speak Alsatian, I did try to speak 'foreign'!"[54] The poem appeared in 1815 under "Songs of Companionship" in his *Collected Works*.

Music

We have plenty of local color in Schubert's (albeit Austrian) folk music setting, including horn-calls and peasant-dance rhythms, in 3/4 time, of course. Capell's disdainful attitude towards Schubert jars at times: "Schubert may have been a rustic," he declares.[55] One wonders if Capell had any idea at all of what cultured Vienna looked like in 1817. Schubert, no aristocrat, of course, was very aware of life by this time and of its adult trials and tribulations. The song was published in volume seven of the Peters edition of 1885.

Setting

There were four stanzas in Goethe's poem: Schubert set them all in strict strophic folk song form, in a jaunty, clichéd, rustic rhythm. The girl can only hint in the fourth stanza at what she and her Hansel were doing. Here, poet and composer were on the same wavelength.

Translation

1. I sat on the mountain, watching the birds; they were singing, hopping about, and building their nests.
2. I stood in a garden watching the bees; they were buzzing, humming and building their hives.
3. I went into the meadow and watched the summer birds there; they were sucking and flitting about, almost too lovely for words.
4. Then along comes Hansel (Jack), and I show him what they are all doing—so we laugh, and we do it too!

54. *Der Goldschmiedsgesell* (D. 560)
(The Goldsmith's Apprentice)
May 1817
F major
14 measures
ca. 2.00 minutes

Text

Although one would not necessarily want to follow current American scholarship and see erotic or Freudian symbolism in the simplest of poems, there is no denying that many of Goethe's works from 1770 to 1775, and of Schubert's from 1817 to 1819, must be placed under that heading. To the pure of mind, this little poem of ca. 1774 can be construed as a cheerful little ditty. A more careful examination of the German vocabulary (particularly of the fifth stanza), reveals the direction of the Goethean mind at the time. Goethe wrote the poem in 1774 when he was twenty-five years old; Schubert composed the music for it in 1817 when he was twenty.

Music

Schubert was obviously working through the 1815 edition of Goethe's works at this time. Many of the poems set appear beside one another in that edition. It is most interesting to observe how he swung between the serious and the trivial poems. This song was published in volume forty-eight of Diabelli's *Nachlass* in 1850.

Setting

In 2/4 time, and again in strophic form, the merry little tune whirls along happily. Singers with good German can emphasize the words of stanzas five and six, if they wish to. Schubert omitted stanzas two and three.

Translation

1. So it's my neighbor, a lovely, dear girl! As soon as I get to my workshop, I look over to her shop.
4. I file away—and probably ruin many a golden chain. The master, a hard man, grunts! He saw that it happened because of that little shop!
5. As soon as work is done, she reaches for her spinning wheel. I know what she wants to spin; the dear little thing keeps hoping.
6. Her little foot spins on and on; I'm thinking of her legs and her garter, too—I gave it to the lovely girl!
7. And my darling lifts the fine thread to her lips. Oh, if only I were in its place, how I would kiss the girl!

55. *Gretchen im Zwinger* (D. 564)
(Gretchen's Prayer before the City Wall) (Fragment)
May 1817
B flat minor
43 measures
ca. 7.00 minutes

Text
This text is the last of the extracts from Goethe's *Urfaust* to be set by Schubert. Gretchen has just met her friend Elizabeth at the well and has been told that their mutual friend Barbara "is feeding two" (that is, is pregnant). Gretchen keeps her secret, but then makes straight to the city wall, where she prays before a statue of the Virgin Mary, set in a niche in the wall.

Music
When the song was published, in volume twenty-nine of Diabelli's *Nachlass*, in June 1838, it was given the title *Gretchens Bitte* (Gretchen's Supplication), but it is usually known as *Gretchen's Prayer* in English. Schubert abandoned the composition after forty-three measures.

Setting
As was often the case, Schubert knew quite quickly when a subject was not his. The setting cannot match the high drama of *Gretchen am Spinn-rade*, and he also failed to give the theme the haunting beauty of his great night songs. More than likely a sense of sin disturbed him much more than it disturbed Goethe in later life, although the poet was never truly free of it either. Just as for the poet in 1788 "there was too much Christianity" in Gretchen, so too for Schubert in 1817.[56] Goethe reduced the number of Gretchen's scenes for his *Faust, a Fragment,* in 1788. Schubert's reasons for not finishing this song might be linked to his great desire to write an opera; this scena certainly has the makings of an aria and the first nine lines would become a Verdi-like prayer, an *Ave Maria* such as Schubert was later to write to Scott's text. In 1943, Benjamin Britten showed his enduring love for Schubert by finishing the composition.

Translation
Gretchen is placing fresh flowers into a vase.
1. Oh, look down, Mother of Sorrows, look graciously down on me in my hour of need! The sword in your heart, you look up with a thousand torments to your Son's death.
2. You look up to the Father and sigh for His and your agony. Who can feel how the pain racks my body? How my poor heart is in

anguish, how it is trembling, what it longs for—only you, you alone know!

3. Wherever I go, alas and alack, what pain is in my bosom! No sooner am I alone than I weep, weep, weep. My heart is breaking . . .

56. *Sehnsucht* IV (D. 656)
(Yearning)
"Nur wer die Sehnsucht kennt" (4)
(Only those who know what yearning is)
April 1819
E major
63 measures
ca. 3.15 minutes

Text and Translation
As for song no. 33.

Music
This setting is Schubert's fourth of Goethe's poem from the novel *Wilhelm Meister*. It was set for a quintet of two tenors and three basses without accompaniment—not technically a Lied, but included for the sake of completeness—a Schubert setting of a Goethe text. It was published by Friedrich Schreiber in 1867.

Setting
Five unaccompanied male voices singing the song of a tiny female (or hermaphrodite?) child might seem almost bizarre, and even Schubert must have sensed the bizarrerie of the effort. On the other hand, yearning was very much part of his persona by 1819; he, too, felt "alone and robbed of all happiness" at times.

57. *Die Liebende schreibt* (D. 673)
(The Beloved Writes)
October 1819
B flat
67 measures
ca. 2.30 minutes

Text
In 1807–1808, Goethe was fifty-eight years old and beginning to feel his age, although it was on 19 October 1806 that, after eighteen years of living together, he finally married the forty-one-year-old Christiane Vulpius. He did this more as a gesture of gratitude than a delayed ex-

pression of love, for on 14 October 1806, two Alsatian *tirailleurs* from the occupying French army had broken into the house in Weimar. Christiana bravely stood in front of her man, preventing the intruders from attacking him, and then calling for help from Weimar's men. Despite that history, this poem belongs to a group of sonnets connected with various other female acquaintances, and particularly with the very youthful Wilhelmine Minchen (Minna) Herzlieb and the sixteen-year-old Sylvie von Ziegesar, with whom Goethe consorted in Jena and Karlsbad in 1807–1808. The sonnets of which this is number eight appeared in his *Collected Works* in 1815 and are regarded as a preliminary to his novel *Die Wahlverwandtschaften* (Elective Affinities). Foreign readers of Goethe, particularly of *Faust*, are never surprised that the very last lines of the long Part II are "Das Ewig-Weibliche zieht uns hinan" (The Eternal-Feminine draws us ever on).

Music
Schubert took this new poem up after a Goethe-less 1818, when some of his intellectual friends were showing a lack of reverence for the "Dalai Lama" as they called Goethe. Although Schubert's manuscript has vanished, the song appeared in 1863 (as Op. 165, No. 1, in A major), via C. A. Spina, and attracted little attention. The first publication had been on 26 June 1832 as a supplement to the *Wiener Zeitschrift* where it was in B flat.

Setting
The poem is a love letter from a girl, begging for a love letter from her lover. Since it is written by an aging man, it reads more like a cry of hope that he still has some machismo left. Minna called Goethe "the dear old gentleman," and in a letter to Zelter on 29 October 1813, the poet admitted that he had loved her when she was sixteen, "more than was proper." Minna was actually ten at the time he met her and eighteen when he declared his love for her; he wisely ceased his visits to her foster-father's house.[57] Schubert found a curiously flat melody in 3/4 time, which suggests that the tone of the poem did not set him on fire.

Translation
1. A glance from your eyes into mine, a kiss from your mouth on my mouth, can he who knows what lies behind these find pleasure in anything else?
2. Far from you, far from my folk, my thoughts go round in circles, but always return to that one hour, the unique one, and I begin to weep.
3. My tears dry at once again; he loves me, I think into my solitude; should you not reach out to me, so far away?

4. Hear the lispings of these pangs of love! Your will is my sole happiness on this earth, your friendship for me; give me a sign!

58. *Prometheus* (D. 674)
(Prometheus)
October 1819
B-flat major
109 measures
ca. 5.30 minutes

Text
Prometheus was the Titan who shaped the human race on earth, stealing fire to aid it. He is the archetypal pagan creator, the genius of Goethe's Age of Genius(es) of the Storm and Stress movement of 1770–1774. It is an anti-Christian polemic, praising the independence of the human spirit, its ability to defy all odds: "I am working up my situation into a drama in defiance of God and men," Goethe said to his friend Johann Kestner (future husband of Goethe's beloved Lotte Buff) in July 1773.[58] The drama *Prometheus* remained a fragment, however. The poem had many admirers in pre–French Revolution days, not least, the passionate Beethoven.

Music
Schubert had set Goethe's companion poem *Ganymed* as D. 544 in March 1817. Goethe always insisted that the poems be printed together; he wanted to set Prometheus' violent defiance of the powers above against Ganymede's gentler praise of the gods, which was now seen as a negative human quality. Was this Goethe's attempt to reach the golden mean, or merely a sitting on the fence? Schubert certainly saw it as a powerful challenge and wrote a heaven-storming Lied. Some older commentators found the setting out of character for what they took to be the mild-mannered little composer. The song was published in 1850 in volume forty-seven of Diabelli's *Nachlass*.

Setting
Prometheus is a powerful dramatic monologue for a full bass voice. We know the turmoil in Schubert's mind in 1819—he was at odds with the world, and his friends were discussing among themselves issues of great moment in political and moral matters. There are torrents of passionate sound in the first stanza, followed by true Schubertian melodic moments: "When I was a child," the speaker says as he remembers the years of innocence when he believed that someone was "up there," looking after him. Schubert might well have been looking back here at his

once secure Catholic childhood. Like *Gretchen*, this Lied broke barriers: "Dramatic music of coming generations owed much to songs such as this," wrote Dietrich Fischer-Dieskau.[59] It is also likely that Schubert's stay in Steyr with Michael Vogl, a fine voice and a powerful personality, influenced the confident writing of the song. He had touched on the theme previously too (in June 1816), when he wrote his cantata *Prometheus* (D. 451) with a piano accompaniment; it was performed in Vienna on 8 January 1819.[60]

Translation

1. Cover your heaven, Zeus, with a cloudy veil! And, as the child does, who knocks the heads off thistles, practice your art on oak trees and mountain peaks. Yet you must leave my earth to me, and my cottage which you didn't build, and my hearth whose fires you envy.
2. I know nothing poorer under the sun than you, oh gods! You feed your majesty wretchedly off sacrificial gifts and breathy prayers, and you would starve, if children and beggars were not such optimistic fools.
3. When I was a child, I didn't know what was what, my confused eye turned to the sun, as if an ear were there to hear my complaints, a heart like mine to take pity on the tormented boy.
4. Who helped me against the Titan's dictatorship? Who saved me from death, from slavery? Did you not do it all on your own, my sacred, glowing heart? And, though deceived, young and good as you were, did you not send glowing thanks for your deliverance to the sleeping god up there?
5. I should honor you? What for? Have you ever eased the pain of him who was suffering? Have you stilled the tears of him in anguish? Is it not almighty Time which has crafted me into a man, along with eternal fate, my masters, and yours?
6. Did you perhaps think I should hate Life, flee into the wastelands because not all my blossoming dreams came to fruition?
7. Here I sit, make men in my image, a race like me, a race which will suffer, weep, enjoy life and be happy, and take no notice of you, as I don't!

59. *Gesang der Geister über den Wassern* III (D. 704)
(Song of the Spirits over the Waters) (Fragment)
December 1820
C major
Less than 139 measures
Less than 6.30 minutes

Text and Translation
As for song no. 47.

Music and Setting
This setting for four tenors and four basses is included for the sake of
completeness. It is accompanied by strings and remained a fragment.[61]

60. *Gesang der Geister über den Wassern* IV (D. 705)
    (Song of the Spirits over the Waters)
    December 1820
    C sharp
    139 measures
    ca. 6.30 minutes

Text and Translation
As for song no. 47.

Music and Setting
This setting for two tenors and two basses is included for the sake of
completeness. It is a fuller version of D. 704 and has a difficult piano
accompaniment. It remained a fragment.[62]

61. *Im Gegenwärtigen Vergangenes* (D. 710)
    (The Past in the Present)
    March 1821(?)
    D-flat major
    155 measures
    ca. 6.45 minutes

Text
The poem is found in *Moganni Nameh* (The Book of the Poet/Singer),
the first book of Goethe's *West-östlicher Divan* (1814–1815). The *Divan*
was a collection of poems fashioned on the translation of the "songs" of
the fourteenth-century Persian poet Hafiz-Hatem, by the Viennese orientalist, Joseph von Hammer-Purgstall. They were, however, really inspired by Goethe's love for Marianne von Willemer, the wife of a Frankfurt banker. This poem was written on 26 July 1814, and the collection
was published in Germany in 1819, and by Carl Armbruster in Vienna
in 1820. In the poem, Hafiz represents Goethe, and Marianne's pseudonym is Suleika.

Music and Setting
Schubert set this love poem (curiously) for two tenors and two basses

with piano accompaniment. Not surprisingly, it is a rarely heard work that Schubert probably wrote after one of the reading-circle evenings with his friends, since the book appeared in 1819. The other settings of poems from the *West-östlicher Divan* have, on the other hand, become extremely popular (songs 63, 79, and 80). The poems were regarded as quintessentially Romantic by Schubert's friends, and this, no doubt, encouraged him to set them. Deutsch found this poem to be "a rare example of serene wisdom in a young man."[63] It appeared in Diabelli's *Nachlass* in 1849.

Synopsis
Roses and lilies are blooming in my garden; a knightly castle rests on the rocks looking out over the forest. And it is just as in the old days, when we were still in love, and I played my zither to charm us both. So, enjoy the woods and let others enjoy what you enjoyed so long ago. Then no one can accuse us of keeping them to ourselves—and, at this point in our song, we are back again with Hafiz, for it is right to be with fellow-spirits at the end of the day.

62. *Gesang der Geister über den Wassern* V / VI (D. 714)
(Song of the Spirits over the Waters)
V: December 1820; VI: February 1821
C major
a: 125 measures (incomplete); b: 172 measures

Text and Translation
As for song no. 47.

Music and Setting
Again, this piece is included for the sake of completeness. It exists in two octet versions, set for four tenors and four basses with string accompaniment. The first version of 125 measures remained a fragment; the second, of 172 measures, was also marked Adagio molto, and is complete. They were published in 1891 and 1858, respectively, and remain a contribution to that enormous musical literature for the glee-clubs that Goethe's friend Zelter had been so conscientious in introducing into German social life. The octet was premièred in the Kärntnertor-Theater on 7 March 1821.

63. *Versunken* (D. 715)
(Lost in Love)
February 1821

A-flat major
125 measures
ca. 2.00 minutes

Text

The poem written shortly before 30 May 1815 appears in *Uschk Nameh* (Book of Love), the third book of Goethe's *West-östlicher Divan* (1814–1815). Goethe did not attempt to reproduce the Persian verse form, the "ghasel," as did the Romantic poets Friedrich Rückert and August von Platen, but gave German poetry the exotic Oriental imagery in its familiar form and rhythm. Thus, his poems became German love lyrics, which was no doubt the reason for their attraction for Schubert in 1821.

Music

Schubert probably found the poem in Carl Armbruster's 1820 Viennese publication of the *West-östlicher Divan*. He transposed the song to F major in July 1825 and it was eventually published in volume thirty-eight of Diabelli's *Nachlass* in 1845. The rushing arpeggios are presumably meant to mirror the lover's excitement as he contemplates his beloved's hair in 2/4 time.

Setting

It is very difficult to fathom Schubert's reasons for choosing this particular poem to set. Although one singer finds it "one of the few erotic poems in Schubert's music,"[64] one would have thought that the line about "the five-toothed comb" alone would have driven any erotic thoughts from the reader. We find the setting both unattractive and undistinguished. Schubert omitted the line "this is not flesh, is not skin" (immediately after "Her ear joins in the game, too"), but kept the rhyme "Haut/kraut." He also omitted the last line, "This you did, Hafiz, we'll begin from the beginning again," and repeated the first line instead. Again, it is difficult to guess why he made these changes.

Translation

A head so round and full of curly locks! And if I may run my hands back and forward through such abundant locks, then I am healthy, to my heart's content. And if I kiss her forehead, eyebrows, eyes and mouth, then, again, I feel the pain. This five-toothed comb, where should it pause? It keeps going back through the curls. Her ear joins in the game, too . . . So delicate a joke, so full of love—yet whenever one fondles this head, one will have to run one's hands through this hair forever—a head so round and full of curly locks.

64. *Grenzen der Menschheit* (D. 716)
(Human Limitations)
March 1821
E major
159 measures
ca. 8.00 minutes

Text
Goethe's poem was written some time between 1778 and 1781, when he was struggling with the concept of Fate as the guiding spirit of human existence; it reminds us therefore of the other great poems, *Prometheus* and *Ganymed*. Here, the poet compares the contemplative attitude of the gods with the turbulent life of humans, and we are insignificant in comparison. The heaven-storming attitude of the earlier *Prometheus* has vanished. For the 1789 *Collected Works* Goethe changed one word of his original poem in the line that read "und viele Geschlechter reihen sie dauernd an ihres Daseins unendliche Kette" (and they [the gods] link many generations on to the endless chain of their existence). He changed the "sie" to "sich," altering the meaning to "many generations *are eternally linked*"; that is, he now believed that humans should decide their own fates.

Music
Peculiarly marked "nicht ganz langsam" (not entirely slowly), the song in ¢ time dates from March 1821 and was intended, like *Prometheus*, for a powerful bass voice. It was published in 1832 in volume fourteen of Diabelli's *Nachlass*.

Setting
If one ever wanted to name a setting that would prove beyond doubt that Schubert had possessed the intellectual capacity not only to understand but also to illuminate a poet's thought process, surely this setting would serve the purpose. From the majestic opening chords that set the grand scene, the composer allows the voice to range over the whole gamut of musical possibilities: the sforzandos that describe the majesty of the gods above the stars, to the quieter tones, as the composer contemplates the difference between humans and the gods. What Goethe would have made of this through-composed, philosophical, musical essay is difficult to imagine. It is certainly light years removed from his, and indeed, from the normal, concept of a Lied, but if perhaps Mendelssohn, instead of Zelter, had undertaken to explain to him where Schubert and modern music were heading, he might at least have tried to appreciate it, as he did Beethoven's Fifth Symphony. One must add that

Chapter Five

even twentieth-century audiences have found it difficult to love this amazing song. Schubert's setting has "deep" in the breast for Goethe's "faithful" breast, another example of the composer's *lèse-majesté*.

Translation

1. When the aged holy Father calmly sows the earth with blessed shafts of lightning from out of the rolling clouds, I kiss the lowest hem of his robes, a childlike shudder deep in my breast.
2. For no man should measure himself against gods. If he reaches upwards and touches the stars with his head, then the uncertain soles of his feet have no firm foundation, and the clouds and the winds will play with him.
3. If, however, he stands with firm strong legs on the eternal, well-founded earth, he will not be able to reach up to compare himself even with the oak or the vine.
4. What distinguishes gods from humans? It is that many waves run on before them; the waves lift us, swallow us up, and we sink.
5. A little ring encompasses our lives, and many generations are eternally linked on a chain of existence.

65. *Geheimes* (D. 719)
(Secret)
March 1821
A-flat major
97 measures
ca. 1.45 minutes

Text

This poem is found in *Uschk Nameh* (Book of Love), Book Three of Goethe's *West-östlicher Divan* (1814–1815). It was written on 31 August 1814 and appeared in the 1819 *Collected Works* as *Glückliches Geheimnis* (Happy Secret). It is one of Goethe's playfully erotic poems to Marianne von Willemer, reminding the listener-reader of those scenes in nineteenth-century novels where young lovers, excited at the thought of later, illicit meetings, exchange shy (or sly) glances—only, in 1814, Goethe was sixty-five, Marianne thirty.

Music

The song was published by Cappi and Diabelli in December 1822, as Op. 14, No. 2. It was sent to the famous soprano Anna Milder (with *Versunken*, D. 715), and dedicated to Franz von Schober, with whom Schubert was exploring at this time the darker side of Vienna. The little turn at the end of each stanza seems to illustrate Schubert's understanding of what really lay behind the little poem: "I am only too well aware what the glances mean!" This was the song (with D. 720, song no. 79) that Marianne von Willemer mentioned enthusiastically in her letter to Goethe on 26 April 1826, but she did not mention the composer's name. If only she had!

Setting
The marking is "etwas geschwind" (quite fast), and this tempo must be retained if the singer is to bring out the playfulness of the words. A coquettish air about Schubert's music matches the poem to a T. The text of Schiller's poem *Laura am Klavier* (Laura at the Piano), which Schubert set as D. 388 in March 1816, depicts just such a scene. The two poems could graphically illustrate the difference between the serious-minded, albeit passionate, Schiller and the playful, much more human Goethe. Schubert set them both in much the same manner, however.

Translation
1. Everyone is amazed at my darling's daring glances; I, on the other hand, who am in the know, am only too well aware of what they mean.
2. For they mean: I love this man—not that one or any other. So, stop wondering, stop hoping, dear friends!
3. Oh yes, she does look around, with such amazing power, yet she is only giving him a foretaste of their next sweet hours together.

66. *Mahomets Gesang* II (D. 721)
(Song of Mohammed) (Fragment)
March 1821
C-sharp minor
39 measures (unfinished)
ca. 1.25 minutes

Text and Translation
As for song no. 51.

Music
A fragment of thirty-nine measures, set for a bass voice. Probably Schubert wrote it under the influence of his work on Goethe's poems in the *West-östlicher Divan*, and maybe even as a treat for the baritone Vogl. For quite a few of his Lieder at this time he had Vogl in mind.

Setting
The onrushing sixteenths remind us of the *Erlkönig* setting, but the simi-

larity ceases there. As in the 1817 version (D. 549, song no. 51) of 114 measures, inspiration seems to have failed the composer here, too.

67. *Mignon* I (D. 726)
  (Mignon)
  "Heiss mich nicht reden" (1)
  (Don't ask me to speak)
  April 1821
  B minor
  59 measures
  ca. 2.40 minutes

Text

Critics' views of Goethe's *Wilhelm Meister's Years of Apprenticeship* vary widely. Lessing (1729–1781), among the first of the classic writers of German eighteenth-century literature, thought it a minor work and believed that "if Goethe ever came to his senses, he would not be very much more than an ordinary person."[65] On the other hand, the leading figure of the Romantic Movement, Friedrich Schlegel (1772–1829), saw it as an example of the world literature by means of which he and his brother August were seeking to break down national prejudices. Mignon has caught the imagination of many readers and composers, however, as the quintessence of mystery, alienation, and abandonment. She becomes almost a transvestite in Goethe's description—she hated female clothes and Wilhelm Meister even speaks of her once or twice as "er" (he). Mignon declaims this poem in chapter twelve of Book Three of Goethe's early novel *Wilhelm Meister's Theatrical Mission* and at the very end of chapter sixteen of Book Five in *Wilhelm Meister's Years of Apprenticeship*, just before Wilhelm leaves on a journey. Goethe mentions it as a poem written by Wilhelm that Mignon "had recited a few times." Its sentiments have led some critics to suggest that Goethe used words that were originally Charlotte von Stein's,[66] for they clearly refer to one of the other female characters, Aurelie, and not to Mignon.

Music

The first draft is headed "Mignon. Goethe," and was published in 1870 by J. P. Gotthard. Although it could be thought of as one of the songs that found Schubert accused of modulation mania, it does not deserve to be forgotten, even though some poetry lovers refuse to accept a musical setting for a poem that was clearly meant to be recited.

Setting

Schubert's ¢ time, his so-called "death-rhythm," marked "langsam" (slowly), was perhaps more tragic than the poem required. The later setting (D. 877, No. 2, song no. 76) seems more suitable.

Translation

1. Do not ask me to speak, ask me to be silent, for it is my duty to keep my secret. I should like to bare my whole soul to you, but Fate will not allow it.
2. The sun will drive away the dark night at the appointed time, and all will be bright; the hard rock will open up its heart and will not deprive the earth of its deep, hidden springs.
3. Every person seeks peace in the arms of a friend, for there the heart can pour out its sorrows; only, an oath keeps my lips closed, and only a god can open them.

68. *Mignon* II (D. 727)

(Mignon)
"So lasst mich scheinen, bis ich werde" (3)
(Let me look like this, until I become like this)
April 1821
B minor
64 measures
ca. 3.45 minutes

Text and Translation

As for song no. 42.

Music

This version is Schubert's third attempt at setting a very difficult poem. It was composed along with "Heiss mich nicht reden" (D. 726) and first published in volume forty-eight of Diabelli's *Nachlass* in 1850.

Setting

Mignon is in a transfigured state when she sings this song in chapter two of Book Eight of *Wilhelm Meister*. The setting does not illustrate this nor does it plumb the emotional depths as does the later, and last, version (D. 877, song no. 77), but it is a song that should be performed more often.

69. *Johanna Sebus* (D. 728)

(Johanna Sebus)
April 1821

D minor
81 measures (unfinished)
ca. 2.30 minutes

Text

Johanna Sebus was a young girl of seventeen who drowned in the
frozen river Rhine near Cleve in northern Germany while trying to save
others in the night of 12–13 January 1809. The brave deed was widely
reported and admired. Goethe wrote the ballad immediately on receiving the news and a request to honor the girl. It was spoken at a memor-
ial service in Cleve and is often mentioned in Goethe's correspondence.[67] It is listed under the heading "Cantatas" in Goethe's *Collected
Works*.

Music

The ballad fragment appeared in the *Complete Edition* of 1895. The
eighty-one measures were completed by Pater Reinhard van Hoorickx
in 1961.

Setting

Schubert set only half the text, but, like the fragment of *Mahomets Gesang*
(D. 549), it was already as long as *Erlkönig,* whose tumbling sixteenth
notes it seeks to emulate in vain. Perhaps it was the success of *Erlkönig,*
published as Op. 1 in 1821, that induced Schubert to undertake what
turned out to be a lost cause.

Synopsis

The ballad tells of the bursting of the dam and Johanna's brave attempt
to save her mother. After setting her mother on dry land, she then
returns to try to save the woman and the three children who shared their
house. The ballad ends with her defiant decision to plunge into the
water to her death.

70. *Der Musensohn* (D. 764) (a/b)

    (The Son of the Muses)
    December 1822
    a: A-flat major; b: G major
    73 measures
    ca. 2.00 minutes

Text

The poem appeared in Goethe's *New Works* in 1800. Erich Trunz believes
that it was likely written just before November 1799, although some editions place it in 1774 because Goethe mentions it in Book Sixteen of *Poetry*

Der Musensohn.

Edition Peters.

Der Musensohn (D. 764), December 1822.

and Truth as an example of his high spirits in those years.[68] This is Goethe as musician, piping his melodies like a Greek god. (He usually depicted himself as a painter.) It is a merry, thought-free piece that shows again Goethe's response to rhythm. The unseen bond between Goethe and Schubert is seen at its strongest here, when Schubert responds to Goethe's musicality and, at the very end, his thought of "lost love."

Music

The tempo direction is "fairly lively," and the song certainly dances along, in Schubert's favorite 6/8 time. It was contained in a manuscript with three other Goethe Lieder (D. 765–D. 767) and was probably written early in December 1822. Schubert mentions the songs when dedicating them to Josef Spaun in his letter of 7 December 1822 and remarks on the *Wilhelm Meister* Lieder, too: "Life in Vienna," he wrote, is now "really pleasant." How soon was that to change.[69] The song was published in July 1878 as Op. 92, No. 1, by M. J. Leidesdorf. That version was in G major, although the original was in A-flat major.

Setting

The song is one of Schubert's most popular. The setting of the five stanzas in 6/8 time can (should) be varied according to the text, but is often not. The composer gives hints with the wonderful modulations at the beginning of the various stanzas. From this song above all comes the clichéd picture of Schubert, the peasant lad with his rustic pipe. Neither the worldly wise Goethe of 1774 or 1799, nor the syphilitic Schubert of 1822, could possibly have matched that description.

Translation
1. Wandering through fields and woods, piping my melody, that's how I go from place to place! And I make them all dance to my beat and my rhythm.
2. I can hardly wait for the first flower in the gardens, the first blossom on the trees, because my songs welcome them. And when winter comes, I still sing that same old dream.
3. I sing it wherever I am, the length and breadth of the frozen lakes—there, winter blossoms so beautifully. But this blossom vanishes too, and I find new joys up on the plowed heights.
4. For, when I find the young folk by the linden tree, I get them moving right away. The dull boy puffs himself up, the stiff young girl twists and turns to my melody.
5. You give wings to my feet, and you drive the loving boy through the vales and the hills far away from home. Dear, divine Muses, when shall I rest on her bosom, oh, when?

71. *An die Entfernte* (D. 765)
(To the Distant One)
December 1822
G major
45 measures
ca. 3.00 minutes

Text
Goethe's close friendship with Charlotte von Stein ended soon after his return from Italy in 1788—particularly after he began his liaison with Christiana Vulpius in that summer of 1788. Nevertheless, many of his poems look back with elegiac sorrow on their friendship: "I had a love," he wrote shortly after their break up, "it was dearer to me than all else! But I have it no longer. Be silent, and bear the loss!"[70] This poem is in the same elegiac mood as that epigram, written in Venice in 1790.

Music
This Lied is one of the four Goethe Lieder mentioned under song no. 70, all four written on the same manuscript of December 1822. They are contained within a few pages of each other in the poems in the 1815 *Collected Works*. The song was published by the Berlin publisher, Wilhelm Müller, in 1868.

Setting
The classic simplicity of the poem is preserved in Schubert's beautifully artless, through-composed setting, although the amazingly varied modulations in the three stanzas in 4/4 time make it anything but simple, either to play or to sing. It is not known whether Schubert was thinking of his lost love; Therese Grob had married in 1820 and the next year he poured out his heart to Anselm Hüttenbrenner about Therese. This Lied is a perfect example of the union of words, emotions, and music, strengthened by the poetic postlude, unusual for Schubert.

Translation
1. So, have I really lost you? Have you fled from me, my fair one? Each word, each note, is still heard in these ears so used to them.
2. Just as the wanderer searches the sky in vain in the morning, when, hidden from view in the ethereal blue, the lark sings, high above him,
3. So too, I look anxiously here and there in the fields, the hedges and the woods; all my songs call to you: Oh, my beloved, come back to me!

72. *Am Flusse* II (D. 766)
(By the River)
December 1822
D major
33 measures
ca. 1.00 minute

Text and Translation
As for song no. 10.

Music
It is strange to observe how often Schubert's last settings of Goethe poems are new versions of earlier attempts. Was this a conscious awareness of the need to make his settings as good as they possibly could be? Was he still hoping for eventual recognition from the great man? *Am Flusse* was one of those early attempts sent to Goethe in 1816. This version was published in 1872, when J. P. Gotthard included it as no. 3 of his *Forty Songs*.

Setting
We praised the earlier setting (D. 160, song no. 10) as "catching the spirit of the poem perfectly." The second setting in ¢ time is even more of a miniature, but still a yearning for a lost love. This time, however, the water, which as a "Bächlein" (brook) was to play such an important role in his *Die schöne Müllerin* cycle of 1823, takes center stage, and the song flits past with a curious lack of emotion. That first version is much to be preferred; Schubert should have left well alone.

73. *Willkommen und Abschied* (a/b) (D. 767)
(Hail and Farewell)
December 1822
C major
a: 104 measures; b: 105 measures
ca. 3.00 minutes

Text
One of the most famous poems in German literature, *Willkommen und Abschied*, first titled *Es schlug mein Herz* (My Heart Pounded), immortalized Goethe's brief affair in 1770–1771 with the simple lass from Alsace, Friederike Brion. All lovers of German poetry know it as the finest love song from Germany's greatest poet of love songs. Less enthusiastic (particularly female) readers see it as the first of many cynical Goethean expressions of guilt at having abandoned a woman after capturing her

Willkommen und Abschied.

Edition Peters.

Willkommen und Abschied (D. 767), December 1822.

affections. In the first version, written at Epiphany 1771, it is the woman
who leaves the man after the night of love; in the second, of 1775, the
more accurate one, the man leaves the woman, albeit with passionate
cries of devotion: "Und doch, welch' Glück, geliebt zu werden" (And
yet, what joy it is to be loved / and, to love, ye gods, what bliss).

Music

This song was among those mentioned in Schubert's letter to Josef von
Spaun of 7 December 1822 as having been completed with the Lieder
from *Wilhelm Meister*.[71] The final version was published in July 1826 as
Op. 56, No. 1, by A. W. Pennauer, with a translation into Italian by J. N.
Craigher. It is sometimes sung by Italian tenors or female singers such as
Cecilia Bartoli. Fischer-Dieskau is of the opinion that it is best suited to
"powerfully voiced" tenors and that it should be sung in the C major
key of the published edition.[72]

Setting

Schubert's two settings (with only minor differences) are grist to the
mills of those who dislike music settings of Goethe's poems. They also
recall Alfred Lord Tennyson's growling comment about those "damned
musicians (who) make me say a thing twice when I said it only once!"[73]
This setting has always disappointed us; the *Erlkönig*-like galloping
accompaniment is fine, but the triple or quadruple repeat at the end of
stanzas and the over-ecstatic Beethoven-like repetitions on "and, to love,
ye gods, what bliss," are a little too heavy for our taste. The original
poem just sounds more genuine, despite its cynicism.

Translation

1. My heart pounded, quick, to horse! It was done, as soon as thought.
    The evening cradled the earth, and the night hung over the moun-
    tains: the oak tree stood in its misty raiments, a huge, towering
    giant, there, where the darkness peeped out of the bushes, with a
    hundred eyes, black as night.
2. From a clouded hill-top, the moon looked down sadly through the
    mist, the wind beat its wings gently, eerily, round my ears; the night
    created a thousand monsters, yet I was bright and happy. In my
    veins, what fire! In my heart, what a glow!
3. I saw you, and a gentle peace flowed to me from your darling eyes;
    my heart was there right by your side, my every breath for you. A
    rosy-colored springlike weather played over your darling face, and
    tenderness for me—ye gods! I hoped for this, yet deserved it not!
4. But oh, with the morning sun, the farewell clenched my heart; in
    your kisses, what joy! In your eyes, what pain! I went, you stood,

looking at the ground, and then looked after me with tear-stained face: And, yet, what joy to be loved! And to love, ye gods, what bliss!

74. *Wandrers Nachtlied* II (D. 768)
   (Night Song of a Wanderer)
   (?)December 1822; before 25 May 1824
   B-flat major
   14 measures
   2.30 minutes

Text
The poem's subtitle, "Ein Gleiches. Auf dem Gickelhahn" (Another of the Same. On the Kickelhahn), refers to Kickelhahn (originally spelled *Gickelhahn*), a mountain above Goethe's favorite village of Ilmenau. In a letter to Charlotte von Stein, dated 6 September 1780, Goethe wrote from the top of this mountain: "The sky is quite clear and I am going to enjoy the sunset. The view is great, but simple. The sun has set. This is the place where I made a sketch of the rising mist for you, now it is so pure and peaceful."[74] He had written that he had climbed the mountain "to escape the desolation of the town, the complaints, the desires, the incorrigible confusions of mankind." As he watched the sun set over the beautiful Thuringian forest, lines of poetry formed in his head, and, before going to sleep in the simple shelter up on the mountain, he wrote them on the wall of the hut. He revisited the hut in 1813 when he was sixty-four and renewed the writing, which was then preserved under glass. Eighteen years later, on his eighty-second birthday on 28 August 1831, he was taken up the Kickelhahn again by a forest ranger, Christian Mahr, who reported that, when Goethe looked at the poem again, tears came into the old man's eyes, and he repeated the last lines in "a gentle, sad voice." "Yes, just wait, you too will soon be at rest." Then he turned and said: "Now we can go back!" The hut was accidentally burned down in August 1870; it has been restored, with a plaque containing the poem on the outside wall, and is Thuringia's number-one tourist attraction. In Goethe's *Collected Works*, the poem follows the first *Wandrers Nachtlied* of 1776 and is titled *Ein Gleiches* (Another of the Same), or *Wandrers Nachtlied* II, but Cambridge academic Peter Johnson has titled it, immortally, an "Ohne-Gleiches" (a nonpareil).

Music
We do not have the original manuscript and therefore cannot date it accurately. Some place it at the beginning of December 1822, others at the beginning of 1823[75]—in troubled times for Schubert. It was pub-

Wanderers Nachtlied.

Edition Peters

Wandrers Nachtlied II ("Über allen Gipfeln ist Ruh," D. 768), possibly before 25 May 1824.

lished in the supplement to the *Vienna Art Magazine* on 23 June 1827, and then appeared as Op. 96, No. 3, in Franz von Schober's Vienna Lithographical Institute in 1828. Later that year, it was published by Probst of Leipzig, as Op. 101, No. 4.

Setting
Not all agree with Jack Stein's oft-quoted opinion that "in this song, if anywhere in song literature, appears the ultimate refutation of the notion that great poems should not be used as texts for art songs,"[76] but we find it difficult not to agree with him. The fourteen measures move serenely in 4/4 time, painting the idyllic scene, it is true, but, at the same time, wonderfully illuminating the poet's thought. Perhaps one has to stand on that mountain and look over the beautiful woods fully to appreciate poem and music, or sit in a concert hall and re-live the moment with a great singer and a sensitive accompanist. It is indeed a mountaintop experience. Schubert repeated the last line in his setting.

Translation
Over all the mountaintops is peace, there is hardly a breath of wind in the treetops. The little birds are silent in the wood. Just wait, you too will soon be at rest. (The last line is repeated.)

75. *Gesänge aus Wilhelm Meister* (D. 877, Nos. 1–4)
(Songs from *Wilhelm Meister*)
Sehnsucht V (D. 877, No. 1)
(Yearning)
"Nur wer die Sehnsucht kennt" (5)
(Only those who know what yearning is)
(?)January 1826
B minor
50 measures
4.00 minutes

Text and Translation
As for song no. 33.

Music
Schubert had returned to Goethe after a break of three troubled years during which he had suffered and partially recovered from his syphilitic infection. The sad, but beautiful, music to *Die schöne Müllerin* (D. 795), of October–November 1823 lay behind him, and he had again tried to make a name in opera, alas, without success. This probably contributed

to the writing of that heart-rending letter of 31 March 1824 to Leopold Kupelwieser, in which he called himself "a miserable, unhappy man." We know that he was unwell in January 1826 when he wrote four songs (nos. 75–78) from *Wilhelm Meister,* so their deep emotional content might well have attracted his basically unhappy mood and might even have brought him solace.[77] This song was published in 1827 by Diabelli as Op. 62, No. 1.

Setting
This Lied is the only one of Schubert's six attempts at the "irregular duet," in chapter eleven of Book Four, between the Harper and Mignon that is set as a duet. It is without doubt the only successful setting of the six. Schubert took the poem from volume two of the 1815 Cotta edition of Goethe's works, where it appeared under the title *From Wilhelm Meister.* Schubert often employed the key of B minor to represent tormented emotions—no more so than in this duet that demands the utmost concentration from singers, accompanist, and audience, for the balance of voices is so fine that the tragedy of the scene might otherwise be lost. Below the title *From Wilhelm Meister* in the edition is a distich: "And hear in the tumult / The songs of those geniuses."

76. *Lied der Mignon* II (D. 877, No. 2)
"Heiss mich nicht reden" (2)
(Don't ask me to speak)
January 1826(?)
E minor
42 measures
ca. 3.30 minutes

Text and Translation
As for song no. 67.

Music
There is, as we have seen, some doubt about the dating of song nos. 75–78. They seem to have been planned and sketched together, but the dates of composition are not known. This song was published as Op. 62, No. 2, in March 1827 by Diabelli.

Setting
A marvelously rich setting in ¢ time for a very good soprano voice. Again, it might be thought to be too rich for the plaint of the child Mignon, but, in 1826, Schubert was not writing a modest song for inclusion in a play, but a vehicle for public performance. The high tessitura

on "and only a god can open them" alone needs the vocal power of an operatic diva.

77. *Lied der Mignon* III (D. 877, No. 3)
"So lasst mich scheinen, bis ich werde" (4)
(Let me look like this, until I become like this)
(?)January 1826
B major
47 measures
ca. 3.00 minutes

Text and Translation
As for song no. 68.

Music
This song was sketched out as were the three other late *Wilhelm Meister* Lieder, and a copy of all four songs is in Dresden. Diabelli published the present song, as Op. 62, No. 3, in March 1827.

Setting
The song is sung by Mignon as, dressed as an angel, she tells Natalie and the children that she wants to become an angel, signifying, for us, that her death is nigh. The strophic-like structure has some remarkable variants—the listener is led from inner speculation to tormented cries that demand an operatic soprano voice. Schubert seems to have known that he could not better this version and, after these songs, he left the Goethe poems alone. Schubert's setting has "dunkle" (dark) house for Goethe's "feste" (secure, safe) house in the last line of the first stanza. Schubert made this change, since Goethe's 1815 edition also has "feste."

78. *Lied der Mignon* IV (D. 877, No. 4)
"Nur wer die Sehnsucht kennt" (6)
(Only those who know what yearning is)
(?)January 1826
A minor
46 measures
ca. 3.00 minutes

Text and Translation
As for song no. 33.

Music
The song was published as Op. 62, No. 4, by Diabelli in March 1827—

along with another setting of the same poem (see D. 877, No. 1, song no. 75).

Setting

It is generally accepted that Schubert adapted for this song the melody and the accompaniment of one of his earlier settings of a poem by J. G. von Salis-Seewis, composed on 27 March 1816 (D. 403). No matter—Mignon's innocent cry of yearning is perfectly matched by the beautiful melody that is slightly adapted, of course, to the new (and immeasurably finer) text. Here, the gentler tone of the whole makes the cry sound like the cry of a little girl. Although written as an "alternative" to the duet (D. 877, song no. 75), this version has long been considered the best of the solo settings.

79. *Suleika* I (D. 720) (a/b)
"Was bedeutet die Bewegung?"
(What does this stirring mean?)
March 1821
B minor/major
a: 142 measures; b: 143 measures
ca. 6.00 minutes

Text

The poem comes from the Book Suleika in Goethe's *West-östlicher Divan*, just before "Ach, um deine feuchten Schwingen" (D. 717, song no. 80). Marianne von Willemer admitted writing these two poems only in 1850, shortly before her death in 1860. This poem was written on her journey eastwards to Heidelberg for a last tryst with Goethe on 23–26 September 1815 and is the companion poem to the one on the west wind (song no. 80). She was not pleased with Goethe's "banal" alterations in the fourth stanza of the published version: "I find mine really more beautiful," she complained.[78] Sadly, although the episode was never forgotten by Marianne, who lived to be seventy-five, it was just another experience for Goethe, which was then to become yet another "fragment of a great confession"—here, another cycle of poems.

Music

Schubert's manuscript is titled "Suleika, Goethe, March 1821." It was published by Cappi and Diabelli in Vienna in December 1822, as Op. 14, No. 1.

Suleika.

Suleika I (D. 720), March 1821.

Setting

Brahms was not the only person to think that this was the loveliest song that had ever been written. From the "windy" beginning, denoted by the ostinato 3/4 rhythm that then dominates, up to the change of rhythm at the beginning of the fourth stanza, the fascinating modulations from B minor to B major underline the change in the poet's emotions. Would Schubert have set these lines in the fourth stanza differently—"and its gentle whisper is a loving message from my lover" —had he known that they were written by a woman deeply in love with Goethe? Moreover, what if Marianne had told Goethe in her letter of 16 April 1825 the name of the composer of the "really lovely melody" to the east wind and to 'Geheimes,' which she had just received from a music-shop, particularly as she was also a friend of Anna Milder-Hauptmann. Would the bond have remained unseen?[79]

Translation

1. What does this stirring mean? Is the east wind bringing me good news? The refreshing movement of its wings brings coolness to the deep wound in my heart.
2. It caresses the dust playfully; chases it up in light, little clouds, drives the happy crowd of little insects into the shelter of the vine-leaves.
3. It allays the burning glow of the sun, and cools my hot cheeks, kisses the vines, which glisten on the fields and hills, as it passes them.
4. And its gentle whisper is a loving message from my lover; before these hills darken, I shall be sitting at his feet.
5. So fly away and serve those who are happy and those who are sad; over there where high walls glow, I shall find my beloved.
6. Ah, the real message of my heart, the breath of love and refreshing life, comes to me from his mouth alone, and only his breath can give it to me.

80. *Suleika* II (D. 717)

"Ach, um deine feuchten Schwingen"
(Oh, how I envy you your rain-dampened wings, oh, west wind)
(?)December 1824; March(?) 1821
B-flat major
186 measures
ca. 4.00 minutes

Text

The poem is found in the Book Suleika in Goethe's *West-östlicher Divan*.

Not until 1850 was it discovered that the poem was actually written by Goethe's paramour, Marianne von Willemer, whose pseudonym is Suleika; Hafiz in the poem represents Goethe. It was written after 23–26 September 1815, when the couple were together in Heidelberg. This poem to the west wind was written on Marianne's return journey to Frankfurt on 26 September. The west wind, the bringer of rain, is here the bringer of tears.[80] Goethe made what he considered to be improvements before publication in 1819. These did not please Marianne, who found them banal.

Music
Schubert's copy for the famous soprano Anna Milder-Hauptmann is all we have of his original thoughts. It was published as Op. 31 by A. W. Pennauer in August 1825 and dedicated to the soprano.

Setting
Anna's letter to Schubert of 8 March 1825 demonstrated what a great singer thought of his Lieder: "The song *Suleika* is heavenly and brings tears to my eyes every time."[81] She was the first to sing the song in public in Berlin on 9 June 1825. The two poems are, of course, more closely related than the two songs. Schubert was not aware that a woman, let alone Suleika herself, in love with Goethe, had written them. The first "east wind" poem brings the woman the messages for which she (Marianne en route to Heidelberg) hopes; the second "west wind" poem, much more erotic, seems to be her response after the tryst. It is much more exultant and passionate, the voice is taken up to a B flat. Did Anna Milder-Hauptmann ever discuss the song with Marianne? She had corresponded at the same time with both Goethe and Schubert. What an opportunity that was to acquaint the one with the other. If only she had!

Translation
1. Ah, how I envy you your rain-dampened wings oh, west wind; for you can tell him how I suffer in our separation.
2. The movement of your wings awakens a quiet yearning in my heart. Flowers, eyes, woods, and hills stand in tears at your breath.
3. Yet your mild, gentle breeze cools my tortured eyelids. Oh, I could die with grief if I did not have the hope of seeing him again.
4. Hurry then to my beloved, speak gently to his heart; yet do not worry him, and hide my agony from him.
5. Tell him—but tell him gently—that his love is my life and his nearness will fill me with the joy of both of us.

Notes

INTRODUCTION

1. Hilmar, *Schubert durch die Brille*, 7: 15.
2. Quoted in Gray, *Goethe: A Critical Introduction*, 29.
3. Capell, *Schubert's Songs*, 2.
4. Brown, *Schubert: A Critical Biography*, 16.
5. John Reed ("Die Rezeptionsgeschichte der Werke Schuberts") has given a useful account of the development of interest in Schubert in the United Kingdom. A rosy-tinted image of Schubert had been given by works such as Rudolf Bartsch's novel *Schwammerl* (1912), which was adapted by Emil Berté as *Das Dreimäderlhaus* (The House of the Three Girls, 1916), which, in turn, became Sigmund Romberg's saccharine *Blossom Time* (1921) in the United States and G. H. Clutsam's *Lilac Time* (1923) in the United Kingdom.
6. Keller, "Goethe and the Lied," 74

CHAPTER ONE

1. Bruford, *Germany in the XVIII Century*, 1.
2. There are claims that a successful performance of the "English opera" *The Devil to Pay* by Charles Coffey, produced in London in 1731 and in Leipzig in 1764, led to the German vogue for the Singspiel (Scholes, *Concise Oxford Dictionary of Music*, 533).
3. Stoljar, *Poetry and Song in Late Eighteenth Century Germany*, 71f.
4. Fischer-Dieskau, *Texte deutscher Lieder*, 9.
5. Smeed, *German Song and Its Poetry*, 237.
6. Most of these songs were written to be accompanied on the clavier. The German word *Klavier* means "keyboard instrument" and is used variously for the harpsichord, clavichord, or pianoforte, according to the period under discussion.
7. Salmen, "Die deutsche Vorklassik."
8. Fischer-Dieskau, *Töne sprechen, Worte klingen*, 152.
9. Feil, *Franz Schubert*, 14.
10. Ritchie, "The Anacreontic Poets," 126.

11. Kinsley, "The Music of the Heart," 126f.
12. Boyle, *Goethe: The Poet and the Age*, 98–99.
13. Georgiades, *Schubert: Musik und Lyrik*, 78.
14. Gottfried August Bürger (1747–1794) wrote a Janus-like ballad *Lenore* in 1773. It looked back to the Scottish ballads in Percy's *Reliques*, such as *Sweet William's Ghost*, and forward to the Scottish border ballads of Sir Walter Scott, who translated *Lenore* in 1797. Few poems have had such a widespread influence on world literature.
15. Smeed, *German Song and Its Poetry*, 23ff.
16. Stoljar, *Poetry and Song*, 30.
17. Geiringer, *Joseph Haydn*, 415ff.
18. Ibid., 419.
19. In Great Britain Haydn showed his awareness of the folk song tradition when, between 1791 and 1805, he undertook the re-working of some 350 Scottish, Welsh, and Irish folk songs for George Thomson and William Whyte, two Edinburgh publishers. The Scottish poet Robert Burns (1759–1796) was even commissioned to deliver new texts for some of these old songs. Haydn's work was to influence the younger Beethoven later.
20. Otto Erich Deutsch, the distinguished Viennese compiler of musical personalities' lives and works, did not accept this point of view and claimed that Mozart was not deceived by the false ascription. He printed a review of 6 January 1790—the song was published as K. 476, one of two German arias for the clavier, on 5 September 1789—which ended: "Would that such songs were studied by many a rising song composer as models for good vocal writing and pure harmony" (Deutsch, *Mozart: A Documentary Biography*, 360–361).
21. Rochlitz, *Für Freunde der Tonkunst*, 112.
22. Scholes, *Concise Oxford Dictionary of Music*, 541.
23. William Mann's praise can be read on the record sleeves of Dietrich Fischer-Dieskau's two Beethoven Lieder LP records, ALP 1317–1318, made in 1954.
24. C.f. Anderson, *The Letters of Beethoven*, 2: 587f.
25. Although Zumsteeg was particularly close to Schiller, he also met Goethe—in Stuttgart in 1797. Zumsteeg made such an impression on the poet that he was sent Goethe's poem *Der Junggeselle und der Mühlbach* (The Young Apprentice and the Mill Stream) to set to music. The Schubert-like theme does not seem to have attracted Zumsteeg as it attracted Reichardt and, later, Wilhelm Müller, whose cycle *Die schöne Müllerin* owes something to Goethe's poem (Youens, *Schubert, Müller and Die schöne Müllerin*, 3f.).
26. Moser, *Goethe und die Musik*, 26.
27. Fischer-Dieskau, *Weil nicht alle Blütenträume reiften*, 175.
28. Stoljar, *Poetry and Song*, 190.
29. Ibid., 191.
30. Ibid., 206.
31. Friedlaender, "Goethe und die Musik," 307.

32. Fischer-Dieskau, *Töne sprechen, Worte klingen,* 41.
33. Moser, *Goethe und die Musik,* 31.
34. Ibid., 91.

CHAPTER TWO

1. There is a sobering assessment of Hans Keller's critical writings by the British composer Robin Holloway in a review of Keller's *Essays on Music* in the *London Review of Books* (3 August 1993): 10–13.
2. Walwei-Wiegelmann, *Goethes Gedanken über Musik,* 55.
3. Ibid., 227–228.
4. Beutler, *Goethe,* 19: 406.
5. Blume, *Goethe und die Musik,* 19.
6. Bielschowsky, *Goethe: Sein Leben und seine Werke,* 1: 7.
7. Sagarra, *A Social History of Germany 1648–1914,* 28–29.
8. Bruford, *Theatre, Drama and Audience,* 297.
9. One of these virtuosi whom Goethe heard with his father and sister Cornelia was none other than the precocious seven-year-old Wolfgang Amadeus Mozart, who played the piano, violin, and glass harmonica during a visit to Frankfurt on 18 August 1763. Speaking to Johann Peter Eckermann on 3 February 1830, Goethe (fourteen in 1763) remembered clearly "the little man with his wig and sword," although we do not know what music Mozart played on the occasion (Deutsch, *Mozart: A Documentary Biography,* 24).
10. All quotations from *Poetry and Truth* have been translated from Richter, *Goethe,* vol. 16.
11. K. E. Goethe, in *Briefe aus dem Elternhaus,* 785.
12. Trunz, *Goethe. Gedichte,* 320, 690.
13. Moser, *Goethe und die Musik,* 12.
14. Grimm, *Goethes Werke,* 33, 176.
15. Beutler, *Goethe,* 18: 162.
16. Boerner, *Goethe,* 43.
17. All quotations from *Werther* have been translated from Richter, *Goethe,* 1.2: 196–299, and are dated.
18. Shelley, *Frankenstein or The Modern Prometheus,* 99.
19. Gerlach und Herrmann, *Goethe erzählt sein Leben,* 101.
20. Richter, *Goethe,* 19, 649f.
21. Moser, *Goethe und die Musik,* 16.
22. Walwei-Wiegelmann, *Goethes Gedanken über Musik,* 65.
23. Georgiades, *Schubert: Musik und Lyrik,* 78.
24. Eckermann and Frédéric Soret conversed regularly with Goethe in Weimar between 1823 and his death in 1832. Quotations from their *Conversations with Goethe* have been translated from Richter, *Goethe,* vol. 19, and are dated.

25. Mommsen, *Goethe-warum?*, 102.
26. Trunz, *Goethe. Gedichte*, 537.
27. Abert, *Goethe und die Musik*, 18.
28. Beutler, *Goethe*, 18: 418.
29. All quotations from the correspondence with Zelter have been translated from Richter, *Goethe*, vol. 20.1 (1799–1827) and from Beutler, *Goethe*, vol. 21 (1827–1832), and are dated.
30. Beutler, *Goethe*, 18: 472–473.
31. Boyle, *Goethe: The Poet and the Age*, 342.
32. Like many poets of that age, Goethe wrote much erotic poetry. Two famous poems concerning Charlotte von Stein are *Der Becher* (The Beaker) and *Nachtgedanken* (Night Thoughts) from 1781.
33. Boerner, *Goethe*, 66.
34. All quotations from the *Italian Journey* have been translated from Richter, *Goethe*, vol. 15, and are dated.
35. He had written on 17 September that the *Liedchen von Marlborough* (Malbrouk s'en va-t-en guerre), which was still being sung all over Europe after the Duke of Marlborough's victory over the French at Blenheim in 1704, was heard in every street. We know the tune as *For He's a Jolly Good Fellow*.
36. Domenico Cimarosa (1749–1801), composer of Italian *opera buffa* such as *Il matrimonio segreto* (The Secret Marriage, 1792), had long been a favorite composer of Goethe's; his nickname, "the Italian Mozart," explains this perhaps.
37. Beutler, *Goethe*, 18: 472–473.
38. Grimm, *Goethes Werke*, 8: 346ff.
39. He had written on 6 January that he was too old for all of this ceremony: "It all flows off me like water off a wax cloth coat."
40. Stoljar, *Poetry and Song*, 196.
41. Fischer-Dieskau, *Weil nicht alle Blütenträume reiften*, 161.
42. Quoted in Hicks, "Was Goethe Musical?" 88.
43. Richter, *Goethe*, 8.1: 126f.
44. Boyle, *Goethe: The Poet and the Age*, 649.
45. Ibid., 652
46. He said to Eckermann on 22 March 1825 apropos the theater: "Everything that was sick-making, weak, tearful and sentimental, everything that was frightening, abhorrent and detrimental to good taste, was excluded. I feared corrupting the actors and the public."
47. Bruford, *Theatre, Drama and Audience*, 304.
48. All quotations from *Wilhelm Meister's Years of Apprenticeship* have been translated from Richter, *Goethe*, vol. 5. Sources are identified by Book numbers.
49. See Schiller's letters of 2, 3, 5, 6, 8, and 9 July 1796, which all contain glowing criticisms of the novel (Richter, *Goethe*, 8.1: 186–211).
50. Gray, *Goethe: A Critical Introduction*, 195 and 186.
51. Bruford, *The German Tradition of Self-Cultivation*, 54.

52. Moser, *Goethe und die Musik*, 33.
53. It is important to remember when discussing a setting of this poem that it refers to Wilhelm's feelings and not (necessarily) to those of the other two.
54. There is a charming letter from Goethe's mother ("Frau Aja," as he called her), dated 9 November 1793, in which she writes from Frankfurt: "There is nothing new here except that *The Magic Flute* has been given eighteen times. No one will admit that they haven't seen it ... they've never known such a spectacle." In another letter (6 February 1794), she asks Goethe to tell her about the Mozart opera *Cosa van Tutti,* as she spelled it! She rarely missed musical or theatrical performances and later, in 1801, gave piano lessons to Goethe's son, August (K. E. Goethe, in *Briefe aus dem Elternhaus,* 643ff.).
55. See, for example, the letter of 9 March 1816 and that of 18 February 1821 in which Goethe regretted that he had spent the entire winter in his room.
56. Moser, *Goethe und die Musik,* 81.
57. Abert, *Goethe und die Musik,* 30f.
58. A selection of Zelter's Lieder can be heard on a Dietrich Fischer-Dieskau CD (*Orfeo*). It will be realized that Zelter's compositional range was much wider than suggested.
59. Grimm, *Goethes Werke,* 11: 13–15.
60. Seidlin, "Goethe's Magic Flute," 58.
61. Bielschowsky, *Goethe: Sein Leben und seine Werke,* 2: 255f.
62. Trunz, *Goethe. Gedichte,* 671.
63. Beutler, *Goethe,* 22: 512.
64. Walwei-Wiegelmann, *Goethes Gedanken über Musik,* 147.
65. Anderson, *The Letters of Beethoven,* 1: 243f.
66. Ibid., 1: 318, fn. 4.
67. It is sometimes overlooked that Goethe and Beethoven met some eighteen times altogether, from the time Beethoven wrote to Bettina on 10 February 1811: "If you write to Goethe about me, choose all the words which will tell him of my warmest regard and admiration" (Anderson, *The Letters of Beethoven,* 1: 312f.). Beethoven actually played for Goethe on 20 and again on 23 July 1812. Goethe wrote afterward in his diary that Beethoven had "played wonderfully."
68. Moser, *Goethe und die Musik,* 35.
69. Lewes, *The Life of Goethe,* 518f.
70. Beutler, *Goethe,* 19: 665.
71. Anderson, *The Letters of Beethoven,* 1: 384.
72. Whether the meetings with Beethoven were the cause or not is unclear, but in 1813 Goethe decided to set to music "In te, domine, speravi et non confundar in aeternum" (In thee, O Lord, do I put my trust; let me never be put to confusion) from Psalm 71, verse 1, in four parts. Then, on 25 December 1813, he asked Zelter to set it, too, so that he might compare both versions. When he heard Zelter's, he was happy to declare himself a "dilettante." His version was presumably destroyed.

73. Richter, *Goethe*, 6.2: 602f.
74. T. J. Reed, *The Classical Centre*, 233.
75. Beutler, *Goethe*, Tagebücher, 344.
76. Johanna, the mother of philosopher Arthur Schopenhauer, wrote to a friend Elisa von der Recke on 25 June 1816: "I saw Goethe today for the first time since his wife's death; for it is his way to let his grief abate in silence, only showing himself to his friends when he has fully recovered. Yet I found him a changed man; he seems to me to be completely devastated in himself" (Beutler, *Goethe*, 22: 859). She had been one of Christiane's fiercest critics.
77. Goethe's favorite was the younger boy, Wolfgang, to whom he gave the nickname "Wölfchen" (little wolf), which his father had given the young Goethe. A typical grandfatherly diary entry was: "Later, Wölfchen sat down beside me and read. I went through his picture book with him." Goethe, however, told Eckermann that the child immediately ruined every conversation (1 December 1823)! Walther became a musician after being coached by Mendelssohn in 1835–1836 and composed an opera *Anselmo Lancia* and a few Lieder. He died in 1885. Wolfgang took a doctorate in law and was known as a poet. Like his father, August, he too died in Rome, in 1883.
78. We have mentioned the role played by Fate in Goethe's life. In 1822, the composer Carl Loewe visited Goethe in Jena, in his pocket a setting of *Erlkönig*, but Goethe had no piano there at the time. What if Goethe had heard the setting and had liked it? That year, Beethoven sent Goethe his settings of *Meeresstille* and *Glückliche Fahrt*, and on 6 August (in Eger) the composer Johann Wenzel Tomaschek handed Goethe eighteen settings of Goethe's poems. Goethe praised them, but thought there was "a certain lack of sensual opulence and colorfulness" (Beutler, *Goethe*, 23: 224). What if Schubert had been able to visit him then?
79. Beutler, *Goethe*, 18: 684.
80. Ibid., 21: 553.
81. Moser, *Goethe und die Musik*, 49.
82. Ibid., 80.
83. Beutler, *Goethe*, 23: 70–78.
84. Friedlaender, "Goethe und die Musik," 322.
85. Richter, *Goethe*, 20.1: 564–577.
86. Friedlaender, *Gedichte von Goethe*, 141ff.
87. On 16 January 1828 the *Allgemeine musikalische Zeitung* of Leipzig reported that a lovely new room of Zelter's Academy of Vocal Music in Berlin had been opened. The report then mentioned that Schubert's *Erlkönig* had been sung by Carl Adam Bader accompanied by Mendelssohn. The song was judged to have been "over-rich in modulations and bizarrerie" and "not as good as Reichardt's or Zelter's." (Deutsch, *Die Dokumente seines Lebens*, 465f.)
88. Beutler, *Goethe*, 19: 344.

89. Walwei-Wiegelmann, *Goethes Gedanken über Musik*, 144.
90. Ibid., 140.
91. J. Reed, *The Schubert Song Companion*, 484.
92. Beutler, *Goethe*, 8, 336.
93. Moore, *Am I Too Loud?*, 178.
94. Eliot, "Goethe as the Sage," 210.
95. Goethe said once that the trouble with living for a long time was that you outlive most of your friends. Käthchen Schönkopf died in 1810, aged sixty-four; Friederike Brion in 1813, aged sixty-one; Charlotte von Stein in 1827, aged eighty-four; and Lotte Buff in 1828, aged seventy-five. Only Marianne von Willemer, in 1860, aged seventy-six, and Ulrike von Levetzow, in 1899, aged ninety-five, survived to tell their friends what they wanted to know about Goethe.

CHAPTER THREE

1. Bauer, *Zwei Jahrhunderte Literatur in Österreich*, 61.
2. Schochow and Schochow, *Franz Schubert*, 6.
3. Dürhammer, "Zu Schuberts Literaturästhetik," 14.
4. Deutsch, *Die Erinnerungen seiner Freunde*, 196.
5. Gramit, *Franz Schubert's Circle* and "Schubert's 'bildender Umgang'," and Dürhammer, "Zu Schuberts Literaturästhetik."
6. Capell, *Schubert's Songs*, 7.
7. Youens, *Schubert, Müller and Die schöne Müllerin*.
8. These are gathered in Deutsch, *Die Erinnerungen seiner Freunde*. The translations in the present volume are mine from the original German edition. The father's remarks are on p. 8.
9. Kreissle von Hellborn, *Franz Schubert*.
10. Deutsch, *Die Erinnerungen seiner Freunde*, 14.
11. Marek, *Schubert*, 13.
12. David Gramit ("Schubert's 'bildender Umgang'," 5) recalls that, from 1805 to 1869, Austrian schoolmasters had to teach from set textbooks and had to ensure that their pupils learned the material by heart, since one could not expect teachers to interpret the texts correctly.
13. Deutsch, *Die Erinnerungen seiner Freunde*, 123.
14. Deutsch, *Die Dokumente seines Lebens*, 12.
15. Schubert scribbled on a chapel score of Peter Winter's first Mass in C: "Schubert, Franz, crowed for the last time, 26 July 1812" (Deutsch, *Die Dokumente seines Lebens*, 21).
16. McKay, *Franz Schubert*, 24. Schubert heard two singers in the Kärntnertor-Theater in January 1813, who were to play an important role in his life: soprano Anna Milder (whom Goethe met as Anna Milder-Hauptmann in 1823), and Johann Michael Vogl. They were the Iphigénie and the Oreste in Gluck's opera, *Iphigénie en Tauride*. For some time after this, Schubert

was engrossed in Gluck's work (Deutsch, *Die Erinnerungen seiner Freunde,* 26).

17. Dürhammer, "Zu Schuberts Literaturästhetik," 16.
18. This may even have influenced Schubert's poetical talents. He wrote a "Klopstockian" ode "Die Zeit" (The Age) in May 1813, which, though not very important perhaps, was proof again that Schubert was alive to poetry and the music of words. It was the first of seven poems that he wrote and which have survived.
19. Bacharach and Pearce, *The Musical Companion,* 376.
20. Deutsch, *Die Erinnerungen seiner Freunde,* 15.
21. Capell, *Schubert's Songs,* 55.
22. Anna Kleyenböck, twenty years younger than Schubert's father, was to give birth to five children, one of whom died as a baby. Thus, the father procreated nineteen children in all.
23. For a full discussion of this topic, see West, "Schuberts Lieder im Kontext."
24. Benedikt et al., *Die Pfarrkirche zu Lichtental.*
25. McKay, *Franz Schubert,* 40.
26. Deutsch, *Die Erinnerungen seiner Freunde,* 49.
27. Ibid., 29.
28. Nägeli, "Die Liederkunst," 765f.
29. Deutsch, *Die Erinnerungen seiner Freunde,* 196.
30. Dürr and Feil, *Reclams Musikführer: Franz Schubert,* 53.
31. Deutsch, *Die Erinnerungen seiner Freunde,* 125.
32. Ibid., 155.
33. Dürhammer, "Zu Schuberts Literaturästhetik," 12.
34. West, "Schuberts Lieder im Kontext," 17.
35. Deutsch, *Die Erinnerungen seiner Freunde,* 45.
36. Deutsch, *Die Dokumente seines Lebens,* 30.
37. Ibid., 43.
38. Ibid., 45.
39. Robertson, *A History of German Literature,* 415.
40. Ibid., 418.
41. Steblin, "Franz Schubert," 34.
42. Deutsch, *Die Dokumente seines Lebens,* 254.
43. Fröhlich, *Schubert,* 39.
44. Deutsch, *Die Dokumente seines Lebens,* 45–46, 49–50, and McKay, *Franz Schubert,* 67.
45. Fröhlich, *Schubert,* 17.
46. A more scholarly investigation by Ilija Dürhammer ("Zu Schuberts Literaturästhetik") revealed the following themes: *Wandering* 20 percent, *Boats/ Water* 20 percent, *Spring* 10 percent, *Love* 50 percent (that is, every second song).
47. Quoted in Deutsch, *Die Erinnerungen seiner Freunde,* 154f. Schubert's first biographer, Heinrich Kreissle von Hellborn (*Franz Schubert,* 35), knew

Therese in 1864 as a "fresh and cheerful woman" who had lost her husband in 1844. Therese's father had been a silk-weaver, not a teacher.

48. Deutsch, *Die Dokumente seines Lebens,* 50.
49. Schubert and Schlegel may have met. That the composer found the German unsympathetic may prove that Schubert was well aware that Schlegel had changed his revolutionary ideas and had made common cause with Metternich. It is thought, too, that Schubert accompanied some of Schlegel's Lieder that were sung at his gatherings. Schubert certainly showed great interest in Schlegel's poetry, setting no fewer than sixteen of his poems, eleven from the cycle *Abendröte* (Sunset Glow) in 1819 and 1820 (such as D. 690–D. 694), which includes the wonderful Italianate *Der Fluss* (D. 693); here is a composer setting poems for their quality, not for their availability.
50. Hilmar, *Franz Schubert in seiner Zeit,* 87.
51. Ibid., 86.
52. All quotations from these letters come from Gramit, "Schubert's 'bildender Umgang'," 6ff.
53. Dürhammer, "Zu Schuberts Literaturästhetik," 29. The group felt inhibited by Goethe's lack of moral purity. Ottenwalt suggested that "selective reading" of Goethe's work would be necessary. The doubts were mainly about *Die Wahlverwandtschaften* (Elective Affinities) and *Tasso,* whereas Schiller's works displayed more "noble" thoughts.
54. Deutsch, *Die Erinnerungen seiner Freunde,* 112.
55. Fischer-Dieskau, *Schubert und seine Lieder,* 134f.
56. Marek, *Schubert,* 61.
57. Deutsch, *Die Dokumente seines Lebens,* 66–67.
58. Deutsch, *Die Erinnerungen seiner Freunde,* 83.
59. Härtling, *Schubert. Roman,* 129. To be fair to Härtling, we must mention two other authors in this context. Eduard von Bauernfeld wrote a little poem later: "Schubert was in love with one of his pupils, one of the young countesses / Yet he gave himself to a quite different girl / in order to forget the other!" (Deutsch, *Die Dokumente seines Lebens,* 256). Wilhelm von Chézy ("Erinnerungen aus Wien," 183), in his memoirs of Vienna, noted that Schubert loved girls and wine, but that this inclination (towards both) had unfortunately taken wrong turnings from which he was unable to extricate himself alive.
60. Deutsch, *Die Erinnerungen seiner Freunde,* 314; and McKay, *Franz Schubert,* 223.
61. Georgiades, *Schubert: Musik und Lyrik,* 132.
62. Dürr and Feil, *Reclams Musikführer: Franz Schubert,* 11.
63. Deutsch, *Die Dokumente seines Lebens,* 77.
64. McKay, *Franz Schubert,* 176.
65. Ottenberg and Zehm, "Briefwechsel zwischen Goethe und Zelter," 564–587.
66. Kreissle von Hellborn, *Franz Schubert,* 60.

67. Some inkling of his eventual fate must have come to Schubert when his Singspiel *Die Zwillingsbrüder* (The Twin Brothers, D. 647), also suffering from a poor libretto, only had six performances at the Kärntnertor-Theater (from 14 June to 21 July 1819). (Zelter must have just missed it.) His next stage-work *Die Zauberharfe* (The Magic Harp, D. 644) had only eight performances and was taken off in August 1819. It seems so sad that, by temporarily abandoning the field in which he was a (if, as yet, unrecognized) genius, he left himself open to disappointment and frustration at his failure in that other territory.

68. Deutsch, *Die Dokumente seines Lebens*, 84.

69. Ibid., 66.

70. Deutsch, *Die Erinnerungen seiner Freunde*, 72.

71. Brown, *Schubert: A Critical Biography*, 121f.; McKay, *Franz Schubert*, 99–132 ("La dolce vita") and 319–331 ("The Final Illness").

72. Härtling, *Schubert. Roman*, 184f.

73. The journal is edited by E. Hilmar. Articles on this topic include Eder, "Schubert und Caroline Esterházy," and Mayer, "Der psychoanalytische Schubert."

74. Porhansl, "Auf Schuberts Spuren in der 'Ludlamshöhle'," 53.

75. Ibid., 54.

76. Deutsch, *Die Dokumente seines Lebens*, 115.

77. *Schubertiade* is the correct word for these events. There seems to be little point in translating it as "Schubertiad," as many do.

78. Deutsch, *Die Dokumente seines Lebens*, 116.

79. Ibid., 118f.

80. Ibid., 174.

81. Ibid., 548; Brown, *Schubert: A Critical Biography*, 127; Walker, "Schubert's Last Illness"; Kiemle, "Woran starb Schubert eigentlich?" (What did Schubert really die of?); and McKay, *Franz Schubert*, 319–340.

82. Solomon, "Franz Schubert and the Peacocks."

83. Deutsch, *Die Dokumente seines Lebens*, 372f.

84. Bielschowsky, *Goethe: Sein Leben und seine Werke*, 2: 241.

85. An entry, for example, in Bauernfeld's diary for September 1825 refers to when Schober, Schwind, and he stayed at an inn in Atzenbrugg: "The three of us slept in a broad bed" (Deutsch, *Die Dokumente seines Lebens*, 317).

86. Card, *Eton Renewed*, 24.

87. Deutsch, *Die Dokumente seines Lebens*, 158f.

88. Mayer, "Der psychoanalytische Schubert."

89. Deutsch, *Die Dokumente seines Lebens*, 159. Ferdinand Schubert gave the story on 7 January 1839 to Schumann, who printed it in his *Neue Zeitschrift für Musik* under the title "Reliquien." (See also Mayer, "Der psychoanalytische Schubert," for an attack on the "psychoanalytical" method of biography.)

90. Fischer-Dieskau, *Schubert: A Biographical Study*, 174.

91. Deutsch, *Die Dokumente seines Lebens*, 207.
92. Youens, *Schubert, Müller and Die schöne Müllerin*, 207, n. 31. *Die schöne Müllerin* has also been the subject of psychoanalytical treatment. Youens' Freudian-orientated study ends with a chapter (159–203) on sex and death in Müller's and Schubert's cycles. Müller's visit to Goethe is documented in Baumann, *Wilhelm Müller*, 27f.
93. McKay, *Franz Schubert*, 137ff.
94. Deutsch, *Die Dokumente seines Lebens*, 203–205.
95. Ibid., 234f.
96. McKay, *Franz Schubert*, 193.
97. Here, too, there is another (albeit ironic) connection with Goethe, since the letter was addressed to Kupelwieser at the "Caffè grecco" in Rome, where Goethe used to meet his artistic German friends.
98. Deutsch, *Die Dokumente seines Lebens*, 258f.
99. Eder, "Schubert und Caroline Esterházy," 13.
100. Deutsch, *Die Erinnerungen seiner Freunde*, 84.
101. Eder, "Schubert und Caroline Esterházy," 16f.
102. Cf. Steblin, *Neue Forschungsaspekte*, 32.
103. Deutsch, *Die Dokumente seines Lebens*, 245f.
104. Ibid., xi.
105. Schubert said to Josef von Spaun once: "Secretly, when I'm alone, I still hope to make something of myself, but, who can do anything after Beethoven?" (Deutsch, *Die Erinnerungen seiner Freunde*, 109). He used to ask of anyone who wanted to join their circle: "Kanevas" (Kann er 'was?—Can he do anything?). This is no doubt what he felt Beethoven would be thinking about him.
106. Deutsch, *Die Erinnerungen seiner Freunde*, 31.
107. Deutsch, *Die Dokumente seines Lebens*, 417.
108. Ibid., 197.
109. Scott had also translated *Erlkönig* in 1797, and it was his translation that Wilhelmine Schröder-Devrient sang with great success in London in 1831. She had sung the ballad to Goethe the previous year. One listener in London, William Gardiner, wrote of "the awful thunder which the piano threw into the bars which had a dramatic effect, purely German!" (Engel, "Schubert's Fame," 469). Cf. Deutsch, *Die Dokumente seines Lebens*, 448.
110. *Die Dokumente seines Lebens*, 322.
111. Ibid., 298f.
112. Ibid., 314.
113. Ibid., 362.
114. Ibid., 176.
115. Ibid., 303f.
116. Deutsch, *Die Erinnerungen seiner Freunde*, 201.
117. Ibid., 117.
118. Capell, *Schubert's Songs*, 239.
119. Deutsch, *Die Dokumente seines Lebens*, 546.

CHAPTER FOUR

1. Panofka (1807–1887) was born in Breslau, Germany, and died in Florence, Italy. He did much to make Schubert's works known in France during his ten years' stay there. His article on Schubert is listed in the bibliography.
2. Walwei-Wiegelmann, *Goethes Gedanken über Musik*, 51.
3. Campe, *Wörterbuch der deutschen Sprache*, 127.
4. Schwab, *Sangbarkeit, Popularität und Kunstlied*, 137.
5. Moser, *Goethe und die Musik*, 94.
6. Schwab, *Sangbarkeit, Popularität und Kunstlied*, 53.
7. Hoffmann, *Schriften zur Musik* (Writings on Music), 43.
8. Finscher, *Lieder für eine Singstimme und Klavier*, 30f.
9. Liszt remained one of Schubert's greatest admirers. He wrote about "the rays of his genius illuminating distant vistas beyond the here and now" (Stricker, *Franz Schubert*, 160f.).
10. Albertson, "Kritik," 236f.
11. Deutsch, *Die Erinnerungen seiner Freunde*, 111.
12. Brown, *Schubert: A Critical Biography*, 46; Fischer-Dieskau, *Schubert und seine Lieder*, 78.
13. Deutsch, *Die Dokumente seines Lebens*, 582.
14. Beutler, *Goethe*, 23: 444.
15. Deutsch, *Die Dokumente seines Lebens*, 165f.
16. Keller, "Goethe and the Lied," 78.
17. McKay, *Franz Schubert*, 220.
18. The great service to Schubert scholarship by Graham Johnson's CD recordings of all Schubert's Lieder (on the Hyperion label) is not least that we can hear all these fragments, some of only a few measures. Others have been "completed" by the Schubert scholar Pater Reinhard van Hoorickx (Johnson, *The Hyperion Schubert Edition*).
19. Deutsch, *Die Dokumente seines Lebens*, 40–41.
20. Dürr and Feil, *Reclams Musikführer: Franz Schubert*, 25.
21. J. Reed, *The Schubert Song Companion*, 465.
22. Goldschmidt, *Franz Schubert*, 89.
23. It has been suggested that Spaun's name on the letter was one of the reasons for Goethe's ignoring it. Spaun's uncle, Franz Seraphicus von Spaun, born in 1754 and living at the time in Munich, had changed from being an ardent Goethe fan into a well-known detractor of his works (Deutsch, *Die Dokumente seines Lebens*, 41).
24. Klessmann, *Goethe aus der Nähe*, 153f.
25. Deutsch, *Die Dokumente seines Lebens*, 43–45.
26. In his diary for 17 September 1815, Goethe's artistic friend Sulpiz von Boisserée wrote that Marianne von Willemer had sung to Goethe settings of his poems *Der Gott und die Bajadere* (The God and the Prostitute), "Schlafe, was willst du mehr?" (Sleep, what more do you desire?), and *Sehnsucht* (Longing), and followed them with the Don Juan–Zerlina duet from *Don*

Giovanni (Give me your hand, my life). Goethe then called her "a little Don Juan." The talk on their way home, we learn, was all about Mozart's music. (The settings were probably Reichardt's or Zelter's.) The anecdote shows how much pleasure Goethe and Marianne had from shared music (Gerlach and Hermann, *Goethe erzählt sein Leben,* 330). The interesting point for our theme is that the singer was also a friend of Anna Milder's. One wonders what Lieder were discussed when they met?

27. Deutsch, *Die Dokumente seines Lebens,* 284.
28. Ibid., 267–268.
29. McKay, *Franz Schubert,* 193.
30. Deutsch, *Die Dokumente seines Lebens,* 288.
31. Grimm, *Goethes Werke,* 10: 68–69.
32. Beutler, *Goethe,* Tagebücher, 447.

CHAPTER FIVE

1. *Faust, A Fragment* was published as volume seven of Goethe's *Works* in 1790. *Faust, The Tragedy, Part One* was published by Cotta as volume eight of Goethe's *Collected Works* in 1808. The *Urfaust* has been called "the one supremely great tragic drama of modern German literature" (Boyle, *Goethe: The Poet and the Age,* 221).
2. Williams, *Goethe's Faust,* 99.
3. This is what H. G. Nägeli ("Die Liederkunst," 765f.) called "polyrhythmic," where "the rhythms of the language, music, and 'play' are merged into a higher artistic whole."
4. Beutler, *Goethe,* 20: 881.
5. Deutsch, *Die Dokumente seines Lebens,* 78.
6. Bielschowsky, *Goethe,* 2: 234.
7. Mason, *Goethe's Faust,* 191.
8. Johnson, *The Hyperion Schubert Edition,* 13: 13–16.
9. Translation of the Latin lines in this work are from O'Connell and Finberg, *The Missal in Latin and English,* 230.
10. Grimm, *Goethes Werke,* 3: 52.
11. Deutsch, *Die Erinnerungen seiner Freunde,* 31.
12. Deutsch, *Die Dokumente seines Lebens,* 43.
13. Albertson, "Kritik," 233.
14. Fischer-Dieskau, *Schubert: A Biographical Study,* 70.
15. Boyle, *Goethe: The Poet and the Age,* 182.
16. Ibid., 369.
17. Johnson, *The Hyperion Schubert Edition,* 10: 15.
18. Beutler, *Goethe,* 18:647.
19. Moser, *Goethe und die Musik,* 95.
20. Boyd, *Notes to Goethe's Poems,* 38.
21. Fischer-Dieskau, *Schubert: A Biographical Study,* 52.

22. Albertson, "Kritik," 233.
23. Beutler, *Goethe,* Tagebücher, 41.
24. Dürhammer, "Zu Schuberts Literaturästhetik," table 6.
25. McKay, *Franz Schubert,* 331.
26. J. Reed, *The Schubert Song Companion,* 194.
27. Fischer-Dieskau, *Schubert und seine Lieder,* 72.
28. Johnson, *The Hyperion Schubert Edition,* 24: 6.
29. Beutler, *Goethe,* 20: 354.
30. Moser, *Goethe und die Musik,* 134.
31. L. L. Albertson ("Kritik," 231) wrote of the *An den Mond* settings and the omitted stanza: "Whichever solution one decides on" (that is, which stanza to omit) "seems not to have been an important question for Schubert."
32. Gàl, *Franz Schubert oder die Melodie,* 104.
33. Capell, *Schubert's Songs,* 104.
34. Johnson, *The Hyperion Schubert Edition,* 7: 123.
35. Deutsch, *Die Dokumente seines Lebens,* 86.
36. Boyle, *Goethe: The Poet and the Age,* 390.
37. Dürr and Feil, *Reclams Musikführer: Franz Schubert,* 129.
38. Beutler, *Goethe,* 23: 221–222.
39. Boyle, *Goethe: The Poet and the Age,* 338.
40. J. Reed, *The Schubert Song Companion,* 222.
41. This is also the reason many lovers of Lieder would prefer Carl Loewe's 1817 setting (*his* Opus No. 1). It seems to them to be truer to the atmosphere of chilling eeriness in Goethe's ballad. Moser (*Goethe und die Musik,* 134) counted seventy-two settings of *Erlkönig* to 1949.
42. Max Friedlaender records Goethe's meeting with the little boy Carl Eckert, who had set *Erlkönig* to music when he was only seven. When Goethe asked him which setting he preferred, the boy answered that he only knew those of "Reichardt and Klein" and he didn't like them, because they made the Erl-King sing so frighteningly. Goethe agreed at once and said that the Erl-King should sing like a "tempter," now gently and flattering, now threatening and angry (Friedlaender, *Gedichte von Goethe,* 142f.). The interesting point here is that, without this knowledge, Schubert changed his original *ff* at "Ich liebe dich" in the seventh stanza to *pp.*
43. Deutsch, *Die Dokumente seines Lebens,* 152.
44. Hartung, *Über allen Gipfeln,* 47.
45. Macdonald, "Schubert's Volcanic Temper," 950ff.
46. J. Reed, *The Schubert Song Companion,* 485f.
47. Einstein, *Schubert,* 58.
48. Beutler, *Goethe,* Tagebücher, 13.
49. Deutsch, *Die Erinnerungen seiner Freunde,* 196.
50. Fischer-Dieskau, *Schubert und seine Lieder,* 117.
51. Johnson, *The Hyperion Schubert Edition,* 24: 46ff.
52. Proof of the justification for the phrase "ordinary sexual instincts" might

be his writing of the obscene fragments *Hanswursts Hochzeit* (Hanswurst's Wedding) in the spring of 1775, just at the time that he had become engaged (ca. 20 April 1775) to Lili (Ammer, *Goethes Erotische Gedichte,* 15–35). Hanswurst was the knockabout jester of many medieval German comedies.

53. Boyle, *Goethe: The Poet and the Age,* 160.
54. Trunz, *Goethe. Gedichte,* 650f.
55. Capell, *Schubert's Songs,* 70.
56. Boyle, *Goethe: The Poet and the Age,* 526.
57. Bielschowsky, *Goethe,* 2: 259.
58. Boyle, *Goethe: The Poet and the Age,* 164.
59. Fischer-Dieskau, *Schubert: A Biographical Study,* 130.
60. Deutsch, *Die Dokumente seines Lebens,* 45, 76.
61. Johnson, *The Hyperion Schubert Edition,* 24: 46ff.
62. Ibid.
63. Reid, "'Dear Brown'," 95.
64. Fischer-Dieskau, *Schubert und seine Lieder,* 272f.
65. Boyle, *Goethe: The Poet and the Age,* 368.
66. Ibid.
67. Trunz, *Goethe. Gedichte,* 667ff.
68. Ibid., 643.
69. Deutsch, *Die Dokumente seines Lebens,* 172f.
70. Richter, *Goethe,* 3.2: 88.
71. Deutsch, *Die Dokumente seines Lebens,* 173.
72. Fischer-Dieskau, *Schubert und seine Lieder,* 219.
73. Prawer, *The Penguin Book of Lieder,* 12.
74. Trunz, *Goethe. Gedichte,* 555–557.
75. Deutsch, *Die Dokumente seines Lebens,* 249.
76. Stein, *Poem and Music in the German Lied,* 73.
77. McKay (*Franz Schubert,* 245) documents Schubert's heavy drinking and smoking during this period, along with his visits to "the seedy sexual underworld of Vienna." The undertones of illicit sex in Goethe's novel would not go unheard by Schubert.
78. Boyd, *Notes to Goethe's Poems,* 203.
79. Of course, Marianne had written to Goethe in June 1821 to say that Beethoven should set the *Suleika* poems: "He would understand them perfectly, otherwise nobody [would]!" (Deutsch, *Die Dokumente seines Lebens,* 284).
80. Boyd (*Notes to Goethe's Poems,* 2: 205) recalled that the old Weimar edition of Goethe's poems added to this point: "The west wind wakens tears, but it also cools the eyes."
81. Deutsch, *Die Dokumente seines Lebens,* 280.

Bibliography

Abert, H. *Goethe und die Musik*. Stuttgart, 1922.

Abraham, G., ed. *Schubert: A Symposium*. London, 1947, 1952.

Aderhold, W., W. Dürr, and A. Feil. *Franz Schubert: Thematisches Verzeichnis seiner Werke in chronologischer Folge*. Neue Schubert Ausgabe, Series 8, vol. 4. Kassel, 1978.

Albertson, L. L. "Kritik an Schuberts Umgang mit Goethe-Texten." *Goethe-Jahrbuch* 102 (1985): 226–237.

Ammer, A., ed. *Goethes erotische Gedichte*. Stuttgart, 1991.

Anderson, E., ed./trans. *The Letters of Beethoven*, vols. 1–3. London, 1961.

Bacharach A. L., and J. R. Pearce, eds. *The Musical Companion*. London, 1977.

Badura-Skoda, E., and P. Branscombe, eds. *Schubert Studies: Problems of Style and Chronology*. Cambridge, United Kingdom, 1982, 1986.

Bauer, R. *Zwei Jahrhunderte Literatur in Österreich*. Vienna, 1977.

Baumann, C. C. *Wilhelm Müller, the Poet of the Schubert Song Cycles: His Life and Works*. University Park, Pennsylvania/London, 1981.

Benedikt, E., et al., eds. *Die Pfarrkirche zu Lichtental*. Vienna, 1978.

Benz, R. *Die Zeit der Klassik*. Leipzig, 1943.

Beutler, E., ed. *Goethe: Gedenkausgabe der Werke, Briefe und Gespräche*, vols. 1–24. Zurich, 1948ff.

Bielschowsky, A. *Goethe: Sein Leben und seine Werke*, 2 vols. Munich, 1905.

Blume, F. *Goethe und die Musik*. Kassel, 1948.

Bode, W. *Die Tonkunst in Goethes Leben*. Berlin, 1912.

Boerner, P. *Goethe*. Hamburg, 1964, 1995.

Boyd, J. *Notes to Goethe's Poems*, 2 vols. Oxford, 1949f.

Boyle, N. *Goethe: The Poet and the Age*, vol. 1. Oxford, 1991.

Braungart, G., and W. Dürr, eds. *Über Schubert*. Stuttgart, 1996.

Brown, M. J. E. *Schubert: A Critical Biography*. London, 1958.

———. *Essays on Schubert*. London, 1966.

———. "The Therese Grob Collection of Songs by Franz Schubert." *Music and Letters* (April 1968): 122–134.

Bruford, W. H. *Germany in the XVIII Century*. London, 1933.

————. *Theatre, Drama and Audience in Goethe's Germany*. London, 1950.

————. *Culture and Society in Classical Weimar*. Cambridge, 1962.

————. *The German Tradition of Self-Cultivation*. London, 1975.

Busch, G., and A. J. Harper, eds. *Studien zum deutschen weltlichen Kunstlied des 17. und 18. Jahrhunderts*. Atlanta, Georgia, 1992.

Campe, J. H. *Wörterbuch der deutschen Sprache*. Brunswick, 1809.

Capell, R. *Schubert's Songs*. London, 1928, 1957.

Card, T. *Eton Renewed*. London, 1994.

Chézy, W. "Erinnerungen aus Wien aus den Jahren 1804–1829." In *Deutsche Pandora*, 167–190. Stuttgart, 1841.

Clive, P. *Schubert and His World*. A Biographical Dictionary. Oxford, 1997.

Cobban, A. *A History of Modern France*. London, 1957.

Deutsch, O. E. *Schuberts Goethe-Lieder*. Vienna, 1926.

————, ed. *Schubert: A Documentary Biography*. Trans. E. Blom. London, 1946.

————, ed. *Schubert: Die Erinnerungen seiner Freunde* (Memoirs by his Friends). Leipzig, 1957; revised 1983, 1996.

————. *Schubert: Memoirs by his Friends*. Trans. R. Ley and J. Nowell. London, 1958.

————, ed. *Schubert: Die Dokumente seines Lebens*. Kassel, 1964, 1980, 1996.

————. *Mozart: A Documentary Biography*. London, 1965, 1990.

Deutsch, O. E., and D. Wakeling. *Schubert: Thematic Catalogue of All His Works*. Cambridge, United Kingdom, 1950.

————. *Franz Schubert: Thematisches Verzeichnis seiner Werke in chronologischer Folge*. Kassel, 1978, 1996.

Dürhammer, I. "Zu Schuberts Literaturästhetik." In *Schubert durch die Brille* (Schubert Through Spectacles), edited by E. Hilmar. Journal of the IFSI, no. 14: 4–99. Tutzing, 1995.

————. "Schlegel, Schelling und Schubert." In *Schubert durch die Brille* (Schubert Through Spectacles), edited by E. Hilmar. Journal of the IFSI, nos. 16–17: 59–93. Tutzing, 1996.

Dürr, W. "Poesie und Musik: Über Schuberts Beziehungen zu Goethe." *Schubertiade* (Feldkirch, 1993): 10–48.

Dürr, W., and A. Feil. *Reclams Musikführer: Franz Schubert*. Stuttgart, 1991.

Dürr, W., A. Feil, C. Landon, et al. *Franz Schubert: Neue Ausgabe sämtlicher Werke* (New Complete Edition). Kassel, 1964ff.

Dürr, W., and A. Krause, eds. *Schubert Handbuch*. Kassel and Weimar, 1997.

Eder, G. "Schubert und Caroline Esterházy." In *Schubert durch die Brille*

(Schubert Through Spectacles), edited by E. Hilmar. Journal of the IFSI, no. 11: 6–20. Tutzing, 1993.

Einstein, A. *Schubert*. London, 1951.

Eliot, T. S. "Goethe as the Sage." In *On Poetry and Poets,* 207–227. London, 1957.

Endter, C. E. *Lieder zum Scherz und Zeitvertreib*. Hamburg, 1757.

Engel, C. "Schubert's Fame." *Modern Languages Quarterly* 14,4 (1928): 457–472.

Feil, A. *Studien zu Schuberts Rhythmik*. Munich, 1966.

———. *Franz Schubert: Die schöne Müllerin, Winterreise*. Stuttgart, 1975.

———. *Franz Schubert: Die schöne Müllerin and Winterreise*. Trans. A. C. Sherwin. Portland, Oregon, 1988.

Finscher, L. J. *Brahms: Lieder für eine Singstimme und Klavier*. 10LP, DGG 2562 479-2562 490. Notes: Songs for Solo Voice and Piano 30–32.

Fischer-Dieskau, D. *Texte deutscher Lieder*. Munich, 1968.

———. *Auf den Spuren der Schubert-Lieder: Werden, Wesen, Wirkung*. Wiesbaden, 1971.

———. *The Fischer-Dieskau Book of Lieder*. Trans. George Bird and Richard Stokes. London, 1976.

———. *Schubert: A Biographical Study of his Songs*. Trans. K. S. Whitton. London, 1976.

———. *Töne sprechen, Worte klingen*. Stuttgart, 1985.

———. *Weil nicht alle Blütenträume reiften*. Stuttgart, 1992.

———. *Schubert und seine Lieder*. Stuttgart, 1996.

Friedlaender, M. *Gedichte von Goethe in Kompositionen seiner Zeitgenossen*. Schriften der Goethe-Gesellschaft, vol. 11. Weimar, 1896.

———. *Das deutsche Lied im 18. Jahrhundert*. Stuttgart, 1902, 1970.

———. "Goethe und die Musik." *Jahrbuch der Goethe Gesellschaft* 3 (1916): 275–340.

Fröhlich, H. *Schubert*. Munich and Vienna, 1978, 1980.

Gàl, H. *Franz Schubert oder die Melodie*. Frankfurt, 1970, 1992.

Geiringer, K. *Joseph Haydn*. Munich, 1986.

Georgiades, T. G. *Schubert: Musik und Lyrik*. Göttingen, 1967.

Gerlach, H. E., und G. Herrmann. *Goethe erzählt sein Leben*. Frankfurt, 1956.

Gibbs, C. H. "Sie wiegen und tanzen und singen dich ein." In *Schubert durch die Brille* (Schubert Through Spectacles), edited by E. Hilmar. Journal of the IFSI, no. 8: 32–38. Tutzing, 1992.

———, ed. *The Cambridge Companion to Schubert*. Cambridge, United Kingdom, 1997.

Goethe, K. E. *Briefe aus dem Elternhaus*, In *Goethe: Gedenkausgabe der Werke, Briefe und Gespräche*, edited by E. Beutler, suppl. vol. 1.

Goldschmidt, H. *Franz Schubert.* Leipzig, 1976.

Graham, H. G. *The Poems of Ossian.* Edinburgh, 1894.

Gramit, D. *The Intellectual and Aesthetic Tenets of Franz Schubert's Circle.* Ann Arbor, Michigan, 1989.

———. "Schuberts 'bildender Umgang'." In *Schubert durch die Brille* (Schubert Through Spectacles), edited by E. Hilmar. Journal of the IFSI, no. 8: 5–21. Tutzing, 1992.

Gray, R. D. *Goethe: A Critical Introduction.* Cambridge, United Kingdom, 1967.

Grimm, H., ed. *Goethes Werke.* Weimarer Ausgabe, Weimar, 1887–1919.

Gülke, P. *Franz Schubert und seine Zeit.* Laaber, 1991, 1996.

Haller, J. *Epochen der deutschen Geschichte.* Stuttgart/Berlin, 1922.

Härtling, P. *Schubert. Roman.* Hamburg/Munich, 1992, 1995.

Hartung, P. *Über allen Gipfeln.* Munich, 1949.

Herder, J. G. *Sämtliche Werke.* Vol. 25, *Volkslieder.* Hildesheim, 1967.

Hicks, W. C. R. "Was Goethe musical?" *Publications of the English Goethe Society* 27 (1958): 73–139.

Hilmar, E. *Catalogus Musicus,* vol. 8, *Schubert-Handschriften in der Musiksammlung der Wiener Stadt- und Landesbibliothek.* Kassel, 1978.

———. *Franz Schubert in seiner Zeit.* Vienna, 1985.

———. *Franz Schubert in His Time.* Trans. R. G. Pauly. Portland, Oregon, 1988.

———. *Franz Schubert.* Hamburg, 1997.

———, ed. *Schubert durch die Brille* (Schubert Through Spectacles). Journal of the IFSI, nos. 1–21. Tutzing, 1990ff.

Hilmar, E., and O. Brusatti, eds. *Franz Schubert.* Vienna, 1978.

Hilmar, E., and M. Jestrowski, eds. *Schubert-Lexikon.* Vienna, 1997.

Hilmar, E., and R. Voit. "Zu Schuberts 'letzten Liedern'." In *Schubert durch die Brille* (Schubert Through Spectacles), edited by E. Hilmar. Journal of the IFSI, no. 6: 48–55. Tutzing, 1991.

Hinck, W. "Goethe: Man of the Theatre." In *Goethe Revisited,* ed. E. M. Wilkinson, 153–169. London, 1984.

Hirsch, M. W. *Schubert's Dramatic Lieder.* Cambridge, 1993.

Hoffmann, E. T. A. *Schriften zur Musik* (Writings on Music). Berlin/Weimar, 1988.

Jacobi, E., ed. *Begegnungen eines deutschen Tenors, 1820–1866: Carl Adam Bader.* Frankfurt, 1991–1992.

Johnson, G., ed. *The Hyperion Schubert Edition* (Complete Songs) CDs, vols. 1–30. London, 1988–1997.

Keller, H. "Goethe and the Lied." In *Goethe Revisited,* ed. E. M. Wilkinson, 73–84. London, 1984.

Kerman, J. L. *Beethoven Studies.* New York, 1974.

Kiemle, H. D. "Woran starb Schubert eigentlich?" (What did Schubert really die of?). In *Schubert durch die Brille* (Schubert Through Spectacles), edited by E. Hilmar. Journal of the IFSI, nos. 16–17: 41–51. Tutzing, 1996.

Kinsley, J. "The Music of the Heart." In *Critical Essays on Robert Burns,* ed. D. A. Low, 124–137. London, 1975.

Klessmann, E. *Goethe aus der Nähe.* Zurich, 1995.

Kreissle von Hellborn, H. *Franz Schubert.* Vienna, 1865.

Krenek, E. *Franz Schubert: Ein Porträt.* Tutzing, 1990.

Lehmann, A. G. *The European Heritage.* London, 1984.

Leppmann, W. *The German Image of Goethe.* Oxford, 1961.

Lewes, G. H. *The Life of Goethe.* London, 1855.

Low, D. A., ed. *Critical Essays on Robert Burns.* London, 1975.

Macdonald, H. "Schubert's Volcanic Temper." *Musical Times* 99 (1978): 949–952.

Mandyczewski, E., J. Brahms, et al., eds. *Franz Schuberts Werke: Kritisch durchgesehene Gesamtausgabe* (Old Complete Edition), 40 vols. Leipzig, 1884–1897.

Marek, G. R. *Schubert.* London, 1985–1986.

Mason, E. C. *Goethe's Faust.* London, 1967.

Mayer, A. "Der psychoanalytische Schubert." In *Schubert durch die Brille* (Schubert Through Spectacles), edited by E. Hilmar. Journal of the IFSI, no. 9: 7–31 and no. 10: 95–96. Tutzing, 1992, 1993.

McKay, E. N. *Schubert's Music for the Theatre.* Tutzing,1991.

———. *Franz Schubert.* London, 1996.

Mitchell, K. "Nur nicht lesen! Immer singen!" *Publications of the English Goethe Society* 44 (1974): 63–82.

Mommsen, K., ed. *Goethe-warum?* Frankfurt, 1984.

Moore, G. *The Unashamed Accompanist.* London, 1943, 1984.

———. *Am I Too Loud?* London, 1962.

———. *The Schubert Song Cycles.* London, 1975.

Moser, H. J. *Das deutsche Lied seit Mozart.* Berlin, 1937.

———. *Goethe und die Musik.* Leipzig, 1949.

Nägeli, H. G. "Die Liederkunst." *Allgemeine musikalische Zeitung* 19 (1817): 765f.

Natan, A., and B. Keith-Smith, eds. *German Men of Letters,* vol. 6. London, 1972.

Newbould, B. *Schubert: The Music and the Man.* London, 1997.

O'Connell, J., and H. P. R. Finberg. *The Missal in Latin and English.* London, 1957.

Ottenberg H. G., and E. Zehm. "Briefwechsel zwischen Goethe und Zelter in den Jahren 1799–1832." In *Goethe: Sämtliche Werke nach Epochen seines Schaffens*, ed. K. Richter, vol. 20.1: 564–587. Munich, 1991.

Panofka, H. "Biografie—Franz Schubert." Trans. Andreas Mayer, from *Revue et Gazette de Paris* (V, 1838, 406–409). In *Schubert durch die Brille* (Schubert Through Spectacles), edited by E. Hilmar. Journal of the IFSI, no. 7: 7–18. Tutzing, 1991.

Porhansl, L. "Auf Schuberts Spuren in der 'Ludlamshöhle'." In *Schubert durch die Brille* (Schubert Through Spectacles), edited by E. Hilmar. Journal of the IFSI, no. 7: 52–78. Tutzing, 1991.

Prawer, S. *The Penguin Book of Lieder*. London, 1964.

Ramler, C. W., and C. G. Krause. *Oden mit Melodien*, Part 1. Berlin, 1753.

Reed, J. *Schubert: The Final Years*. London, 1972.

———. *The Schubert Song Companion*. Manchester, 1985, 1986.

———. *Schubert*. London, 1987, 1997.

———. "Die Rezeptionsgeschichte der Werke Schuberts in England während des 19.Jahrhunderts." In *Schubert durch die Brille* (Schubert Through Spectacles), edited by E. Hilmar. Journal of the IFSI, no. 5: 43–50. Tutzing, 1990.

Reed, T. J. *The Classical Centre*. London/New York, 1980.

Reid, P. "'Dear Brown': Briefe von Otto Erich Deutsch an Maurice J. E. Brown." In *Schubert durch die Brille* (Schubert Through Spectacles), edited by E. Hilmar. Journal of the IFSI, no. 19: 81–98. Tutzing, 1997.

Richter, K., ed. *Goethe: Sämtliche Werke nach Epochen seines Schaffens*, vols. 1–20.1. Munich, 1985ff.

Ritchie, J. M. "The Anacreontic Poets." In *German Men of Letters*, eds. A. Natan and B. Keith-Smith, 6: 123–145. London, 1972.

Robertson, J. G. *A History of German Literature*. Edinburgh/London, 1947.

Rochlitz, J. F. *Für Freunde der Tonkunst*. Berlin, 1832.

Sagarra, E. *A Social History of Germany 1648–1914*. London, 1987.

Salmen, W. "Die deutsche Vorklassik." In *C. P. E. Bach: Oden, Psalmen und Lieder*, L.P. 2523 058, Archiv Produktion, D.G.G., 1969.

Schochow, M., and L. Schochow, eds. *Franz Schubert: Die Texte seiner einstimmig komponierten Lieder und ihre Dichter*. Hildesheim/New York, 1974.

Scholes, P., ed. *Concise Oxford Dictionary of Music*. London, 1952, 1978.

Schulz, J. A. P. *Lieder im Volkston*. Berlin, 1782–1790.

Schulz, M. *Academic Illusions in the Fields of Letters and the Arts*. Chicago, 1933.

Schünemann, G., ed. *Lieder von Goethe komponiert von Franz Schubert*. Berlin, 1943.

Schwab, H. W. *Sangbarkeit, Popularität und Kunstlied*. Regensburg, 1965.

Seidlin, O. "Goethe's Magic Flute." In *Essays in German and Comparative Literature*, 45–59. North Carolina, 1961.

Shelley, M. *Frankenstein or The Modern Promethus*. London, 1818, 1993.

Smeed, J. W. "The Composer as Interpreter." *German Life and Letters* 35,3 (1982): 221–228.

———. *German Song and Its Poetry, 1740–1900*. London, 1987.

Solomon, M. "Franz Schubert and the Peacocks of Benvenuto Cellini." *19th Century Music* 12 (1989): 193–206.

Spaethling, R. *Music and Mozart in the Life of Goethe*. Columbia, South Carolina, 1987.

Staiger, E. *Musik und Dichtung*. Zurich, 1947ff.

———. *Goethe*. Zurich/Freiburg, 1952ff.

Steblin, R. "Franz Schubert und das Ehe-Konsens-Gesetz von 1815." In *Schubert durch die Brille* (Schubert Through Spectacles), edited by E. Hilmar. Journal of the IFSI, no. 9: 32–42. Tutzing, 1992.

———. "Neue Forschungsaspekte zu Caroline Esterházy." In *Schubert durch die Brille* (Schubert Through Spectacles), edited by E. Hilmar. Journal of the IFSI, no. 11: 21–33. Tutzing, 1993.

———. "The Peacock's Tale: Schubert's Sexuality Re-considered." *19th Century Music* 17 (1993): 5–33.

Steiger, R. *Goethes Leben von Tag zu Tag*. Zurich/Munich, 1982f.

Stein, J. M. "Was Goethe Wrong about the Nineteenth-century Lied?" *PMLA* 77 (1962): 232–239.

———. *Poem and Music in the German Lied from Gluck to Hugo Wolf*. Cambridge, Massachusetts, 1971.

Steiner, G. *After Babel*. Oxford, 1975–1976.

Stoljar, M. *Poetry and Song in Late Eighteenth Century Germany*. London, 1985.

Stricker, R. *Franz Schubert*. Paris, 1997.

Susman, M. M. *Deutung einer grossen Liebe*. Zurich, 1951.

Trunz, E., ed. *Goethe. Gedichte*. Munich, 1981, 1988.

Waidelich, T. G., ed. *Franz Schubert: Dokumente 1817–1830. Band 1: Texte*. Tutzing, 1993.

———. "Begegnung eines deutschen Tenors." In *Schubert durch die Brille* (Schubert Through Spectacles), edited by E. Hilmar. Journal of the IFSI, no. 13: 55–66. Tutzing, 1994.

Walker, F. "Schubert's Last Illness." *Monthly Musical Record* 77 (1947): 220–236.

Walwei-Wiegelmann, H., ed. *Goethes Gedanken über Musik*. Frankfurt, 1985.

West, E. "Schuberts Lieder im Kontext." In *Schubert durch die Brille* (Schubert Through Spectacles), edited by E. Hilmar. Journal of the

IFSI, no. 12: 5–19. Tutzing, 1994.

Whitton, K. S. *Dietrich Fischer-Dieskau, Mastersinger*. London, 1981.

―――. "Krämerspiegel" (Richard Strauss/Alfred Kerr), "A 20th Century Musical *Komödie:* A Footnote to a History of German Satirical Writing," *New German Studies* 12,2 (1984): 107–126.

―――. *Lieder: An Introduction to German Song*. London, 1984.

―――. "Humour in the German Lied," *New Comparison* 3 (1987): 160–173.

―――. "Grosses wirket ihr Streit, Grösseres wirket ihr Bund": "On the 'Wort/Ton' Problem in the German Lied," *German Life and Letters* 42,4 (1989): 395–410.

―――. "Robert Schumann, Robert Burns und der Myrthen-Zyklus," *4.Schumannfest*, Düsseldorf (1991): 64–69. (In German.)

Wilkinson, E. M., ed. *Goethe Revisited*. London, 1984.

Williams, J. *Goethe's Faust*. London, 1987.

Youens, S. *Schubert's Poets and the Making of Lieder*. Cambridge, United Kingdom, 1996.

―――. *Schubert, Müller and Die schöne Müllerin*. Cambridge, United Kingdom, 1997.

Young, P. M. *The Bachs 1500–1850*. London, 1970.

Index of Names

Index of Goethe's Poems
and Other Works

(Only works mentioned in the text are listed below.)

Index of Schubert's Lieder and Other Works

(Only works mentioned in the text are listed below.)